THE JEWS
IN THE BYZANTINE EMPIRE
641–1204

TEXTE UND FORSCHUNGEN
ZUR BYZANTINISCH-NEUGRIECHISCHEN PHILOLOGIE
Zwanglose Beihefte zu den „BYZANTINISCH-NEUGRIECHISCHEN JAHRBÜCHERN"
Herausgegeben von Prof. Dr. **NIKOS A. BEES** (Béης)

Nr. 30

THE JEWS
IN THE BYZANTINE EMPIRE
641–1204

BY

JOSHUA STARR, Ph. D.

ATHEN
VERLAG DER „BYZANTINISCH-NEUGRIECHISCHEN JAHRBÜCHER"
Averof-Str. 16.
1939

S.B.N. - GB: 576.80131.3

Republished in 1969 by Gregg International Publishers Limited
Westmead, Farnborough, Hants., England.

Printed in England

TO ANN

FOREWORD

The history of the Jews in the Byzantine Empire begins, of course, in the fourth rather than the seventh century, where the present study opens. Inasmuch as no monograph on Byzantine-Jewish history from Constantine to Heraclius has yet been produced, it may seem strange that I have preferred to treat a portion of the subsequent epoch, from the death of Heraclius to the Fourth Crusade, the middle period of Byzantine history. The choice is due to the realization that the fourth to seventh centuries have received and are continuing to receive a considerable degree of attention on the part of both historians and archaeologists, whereas the later age remains relatively neglected. Accordingly, after having made a preliminary survey of the whole Byzantine-Jewish field, at the suggestion of Prof. Salo W. Baron, I considered it best to start with the changed situation which began with the period of the Arab conquest.

The nature of the source-materials has made it imperative to spare no pains in making an exhaustive collection of them and to present these texts and the pertinent apparatus *in extenso,* as Part Two, rather than adopt the usual and normally commendable footnote system. I hope that the reader who will find himself inconvenienced by the separation between the discussion and the documentation will, nevertheless, have occasion to rejoice in the advantages which accrue from this arrangement in the present instance.

I would not conceal my awareness that in my desire to include the cultural aspects of this phase of Byzantine-Jewish history I have had to venture into certain fields, the liturgical poetry, the Biblical commentaries, the rabbinic writings, and the Karaite literature, each of which is almost a special discipline in itself. For that reason, while I have striven to collect the essential facts in order to indicate how the Jews of the Byzantine Empire shared in the cultivation of these medieval interests, I have made no effort to go beyond the results of the specialists in these fields.

Among the scholars who have permitted me to consult them while I was pursuing my research, it is a pleasure to name Prof. Simcha Assaf of the Hebrew University in Jerusalem, who gave me of his time and of his vast erudition most generously. For assistance in solving detailed questions I take this opportunity to thank the following: Prof. A. A. Vasiliev (University of Wisconsin), Prof. Wm. L. Westermann, Dr. A. S. Halkin, Dr. R. Marcus (Columbia University), Prof. G. Scholem (Hebrew University), Prof. U. Cassuto (University of Rome), Prof. N. A. Beés (University of Athens). The encouragement and criticism of the late Prof. A. M. Andréadès of Athens, as well as that of Professors A. P. Evans and L. Thorndike (Columbia University) have likewise been of great value.

It would be difficult to give adequate expression of my indebtedness to my teacher Prof Baron, who after seeing me launched on this undertaking guided my progress until the work was completed. This expression of gratitude for his aid and that of others should not, however, be construed as shifting any part of the responsibility for deficiences in this book to any person other than myself.

My thanks are extended to Mrs. Florence B. Freedman who read the manuscript and assisted me in eliminating various errors of style.

It is appropriate, finally, to record that a large part of the work involved was accomplished during my academic residence as Nies Scholar of the American School of Oriental Research in Jerusalem, from 1933 to 1935, a period in which I enjoyed the stimulating instruction and delightful company of Prof. Wm. F. Albright (Johns Hopkins University), whose sympathetic interest in my work was most gratifying, and then during my term as Miller Fellow at Columbia University the following year.

J. S.

New York City,

March, 1938.

CONTENTS

Tombstone in the Museo Civico, Brindisi
Dated 832

CHAPTER I

PERSECUTION AND INTOLERANCE

It has long been known that the period of five and one-half centuries to which this study is devoted was not one of undisturbed toleration for the Jews of the Byzantine empire. At its opening they were still under the shadow of the forcible Christianization decreed by Heraclius (610-41), in a vain effort to establish a solid front against his Moslem enemy. Thereafter, each of the following three centuries produced an emperor who outlawed Judaism. However, a mere enumeration, ominous as it is, does scant justice to the total historical situation, for, besides attempting to recover the course of events itself, it is necessary to see these spasms of intolerance in the perspective furnished by materials of a rather different tenor. Accordingly, it is proposed here first to review the treatment of the Jews by the intolerant emperors, and then to measure the duration of these situations against the remainder of our period.

We have no definite proof as to the continuation or abandonment of Heraclius' policy by his immediate successors. But in a period in which Constantinople itself was repeatedly threatened by Moslem attacks, it is rash to assume that the necessary attention could be spared for the suppression of Judaism (2).* However, according to a late source, about the year 680, «many Jews» were converted to Christianity somewhere in Asia Minor. This event (if historical) is assignable to the empire, and while it may refer to a voluntary act, the omission of all reference to a missionary as responsible for it suggests that it was not such. However,

* Numbers enclosed in parentheses refer to the source-extracts in Part Two.

1

there is no way of determining whether it was simply a local affair or whether it points to the survival of Heraclius' policy (7).

Leo (III) the Isaurian, who decreed the next persecution, has gone down in Byzantine history, as a great and energetic ruler. In the sphere of religion the earliest recorded expression of his desire to enforce reforms, is the edict issued in his fifth regnal year (721-2), which prescribed baptism for all Jews and Montanists. In contrast to the latter, who are said to have burnt themselves in their churches as in Justinian's time, the former in part fled the empire, and in part submitted outwardly. These converts bore a special designation, which in one source is given as identical with that of the *Nuevos Cristianos* in Spain centuries later, while another has the variant term «New Citizens» (11). So garbled did this fact become in transmission that we find one chronicler asserting that the converts were called Montanists! (12) And the repetition of this confusion in a scholium to the «Formula of Abjuration» (published by Beneshevich), by no means weakens the absurdity (121). As for the refugees, there is reason to believe that they settled not only in the neighboring Moslem states but continued their journey until they reached distant Khazaria, where, however, the contemporary situation is extremely obscure (13).

Ordinarily one would assume that the edict remained in full force at least until the close of the emperor's reign. It so happens, however, that there is a clause in the Ecloga, a product of this administration, which provides capital punishment for Montanists and «Manichees» (Paulicians), whereas nothing is said in the code with regard to the Jews. Although the inherent weakness of an *argumentum e silentio* is not to be overlooked, it seems a reasonable hypothesis to take the date of the promulgation of the Ecloga (726 or 740 at the latest) as the *terminus ad quem* for the enforcement of the edict of 721-2, as affecting Jews. Indeed, it would be difficult to see how in a time filled with foreign attacks, and with domestic revolts due to the adoption of the iconoclastic policy in 725, sufficient administrative energy could be spared for the purpose (15). Nevertheless, the secret Jews against whose hypocrisy the eighth canon of the council of 787 was directed, were undoubtedly the descendants of the victims of Leo's edict, who apparently were inhibited by fear of the penalty for apostasy as well as by extra-legal forces. This reluctance of the children of the forced converts to revert to the open observance of their religion is understandable also on obvious psychological grounds, and by the analogy of the Marranos several hundred years later; some of the forced converts who left Spain found it to their economic advantage to retain their nominal Christianity. Similarly, judging from the canon of 787, some secret Jews of Byzantium used their cloak to carry on the slave-trade, which was forbidden to non-Christians (18).

A peculiar historiographical error is responsible for the notion that sometime during the years 786-809 a Byzantine emperor expelled his Jewish subjects. The source for this is ad-Dimashqī, who gives it in the name of Ibn al-Athīr. The latter's chronicle, however, says not a word of this matter and as has been shown by Marquart, the former writer really mis-cites al-Masʿūdī's statement regarding a tenth-century event. One need only compare the two passages to see that the later writer's chronological error is due to his telescoping of a point relating to the time of Hārūn ar-Rashīd with the subsequent Byzantine event, both of these occurring contiguously in his source (91).

The wave of missionary zeal which characterizes Byzantine history in the latter ninth and tenth centuries, as exemplified by the conversion of the Slavs, affected the internal situation of the empire as well. In the present study we are especially concerned with the efforts of Basil I to make his realm thoroughly orthodox. It is noteworthy that whereas he took violent measures against the Paulician heretics and shed much of their blood, his procedure as regards the Jews was much less drastic. First, in consonance with the spirit of the times, disputations were ordered

by the emperor, and his biographer leaves no doubt that atten-
dance on the part of the Jewish representatives was compulsory (69). That is the kernel, likewise, of the tradition which
relates that a Jewish scholar and communal leader, Shefatiah of
Oria, received a chrysobul from the emperor inviting him to call
at the palace (63).

It occasions little surprise to find that no pretense was made
of testing the respective claims of the two religions, but that the
emperor demanded rather that the Jews show cause why they
should not become Christians. In other words the «disputation»
was a formal prelude to the inauguration of the new policy. Our
Jewish chronicler, Ahima'as, has preserved the legendary memo-
ries of this phase of Basil's operations in his accounts of Shefatiah's experiences as a guest in the imperial court, (64-5) and of
the attempt made by the «bishop» of Oria to convert his (Shefatiah's) brother (68). But despite the unfair character of the disputation, it is nevertheless remarkable to what lengths Basil went,
offering appointments to office and exemption from taxation to
all voluntary converts, before resorting to the secular arm. Of
course, one should not be misled by the tendencious emphasis on
this short-lived policy of persuasion and the glossing over of the
subsequent, less palatable measures, which certain sources (69-70)
reveal. Yet it is entirely plausible that the emperor and his ad-
visers should first have hoped and worked for a conversion by
persuasion, accompanied by material rewards, which are, indeed,
well paralleled by the advantages proffered by law to converts
from Islam (69 n.), as well as by the advice once given by Pope
Gregory I. It is relevant also to note that this element of voluntary acceptance of Christianity is given a prominent role in a
Western writing, though only as a romantic sequel to the baptism *per vim* (72).

The contemporary tract by Gregorios Asbestas, then metropolitan of Nicaea, indicates that the Jews who actually accepted
the emperor's proposition were sufficiently numerous to evoke

this lengthy document protesting against the entire procedure. In view of the fact that both Church and State had had previous experience with Jews who by force of circumstances outwardly professed Christianity, the writer has little difficulty in showing that the current policy was utterly at variance with the civil and ecclesiastical law. But who would heed an exposure of official hypocrisy, when the only alternative was a policy of toleration which had been definitely repudiated for the third time in Byzantine history? (74) Indeed, when two centuries later it was deemed expedient to convert the Bogomiles, the emperor Alexios achieved his aim by means of the same inducements (69 n.).

There is some disagreement in the sources as to the precise year in which the policy of compulsion was inaugurated. According to Ahīma'as, it took place in 868, which is a suspicious figure since it marks the year 800 of the era of the fall of Jerusalem, as the chronicler himself notes (63). Moreover, how could the government even attempt to enforce such a policy in southern Italy, the region to which that writer has particular reference, since it was dominated until 871 by a strong Moslem chieftain, Saudan by name? (56) A Greek chronicler puts the decree ambiguously in the seventh and eighth regnal years (874-6), and this agrees substantially with the more precise annalist of southern Italy or Sicily who succinctly records the baptism as of 873-4 (61).

The inaccuracy noted in our Hebrew chronicler is not the only one respecting this period. Thus, he is content with the approximate figure of twenty-five years as the space of time which elapsed between 868 and Basil's death in 886 (76). But the tradition on which he was dependent took even greater liberties with the facts, for he does not scruple to assert that the emperor exempted Oria from the persecution, in compliance with a request from Shefatiah (66, 76). This gave rise to a derivative tradition, known before the publication of the chronicle Ahīma'as by Neubauer, which expanded this exemption to include five communities, and one is not surprised to see that the entire story was long ago rejected by Graetz (67). Curiously enough, the chronicler elsewhere inconsistently allows allusions, oblique yet unmistakable, to the outward acceptance of Christianity by the Jews of Oria to slip into his narrative (76, 80). It is only recently that the tenor of this material was made clear by Sonne, who also brought it into relation with certain lines in two recently published poems by Shefatiah's son Amittai, where the reference to the enforcement of the persecution is in no way open to question (62). Indeed, there can no longer be the slightest shadow of a doubt as to the unhistorical content of the tale of Oria's exemption.

The tendency of tradition to exaggerate, of which a sample has just been cited, also manifests itself in a late description of the great physical cruelty with which the emperor's orders were executed upon recalcitrants, who are said to have been crushed in an olive-press (67). And in another, less remote source we read that Basil first baptized the Jews against their will and then sold them into slavery. This, a late Byzantine-Jewish tradition, seems to indicate that many of the converts were punished for their insincerity by being made *servi pœnæ* (71). But if this be historical, why is there no hint of it in the earlier source-material, which is relatively abundant? Despite the willingness of certain scholars to take it as literal fact, this particular item is most likely another traditional exaggeration.

The remaining problem in this connection is that of duration: did the death of Basil in 886 mark the discontinuance of his policy? There is, indeed, a formal enactment among the Novels of his son and successor Leo VI, which is intended to perpetuate the outlawry of Judaism (84), but its purely legalistic import becomes apparent when it is confronted by contradictory evidence from both sides. The relapse of the forced converts after the death of Basil is noted by his biographer, who is believed to be the son of Leo (77), and the Jewish sources go so far as to say that the new emperor explicitly revoked his father's decree (78-79). In the first half of the tenth century there occurred a fourth imperial attempt to enforce conversion. It was initiated by Romanos I (919-44), who is said also to have persecuted the Armenians and to have christianized his Moslem captives (91). His policy was continued into the reign of his successor, and was apparently initiated about the year 930, although it must not be overlooked that this chronology is derived from a source of dubious character. According to this Latin account the emperor's decree was inspired by the patriarch of Jerusalem, and he would, moreover, have us believe that the miracles related in his letter effected a voluntary conversion of the Jews. A more sober notice than this occurs in al-Mas'ūdī, who wrote, however, in the final year of Romanos' reign without furnishing us with the initial date of the event. It is known both from this historian and from a Jewish source that the emperor's policy caused a considerable migration to Khazaria (91-2), and it is the aspect of expulsion only which is recorded by a late Jewish writer, who, moreover, credits the emperor with «mercifulness» in his procedure (93).

Inasmuch as Ahīma'as says nothing of this, one would have assumed that it affected Byzantine Italy little, if at all. But the local situation is fortunately illumined by a contemporary letter which the community of Bari sent to the distinguished Jewish figure at Cordova, Hasdai Ibn Shaprūt, in response to his inquiry. The document relates the sorrowful events of the two days in which the emperor's decree was executed in Bari and Otranto, then the leading Jewish centers of that region. Prominent Jews were put to death in both places, and Hebrew writings were burned in the former, from which a timely warning was despatched to the latter (84). After receiving such news, one would *a priori* assume that the influential Hasdai, whose government is known to have had relations with Romanos, interceded on behalf of his coreligionists. And, indeed, Mann has lately published a letter which fits the situation remarkably well, although its chronological relationship to the previous one is problematic. Both salutation and signature are lost, but it is clearly written by a man in authority in Cordova to a Christian female ruler, requesting that the practice of the Jewish religion be permitted in the latter's realm as was that of the Christian faith in the writer's state. What interpretation can be offered other than Mann's?—viz., that this was sent by Hasdai to the Empress Helena, whose husband, Constantine VII, nominally assumed the control of the state after Romanos, and to whose intellectual interests the document alludes? (99)

If this astounding discovery be accepted, we shall be in a position to understand the commendation of Constantine for his conversion of Jews in a passage hitherto unnoticed. This achievement of his was clearly of a different order from the attempts to convert the heretics, for which he is likewise lauded there (96).

The foregoing material represents all that is known at present with regard to the spasmodic withdrawal of the status of toleration which, in greater or lesser degree, the Jews of the empire normally enjoyed during this period. The sum of the years in question does not exceed fifty out of the three hundred which elapsed between the death of Heraclius and the probable time of the discontinuance of the persecution initiated by Romanos. This was followed by a stretch of more than two and a half centuries of undisturbed toleration, generally speaking, before the arrival of the Latins in 1204 and the vicissitudes of the ensuing generation brought still another imperial attempt to drive Judaism out of Byzantium. With respect to the period falling within the direct scope of the present work, it is thus clear that 90% of it was free from general and serious persecution. It has, moreover, been seen that the three emperors who manifested anti-Jewish tendencies, did not single out their Jewish subjects as most deserving of oppression, but treated other dissident groups, such as the Paulicians, with at least an equal degree of harshness.

Another and less serious form which intolerance occasionally assumed, is the expulsion or the exclusion of the Jews from some locality. The eminent Byzantine examples of this phenomenon, however, occurred in the period preceding the seventh century in Alexandria, Antioch, and Constantinople proper. The few record-ed instances after the sixth century seem to have been rather less serious. In the latter tenth century the monk Nikon came to Greece from an eastern province and persuaded the residents of Sparta to expel the Jews. But this was considered an extraordin-ary step, and did not meet with the unanimous approval of the townsfolk (115). In Chios in 1062 it was found desirable for reasons unknown to exclude any new Jewish settlers, although at the same time those already resident there were forbidden to leave (147). In the next century the archbishop Niketas of Kho-nai (Phrygia) refused to tolerate Jews in his city. For this he was commended by his eulogist, the illustrious Michael Choniates, a native of that place, and later archbishop of Athens, which was likewise a city without Jews (176).

Much less clear is the Slavonic monastic tradition, according to which the emperor (Alexios I?) was provoked at the end of the eleventh century by the unbridled behavior of the Jews of Cher-son so that he ordered drastic measures against them. For one of these Jews is said to have crucified his slave, the monk Eustratios, and the local eparch, a false convert from Judaism, winked at this as well as at the illicit possession of Christian slaves in general. In consequence thereof these two men were put to death to-gether with the elders of the community. All the other Jews were banished from Cherson and their property confiscated (155).

Summing up the external history of Byzantine Jewry during these centuries, it will be recalled that they suffered three serious waves of persecution and a number of more frequent local diffi-culties. How in the latter tenth century the various communities proceeded to rehabilitate themselves, we are not informed. Doubt-less the general attitude of the surrounding population was a distinct hindrance in this process. Yet the situation, far from being hopeless, was entirely comparable to that prevailing in other parts of the world. In the ensuing chapters it will be seen that the Jews of the empire successfully adapted themselves to their opportunities as well as to their limitations and led, on the whole, a «normal» medieval Jewish life.

CHAPTER II

TAXATION

There is no doubt that as far as the early Byzantine empire is concerned the Jews were required to pay a special tax. However, following the interruption in this discrimination under Julian the Apostate there is a lacuna in our information. Then Theodosius II while abolishing the office of the Patriarch by the act of 429 provided that the collection of the revenue enjoyed by that dignitary, the *aurum coronarium,* be continued for the benefit of the fisc. This imperial constitution was included as a matter of course in Justinian's *Corpus* and again three centuries later in the Nomocanon (**14 n.**). But neither of these repetitions is convincing evidence that the act of 429 was enforced in the seventh century and later.

Generally speaking, it was the normal thing for Jews during the Middle Ages to be required to pay a special tax, such as the *Jizyah* in the Islamic world, or one of the various levies collected in the domains of Latin Christians. With regard to the Byzantine Empire the question has been debated at some length by the late Prof. Andréadès and by Dölger. The discussion resulted in the former scholar's acceptance of the latter's theory that the situation in the empire was demonstrably no different in this respect from that obtaining elsewhere. Nevertheless, the existence of a special Jewish tax *within the limits of the period 641-1204* is still open to question. It is significant that Dölger, while arguing in the affirmative, does not maintain that this tax, unlike those collected from Jews elsewhere, was always designed to bring in revenue; it was upon occasion, if not regularly, a mere «Rekognitionsabgabe». Furthermore, both of the scholars named have fallen into the serious error of neglecting to separate the material relating to the period prior to the advent of the Latins from that of the thirteenth to fifteenth centuries. Thus, in citing the later evidence they failed to allow for the greatly changed conditions which distinguish the two periods from one another, so that even if it be true that a special Jewish tax was collected after the Fourth Crusade and the infiltration of the Latins, it need not have been so under earlier Byzantine rule. Indeed, if, in accordance with the limited scope of the present study, we confine our reconsideration of the evidence to the years 641-1204, we shall see that there is at present no sound basis for Dölger's theory.

The earliest item is a tendencious passage concerning the iconoclastic emperor Michael II (820-9), who is accused of having so loved the Jews that he exempted them from taxation (28). An adequate interpretation of this calumny would involve us in a digression on the relation of the Jews to the iconoclastic movement (9) and to the sect of Athinganoi, from whom this emperor sprung, (20) all of which is discussed in more appropriate connections. Critical study shows that such material is quite untrustworthy, but aside from that question, both the wording and general context of the passage under consideration indicate that the writer is thinking of nothing other than the usual taxes to which the general population was then subject. As for Dölger's contention that it refers to the abolition of the special tax, such an interpretation fails to explain the unqualified use of the common φόροι. Moreover, it is precisely the same word which is used in connection with the offer of Basil I to the voluntary converts (62). Asbestas, a contemporary prelate, describes and undoubtedly exaggerates the heavy burden which the unconverted Jew had to carry, but he too employs a colorless term, δημοσιακᾶ, apparently denoting the same oppressive taxation to which all were subject. For with any other interpretation, how is one to account for the tax-free life led by the convert, so glowingly described by the same writer? If conversion carried with it exemption only from the special Jewish tax, what of the regular and irregular levies to which every ordinary Christian was subject? It was rather immunity from the latter which Basil held out to the Jews, and he apparently rewarded the converts (or merely some of them?) by placing them in the privileged class which drew an income from the state and paid no taxes (74).

We have, however, for the same century contradictory evidence in the well-known description of the empire by Ibn Khurdādhbah. The lost source on which he drew, (a certain al-Jarmī, who had spent some years in the country) manifests its reliability in mentioning the existence of a general hearth-tax, the καπνικόν, which amounted to the equivalent of six dirhems *per annum*. But directly preceding this statement there occurs the rather amazing remark that the government levies an additional annual tax of one *dinar* ($^1/_2$ nomisma?) not only on the Jews but on on the Magians as well! No suspicion has heretofore been cast on this statement, with the exception of Ostrogorsky's casual rejection of it, chiefly because the study of it has been hampered by an antiquated translation in which *majūs* was rendered «pagans». Although even in that form its value might well be challenged, its affinity to an extra-Byzantine principle is thereby obscured. For in the original text and in de Goeje's accurate rendering, one cannot fail to recognize the widely known law of Islam which prescribed that a poll-tax *(jizyah)* be paid by Christians, Jews, and Magians. In our passage it appears simply to have been projected into the empire, *omisso omittendo* (44). One may, of course, argue with considerable justification that despite the suspicious form of the statement, it does have real value for our purpose in indicating that our author or his source was aware of a special tax on non-Christians, considerably greater than the *kapnikon*. But this type of evidence is ambiguous at best, and the confirmation or rejection of our passage consequently depends on the relevant material from other sources, to the continued discussion of which we may now proceed.

We must skip to the middle of the eleventh century for further data. When Constantine IX founded a monastery ('H Νέα Μονή) on Chios, he took care to endow it with an ample and regular income, effectively safeguarded by chrysobuls of unequivocal content. Thus, when he assigned to it the *kapnikon* payable by the local (Christian) serfs (πάροικοι), he at the same time prohibited any official from collecting any other levy from them. Then, since the island contained fifteen Jewish families, who are explicitly referred to as free here as were the rest of their coreligionists in the empire, and who had been paying, presumably to the fisc, a family-tax termed κεφαλητιῶν (capitation-tax), he transferred this income also to the monastery, and provided the same safeguards (**143**). Thereafter, successive emperors renewed this grant, and in one instance this was done in response to the monks' request (**147, 151**). It is very likely, moreover, that the *gulgolet* paid by the contemporary Jews of Thessalonica, refers to the *kephalétiôn* also (**153**). Once again we find an oblique allusion to a tax so-named in a peculiar passage written in the early twelfth century by Zonaras. He states that Leo III once imposed new taxes on the Calabrians and Sicilians, compelling them to pay the *kephalétiôn* «like the Jews». The chronicler's source is known to be a parallel passage in Theophanes where however, no such term is employed. Here instead of the contemporary Jews only Pharaoh's Hebrew slaves figure, so that no one has been tempted to apply Zonaras' words to the Jews of the eighth century. But does it prove, as Dölger maintains, when combined with the Chios documents, that *kephalétiôn* by the eleventh century had come to denote a special Jewish tax?

As has been seen, Zonaras' statement calls for some literary criticism before it can be used, and if the second step in that process be taken, we shall see that it undermines Dölger's theory completely. For the chronicler's *kephalétiôn* is borrowed from the parallel passage in Kedrenos, his older contemporary, who uses it, as do some others, unequivocally in the sense of capitation-tax, and who omits Theophanes' Biblical reference. It is clear then that since the term connoted nothing pertaining to the Jews to the earlier of the two who drew on that chronicle, we have no reason to assume that it was known to the slightly later writer as the designation of a special Jewish tax. Thus, the *prima facie* value of Zonaras' testimony, once it has been properly analyzed, vanishes into thin air. It represents nothing more than the artificial combination of a phrase in Theopanes with one in Kedrenos (**14**).

But this does not dispose of the application of the term in question to the tax paid in Chios, which, it should be noted, was assessed per family, rather than per head, notwithstanding the etymology. Dölger has laid a certain amount of stress on the fact that it recurs in both the renewals of the original grant of Constantine IX, although the repetition in all likelihood indicates simply that the notary was following the line of least resistance. That scholar has, however, a stronger argument in the fact that the official documents use a large variety of fiscal terms, among which *kephalétiôn* fails to appear except in the chrysobuls given to the Nea Moné. The difficulty caused by this specialized use is a serious one, yet Dölger's solution, as has been seen, fails to check with the other relevant data. It is, moreover, of some significance that when the Jews of Zichna in 1333 paid a *collective* annual tax to the local monastery, no technical name was bestowed upon it (**151n.**). Similarly in the middle of the twelfth century the tax due from the (individual) Jews of Strobilos, was re-assigned to the famous church of St. Sophia in Constantinople, and was payable even by those who had removed elsewhere. But this is given merely as a brief item in the course of a long enumeration and not even the simple word «tax» appears in it (**181**). Although these two instances are of opposite import, they equally expose the weakness of Dölger's position. Finally, reverting to the case of Chios, it is not likely, as he believes, that the *kephalétiôn* was but a small sum paid as a formality. The exemption of these

Jews from outside exploitation precisely as the local *paroikoi*, indicates that like the latter's *kapnikon* it was a genuine source of revenue.

The recent publication of a source which illuminates the fiscal situation in Cyprus in the first two decades of the twelfth century, has afforded Dölger another opportunity to adduce evidence in support of his thesis. It appears that the incumbent Dux of that theme, with the διοικητὴς as adjutant, did not scruple to force taxes out of the local clergy. Undoubtedly such an undertaking would not be relished by the minor officials, who as pious Christians would be prone to spare their priest and bishops. In order to overcome this obstacle the Dux is said to have resorted to bringing in Jews from elsewhere into the island to help in the tax-collecting. Now the foregoing data are derived not from a matter-of-fact prose account but from a composition in verse in which the meaning is veiled and obscured by rhetoric. The resultant ambiguity is particularly troublesome in the lines alluding to the work of these Jews, in which the writer complains that the administration heaps huge tax-assessments upon «them», and leaves his reader somewhat perplexed as to whom he means. The general tenor, however, requires the clergy to be considered the sufferers here, yet Dölger claims that the Jews were the ones meant by our author, and since they were «mit unzähligen Gelden von dem Steuerbeamten bestochen», they worked toward the prosecution and punishment of the clergy. Although it is difficult o see how this would have lessened the former's burden, such at situation is perhaps conceivable where resident Jews are involved, but can hardly be true where specially employed persons are brought in from outside for the specific function of executing orders on the clergy. Once more Dölger has supported his theory with an unsound interpretation (**165**).

In addition to the foregoing material there are in our sources, a handful of references to taxation which have no bearing on the problem just discussed. In the latter part of the twelfth century

Benjamin of Tudela, in his description of the capital of the Empire, notes that the annual tax which is delivered there every year consists not only of gold but also of garments of silk and purple. Elsewhere he tells us that the Jews of Thebes, Thessalonica and Constantinople, were engaged in the manufacture of this expensive apparel, which, incidentally, certain scholars believe was made under the emperor's monopoly. At any rate, we have here evidence of a tax in kind paid by the Jewish artisans of those cities, in common with their Christian fellow-craftsmen (182). There are also allusions to the special levy, ἐπήρεια, which some official would collect upon occasion in the locality under his jurisdiction, and which would, of course, be paid by the Jews there (111, 143).

There has recently been published by Mann an incomplete letter which tells of an internal disturbance in an unnamed community between the Rabbinites and Karaites. The latter are said to have slandered their opponents to the civil authorities, as a result of which the Rabbinites were fined about 1000 ὑπέρπερα (? 125). It is also necessary to note in this connection that the word 'onashim, which occurs in a document referring to Thessalonica, has been taken by some to denote a penal payment of this type. But although this meaning accords with the etymology of the word, it must not be overlooked that for Arabic-speaking Jews, among whom the writer in question is to be included, 'onashim signifies simply tax in general (153).

In the light of the foregoing discussion it seems appropriate to infer that the Jew's tax burden during these centuries was no greater than the Christian's. Apparently his economic position under Byzantine rule (see Ch. IV) did not invite special exploitation by the fisc.

CHAPTER III

LEGAL ASPECTS

The status of the Jews, insofar as their rights and disabilities *de iure* were concerned, had been fixed before this period by a considerable number of laws. These had been enacted from time to time by successive emperors since the empire's inception, and were transmitted to later generations as part of Justinian's great Corpus. During the various phases of the history of later Byzantine law, undergone subsequently, the individual provisions governing the position of the Jews were for the most part repeated in various codes and manuals, as will soon appear. As for the minor changes which inevitably occurred, traces are found to some extent both in those sources and in the extra-legal materials as well. Thus, it will be possible in some degree to check, supplement, and modify our information on the *de iure* status with the aid of sources bearing on the state of affairs *de facto*.

We may begin by considering the several political and economic restrictions known to us. Although the contemporary Islamic states and some of the Latin ones, overcame their scruples against admitting Jews to public office, Byzantine law did not relax this prohibition (**19, 75, 83**), nor do any genuine instances of its evasion appear. Some have, indeed, assumed Manuel Commenus' adviser and Latin secretary, Aaron Isaakios, to be a Jew because of his name, which, however, is no proof whatever. (Exc. D) As for the contemporary tax-official, Astafortis, whom the emperor brought with him from Hungary, it is true that he was by birth a Jew, but he appears on the scene only after his conversion. (Exc. F) The employment of Jews as tax-collectors in Cyprus earlier in the century is an isolated phenomenon, and in view of the special circumstances discussed above, need not be considered a real violation of the law on the part of the administrative officials (165).

Another disability affected the ownership of and traffic in Christian slaves (19, 83). This seems to have been more successfully suppressed in Byzantium than in the other Christian states of the early Middle Ages, since there are but two references to its circumvention, viz., on the part of the secret Jews of the latter eighth century (18), and in distant Cherson toward the year 1100 (155). If there were any other restrictions directed against the Jews *per se,* they have yet to be found, for the remaining few which affected them, included orthodox Christians as well. Thus, in the prohibition of the sale of raw silk to merchants who might export it from the capital, the Jews are specifically included, but obviously because they were so prominent among the illicit exporters of this material (108). The situation is even clearer with respect to the chrysobul of 992, in which the Venetian ships were forbidden to carry Jewish traders from Bari in order to prevent the defrauding of the customs, for the law explicitly applied to the Christian merchants of Italy as well (117).

As far as is known, freedom of occupation was but rarely denied. The Church occasionally attempted to deprive Jewish physicians of their Christian clientele, notably by a canon passed in 692 (8), but there is reason to doubt its effectiveness. Our evidence regarding its violation is limited, however, to two instances, both involving practitioners of extraordinary ability who served an important official in Italy (107) and the emperor Manuel I (182), respectively. Apart from this restriction there is only to note that a twelfth-century prelate in Phrygia seems to have forced the Jews into certain lower types of work (176).

The sole restriction on the ownership of real estate was the law prohibiting the possession or management by a Jew of a plot on which a church stood (83). The contrast with feudal Europe in this respect will be evident to all students of medieval history.

Juridically we have a larger body of indications of the Jew's inferior status. His person and property were protected by law, but whereas a Christian plaintiff against a thief would be awarded three or four times the amount of damages, the Jew was entitled only to twice the value (83). Undoubtedly in practice, there were cases where the local court refused to enforce the law, as happened in Bisignano in the latter tenth century. Here a Jewish merchant was robbed and murdered, but the criminal got away. Thereupon a relative of his, as proxy, was turned over to the Jewish authorities for execution. But under the moral pressure of the revered monastic figure, Nilos, the sentence was annulled. However, we need hardly take seriously his alleged demand that seven Jews must die before a Christian could be executed for this crime. It is an interesting speculation whether Nilos would have interceded in the same manner on behalf of the murderer himself, and if he had, whether it would have had the same effect (105). We get a rather different impression from a civil case of the twelfth century in Attaleia. Here the plaintiff, a convert, sued certain local Jews who had seized his father's home and its contents, and recovered the former only after appealing to the emperor. By that time the articles it once held were gone (167), and the πράκτωρ before whom the second phase of the case was tried, dismissed the complaint, accepting the defendants' denial of the charge of having taken possession of them. Again the plaintiff appealed to the emperor, but the rescript he received was not such as to be of much service to him. He does accuse the *praktôr* of having been bribed, but while that is one explanation of his failure to win the suit, it is not necessarily the most likely one (171).

The testimony of a Jewish witness was not admitted against a Christian (83). The Byzantine jurists, moreover, are to be credited with the introduction of the oath *more Iudaico* into Christian court procedure, where it survived well into modern times. There is no definite proof that the Greek text and its Latin derivatives are earlier than their Islamic counterpart, which is reputed to have been drawn up *ca.* 800, yet there is no reason to believed that the Christian oath is traceable to foreign influence. The original form prescribes that the litigant gird himself with bramble and pronounce, Torah-scroll in hand, a brief and restrained declaration of his honesty. The maledictions with which it concludes have their parallels in other contexts, and the entire formula may be as old as the latter sixth century. Actually, however, it does not appear until the twelfth, by which time it had already made its way westward. It comes as a citation from the Ἐπαρχικὸν Βιβλίον, which is an indication of its antiquity, although it is not included in the well-known writing so named which was discovered by Nicole, and which in its extant form is usually assigned to the tenth century (**108, 109**). It appears that outside of the area under the jurisdiction of the prefect of Constantinople, the oath was known in modified form. The one preserved in a manual compiled for southern Italy during the Norman regime, is somewhat more abusive than that just mentioned, but the longer one which the convert of Attaleia proffered the defendants, is drafted in a much more insulting style. Indeed, the emperor in his rescript refrained from supporting the demand that this oath be pronounced by the Jews, but directed the petitioner to substitute instead the one known in the capital (**171**).

In this connection it should be noted that in the eleventh and a good part of the succeeding century, cases involving Jews in Constantinople were by custom tried only by an official of the suburb in which they resided, the στρατηγὸς τοῦ Στενοῦ. It is easy to see why the custom should have grown up, and we may infer from the title of the officer that it is not older than the latter tenth century, i. e., the generation following Romanos' persecution. This limitation of judicial access was abolished by the emperor Manuel Comnenus, apparently as part of his reform of the administration of the courts in the capital, which he instituted in 1166 (**172**). This seems to be a more likely explanation than an hypothesis which would view the change as prompted by some

special consideration directed either in favor of or against the Jews.
We have a few instances in which the authorities are known
to have taken advantage of the Jews' weaker position, as in the
Bisignano affair cited above. In the same region, somewhat over
a century earlier, there is a story of the cruel fate of Teofilo at
the hands of the governor of Oria. The two men had entered into
an informal contract, whereby the official saved the Jew's life on
the promise that he would undergo conversion. Then when the
latter proved recalcitrant, he was flogged, mutilated, and finally
cast into prison to die (52). As for the two additional occasions
on which we find Jews in prison, we know nothing whatever
regarding the circumstances surrounding one of them (125), while
the other one, a certain Israel b. Nathan from Egypt, was apparently arrested in the capital as were other aliens who could not satisfactorily account for their presence to the bureau concerned (146).

The individuals connected with the central government
showed themselves now and then apt to trample on one or the
other of the rights of the Jews, when it suited their purpose. This
is well illustrated in the closing generation of this period by the
burial in the cemetery of the Constantinople Jewish community
of one who was not only outside the faith, but who had been
executed as a criminal (190). Of greater significance is the
procedure of the agents of Michael VII, successor to the ill-
fated Romanos IV. As is well-known, the latter was seized at
Kotyaion upon his liberation by the Seljuqs, to be rendered
harmless to the new emperor by being blinded, in the traditional
Byzantine manner. For this purpose a local Jew was drafted, and
he, being without previous experience in such operations, carried
out the imposed task in a manner that caused great pain to the
victim, as had occurred on many similar occasions. Now it happens
that for the thirteenth to fifteenth centuries there are an impres-
sive number of parallels to this procedure, in which Byzantine
Jews and others in neighboring countries, were customarily compelled to execute mutilations and death-sentences. Certain scholars

have expressed the opinion that this originated in the empire and was thence adopted by the surrounding Christian and Moslem states. A full discussion of this problem extends chronologically beyond our scope, but as far as the earlier period is concerned, there is no basis for assuming that Jews were regularly drafted for this gruesome business. But on the other hand, when a high official chose to perpetrate this as well as other abuses, there was evidently no redress (151).

The social and religious aspects of the Jewish problem also concerned the legislators, both civil and ecclesiastical. The council of 692, while repeating the older prohibition of participating in the Passover celebration, also forbade associating with Jews in general, and the use of Jewish physicians and the practice of joint bathing in particular (8). Intermarriage had before this time been made tantamount to adultery, i. e., subject to capital punishment (83). These restrictions are all bound up with the fact that Judaizing was a crime not only for the Jew involved as missionary, but for the apostate as well. The former is threatened with death in some texts for a mere attempt in this direction, but this is effectively contradicted by the law which prescribed nothing more drastic than confiscation of property and banishment for him who actually made a convert. The circumcision of a Christian infant was, however, punishable by death. As for the apostate, his penalty continued to be confiscation (19, 83). The punishment of the convert from Judaism who relapsed, a problem that goes back perhaps to the reign of Constantine the Great (84 n.), is held out as an indefinite threat (84, 121); hence, it might be presumed to be the same as for simple apostasy, (witness Justinian's law respecting the Samaritans) but there is evidence in the legal sources that it was more severe. In the late sixth century Theodoros of Hermopolis ruled that to the confiscation of property must be added banishment, and in Leo VI's Novel 65 the penalty is specified as death, although there is no explicit reference to the Jews (84 n.).

The status of the Jewish cult had aspects some of which were unfavorable, but in general it was superior to the lot of the heretical sects. Thus, it had always been forbidden by law to disturb a synagogue, and like a church, it was exempt from the quartering of soldiers. On the other hand, the prohibition of the construction of new synagogues threatened to prevent the expansion of the Jewish population (83). At the beginning of our period the enforcement of this law by the archbishop of Syracuse is related (4), but it stands out as an act of great piety on his part, and we have ample reason to believe that, on the whole, it remained a dead letter. For otherwise the effects would not have passed unnoticed in the history of the Jews in the empire. Moreover, in the eleventh century Elisha bar Shinaya, a Nestorian theologian in Nisibis, emphasized the freedom of these Jews to erect synagogues, in contrast to the suppression of his own sect (131). As for interference in the system of worship, for which Justinian had set the precedent in Novel 146, no hint of this appears, with the exception of the archaistic inclusion of that law in a later code (83).

The observance of the Sabbath and the holidays took precedence over the rights of the court authorities, and from the standpoint of the law even the practice of circumcision was a privilege. On the other hand, polygamy, which was permitted and under certain circumstances prescribed by Jewish law, was not tolerated (83).

The various local and general persecutions to which Byzantine Jewry had been exposed between the fourth and tenth centuries, had created for the law and the Church the problem of regulating the admission of converts. Since the end of the fourth century (397) the secular law had declared that any ulterior motive disqualified a Jew seeking conversion (83). One might have expected with time that an extended catechumenate would have been prescribed in order to ensure sincerity, as was the case with regard to the Samaritans, of whom Justinian and his successor demanded a two-year period (**3 n.**). The Church, indeed, had by the sixth century developed a brief formula of abjuration to be recited before the sacrament of baptism was performed, and which contemporaneously or somewhat later was required of various types of converts other than Jews as well (**121 n.**). But on the whole it appears that the trend of the times was otherwise, and, as we have seen, some of the later emperors showed themselves determined to bring about mass-conversions with complete disregard of the hypocrisy on both sides. It is likely, however, that by the end of the tenth century the ecclesiastical party which was opposed to this procedure (**18, 74**), finally won out. And it is in this period that we find a more elaborate formula prescribed for converts from Judaism. The discussion of the contents of this document belongs, however, to a different division of our study (**121**). (See Ch. VII.)

Another provision with respect to converts, was the law which protected them against mistreatment by their former co-religionists (**83**). That there was occasional necessity for such protection is attested in the life of the ninth century convert, Constantine, who resided in Asia Minor (**54**).

All these details taken together enable us to arrive at a generalized view of the extent of the toleration of Jews in the empire. It is clear that the restrictions and disabilities both *de iure* and *de facto* were relatively numerous, although not invariably of great significance. Dölger has attempted to sum the matter up by calling attention to the term ἄτιμοι, which the biographer of Basil I applies to the Jews (**77**). It implies, he asserts, that their status was comparable to that of the Roman citizen who had suffered by *capitis deminutio (media)* the loss of his major rights. In a word, the Byzantine Jew was declassed. This view comes perhaps as close as any generalization can, to doing justice to all the facts, although it does require some modification. The word ἄτιμοι, in the first place, appears from the context to be used in a limited sense, viz., «disqualified for public office» (τιμή). Indeed, the cognate verb is employed in the legal texts bearing on the matter (75). Secondly, in normal times, i. e., throughout 90% of our period, there was no interference with the fundamental rights of freedom of economic and communal life, as will appear from the discussion in the succeeding chapters. From the comparative viewpoint, if the lot of the Jew was here generally more difficult than under contemporary Islam, it was with certain exceptions limited in extent both in time and space, rather more attractive than the situation prevalent throughout Latin Christendom during these — and later — centuries.

CHAPTER IV

ECONOMIC ACTIVITIES AND POPULATION

The right of owning real property, a basic economic factor, came within the chronological span of this study to be entirely denied to the Jews of western and central Europe, and later even with respect to the Ghetto assigned to them in cities such as Frankfort and Venice. The material bearing on this factor for the empire is not abundant, but because the occurrence of Jews who own their estates and homes is random and casual, it is entirely safe to conclude that neither law nor custom withheld the right from them. The earliest instance of a family in possession of its urban dwelling appears in Mastaura in 1022 (**130**). Half a century later we find the community in Constantinople living in what were apparently their own wooden homes, which were destroyed by a conflagration during one of the frequent internecine conflicts (**150**). The evidence with respect to their contemporaries in Thessalonica is quite explicit (**153**), as it is also in twelfth-century Attaleia, where the litigation over a dwelling-house, recounted above, took place (**167**).

A similar situation exists in the matter of rural property. The wealthy and celebrated Amittai II at the beginning of the tenth century had a vineyard estate near Oria, to which he would retire in the manner of a Roman patrician (**81**). In the vicinity of nearby Taranto, we have two deeds of sale whereby a Theophylaktos-Shemariah in the fourth decade of the following century acquired two adjoining parcels of the same type of land from a Christian owner (**137, 138**). Finally, in Benjamin's time there lived a community of farmers on their own soil in Krisa (**182**).

With regard to occupational pursuits, the sources yield but a limited variety, considering the freedom of choice which seems to have prevailed. The ownership of land outside the towns implies, of course, some degree of agricultural activity, but Benjamin's note on the Jews of Krisa, nevertheless, cannot be duplicated. However, the villagers who in the ninth century came in their wagons to Venosa to spend the Sabbath there, were presumably farmers also (22). A general reference to the possession of domestic animals is perhaps another relevant hint (121).

It may be inferred that only a small percentage of the Jewish population lived and worked in rural districts, and, accordingly, considerably more information is available concerning their activities in the towns and cities. In view of the tenor of the canon of 692 in its protest against the consultation of Jewish physicians, the handful of later references to such occurrences is rather surprising. However, in the latter part of the tenth century, Shabbetai Donnolo seems to have been the leading practitioner in Byzantine Italy, and he apparently was in demand among the Christians (106), including Eupraxios, a resident official of high rank (107). One of his contemporaries, Abraham b. Sasson, was a prominent communal figure in Bari (95). It appears that the physician who was taken captive in the following century by Mediterranean pirates, was also a Byzantine Jew (129). Manuel's medical attendant, Solomon «the Egyptian», seems, however, to have been an immigrant (182).

Among the artisans of whom we have information, a limited number of crafts are represented. A rare example is that of the silversmith, Obadiah by name, who lived probably in Constantinople in the eleventh or twelfth century (125). The most frequent instances are branches of the textile industry. John Aratos of Sparta employed Jews as finishers of woven material in the latter tenth century (115). In Corinth, about the same time, there lived a certain Caleb the dyer (85), member of a craft which in other parts of the Mediterranean world attracted Jews to a remarkable extent. With regard to the related industry of weaving, no definite information is at hand, although it has been plausibly inferred that the group of Jews transplanted by the Normans to Sicily as a result of the raid of 1147, included silk-weavers, as did their Christian fellow-captives (173). However, when Benjamin speaks of the Jews of Thessalonica and Constantinople as being *'umanim shel meshi* and as engaged in *mele'ket ha-meshi,* he means not that they manufactured silk, as one would naturally suppose, but that they made garments of that stuff. For there is good reason to believe that the phrases in question are abbreviated from the complete form used by him with reference to the outstanding ability of the Jewish manufacturers of silk and purple garments in Thebes. It seems, moreover, that these were the goods which the Genoese vainly sought from the emperor for export. It should be noted finally that Michael Choniates alludes to the industry as practiced here about two decades later (182).

Dölger believes that he has detected in a passage in the tract of Asbestas evidence that the Jews were somehow driven into the loathsome occupation of tanning (74). This happens to be true of the region dominated by an antisemitic bishop of Chonai in the twelfth century (176), and had Dölger known of this situation he would no doubt have considered it a corroboration of his idea. Yet the superficial connection between the two seems quite illusory, for the language of Asbestas is clearly of a piece with the tone of utter contempt and disgust with which orthodox writers were wont to denounce both Jews and heretics. Other, even less complimentary, metaphorical allusions to the Jewish faith are made by that writer. Of a totally different tenor are the remarks of Benjamin on the tanners among the Jews of Constantinople, who committed the nuisance of spilling their stinking liquid into the street, thereby provoking the neighboring Christians to attack them. (182) Peculiarly enough in the garbled form which this assumed in Ibn Verga's *Shebet Yehudah,* the occupation of tanning is imposed by an emperor after a futile attempt at conversion by force. (176 n.)

Commercially the Byzantine Jews seem to have been fairly

active, although far less than those of other Christian countries, where the well-known restrictions caused such pursuits as banking and the used clothing trade to assume a role which is as a matter of fact alien to the scene which we are considering. The merchants who appear in the sources are of both the type which limits its trading to a short radius, and that which is concerned with commerce over long distances. Representatives of the former are found in the ninth century in such widely separated points as Nicaea (54) and Oria. In the latter instance we are told of a business trip which Shefatiah and his brother once made to Benevento (57), but in neither one do we find more concrete data. It is, however, relevant to note that Shefatiah is said to have been quite wealthy (76). For the same region we note during the following century, Elijah of Otranto (94), and the merchant of Bisignano who transported his goods on an ass (105). Benjamin tells somewhat of the merchants of Constantinople, including some who were rich, who would cross the Golden Horn to trade in the city proper (182). With regard to the other commercial centers which he visited and in which he found Jewish communities, one is obliged to fall back on conjecture with regard to their economic activities. There is a certain significance in the fact that the Jews are mentioned chiefly in the larger towns and in the cities of some commercial importance; to those mentioned above we may add Bari, Chalkis, Harmylos, Amorion, Synnada, Attaleia, Strobilos, Ephesus and Cherson. The only name conspicuous by its absence is Trebizond (45 n.). There is no doubt, however, that even if a large proportion of the Jewish population actually resided in the less important places, the sources would still probably refer more frequently to those in the larger towns.

In the latter seventh century certain Jews from Cappadocia (?) appear in Damascus, but we have no clue as to whether they were immigrants or merchants (7). Not until the twelfth century is there definite evidence of long-distance commerce, more hazardous and correspondingly more lucrative than the activities hitherto noted. A possible exception is indicated in the rule laid down by the prefect of Constantinople whereby the guild of dealers in raw silk were forbidden to sell that commodity either to Jews or to any other merchants who might smuggle it out of the city. The juxtaposition of simply « Hebrews » with « merchants » is significantly reminiscent of the phrase « Iudei et ceteri mercatores », which figures in the Frankish sources, but we have no way of determining whether the former refers to those who came to Byzantium from elsewhere, or whether it is directed against some local traders who exported the precious stuff when they could (108).

Reference has already been made to the apparent suppression of the traffic in slaves, and in this connection attention should be called to certain hagiographic and other sources in which Jewish slave-dealers appear on the periphery of the empire, viz., in Bulgaria and Venice at the close of the reign of Basil I, (136 n.) as well as in Bohemia in subsequent centuries. Thus a certain merchant is known to have been in Prag, a famous center for this traffic, in the early eleventh century. However, although he is designated in our Hebrew source as a « Greek » Jew, that term happens to be an amazingly ambiguous one in the vocabulary of the central and western European writers, and the individual in question may have hailed from some Slavic land, rather than from the empire. Again, although he figures as the ransomer of a Jewish slave, his proper work may have lain in some other branch, such as the trade in skins (136). At the end of the eleventh century the Jews of Cherson seem to have bought and perhaps sold Christian slaves with impunity. At any rate a group of 50 taken captive in the Polovtzian raid on Kiev in 1096 were sold to a Jew living in Cherson. This is recorded in connection with the martyrdom of Eustratios and the failure of the officers of the state to stop the illicit traffic is attributed to the fact that the local eparch was a secret Jew (155). It seems reasonable to conclude from the foregoing material that, whereas the slave-trade was not entirely unknown among Byzantine Jews, it could not be carried on by them within the empire except under rare circumstances. Just how prominent they were in this traffic in neighboring states is not yet clear.

With regard to another type of commercial activity rather firmer ground is furnished by certain letters from the Genizah in Cairo. All of the material relevant to this aspect of our subject has been treated by Mann, whose publications have made most of them available for the first time. These are practically all communal documents written in Alexandria, and are devoted to one pressing task, the ransom of captives from the Moslem pirates of the Mediterranean. Ordinarily some information regarding these persons is included, and in a number of instances it is either stated or implied that they were merchants. Relatively well represented are the Jews of Attaleia, although the form in which the name occurs, « the land of *Antāliyah* », has somewhat disguised the identity of their residence up to the present. During the third decade of the eleventh century ten of them were taken and deprived of their funds (128). The similar plight of another group of merchants is dated in the year 1028 (132). A third group whose number is unspecified was ransomed within the ensuing few years (133). Somewhat later, presumably, when some captives from Mastaura were in need of assistance, the resources of the Egyptian communities had given out, and a messenger was dispatched to their home-group to get the required funds (139). Another group of five youths came from a city *Istasbilo,* which may be the Arabic form of Pylae (εἰς τὰς Πύλας; 128 n.). At any rate, the existence of the foregoing specific references renders it highly probable that the documents in which the captives' provenience is given ambiguously as « Edom », i. e., Christendom, intend thereby to designate the Byzantine empire (129, 135, 148). Indication of the continuation of the same general situation is furnished by a twelfth-century account of the sum collected in ten Egyptian localities for the ransom of captives from *Rūm* (170).

It is relevant to note the strain which the Jewry of this region suffered as a result of all this. That it occasionally became too much for then is attested by the messenger sent to the home-community mentioned above. Even more illuminating is the remark of a certain Malīhah, who wrote to her brothers in Egypt, apparently in the twelfth century, to the effect that, as they well knew, a Byzantine Jew would quite frequently set out across the sea for the purpose of ransoming a relative (162).

The significance of this material in the present connection lies in the hints it affords of the extensive commercial travelling done by Byzantine-Jewish merchants across the Mediterranean, an aspect of our subject which had otherwise been unknown. Moreover, in the light of the fact that the dangers involved in it failed to deter them from this activity, we may infer that the economic inducement was a substantial one.

It is necessary, finally, to give some attention to the foreign Jews who are known to have traded in Byzantium. The well-known *Rādāniya* were apparently Orientals, some of whom would take their cargo of exotic commodities from China, and bring it to Constantinople. From that city they evidently carried out, legitimately or otherwise, the forbidden silk (45). We hear also of Jewish merchants who used the Venetian ships in transporting their goods from Bari to the capital, but together with the other competitors of Venice they had to abandon this route before the close of the tenth century, on account of the special arrangement between the empire and the republic (117). There was a section of the waterfront of the Golden Horn which appears at a late date under the style of « Hebraic wharf». The term σκάλα so qualified seems to indicate that before the eleventh century the foreign Jewish merchants used this area in the same manner as others nearby were utilized by Gentile merchants of various geographical groups, notably Italians and Russians (152). For the subsequent period we note how the aforementioned Malīhah invites her brothers to bring merchandise with them from Egypt, on their trip to her (162), and in another document the merchants from Russia, who appear in an unnamed city (125).

A legend concerning the conversion of a wealthy Jew in Constantinople during the reign of Heraclius is sometimes cited as evidence that money-lending as a pursuit was not unknown among the local Jews. However, in this narrative it is simply related that the Jew Abraham lent money to Theodore, a Christian shipmaster, and no interest is stipulated. Apparently the men were to share in the profits of the voyage, the cargo for which was purchased with the loan. Moreover, it must not be forgotten that under Byzantine law a legal rate on loans was prescribed, so that there was nothing to hinder banking operations without the services of non-Christians. The significant point of our legend, which seems to be of eighth-century authorship, is the fact that Theodore resorted to association with the Jew only when every other possibility had failed him (3 n.). Although the writer of this narrative was probably a clergyman rather than a merchant, we have as yet no reason to reject this indication that business partnerships with Gentiles were practically non-existent.

The problem of the approximate extent of the Jewish population in the empire, has been discussed by Andréadès, who was eminently qualified for the task because of his research both in a number of aspects of Byzantine-Jewish history, and in the statistical problem of the empire in general. We have ample reason to infer that the number of Jews reached its nadir during the persecution of Romanos I, which caused a migration for the third time in about two centuries. Hence, we need not place much stress on Elisha of Nisibis' statement that the empire within the following century tolerated a remarkably large Jewish population (131). In the meantime the relatively strong proportion which they undoubtedly constituted in Apulia, e. g., in Oria, and later in Bari and Otranto, must also have diminished during the ninth and tenth centuries, primarily as a result of the emigration and destruction caused by the Moslem invasions. Moreover, by the middle of the following century, the Jewry of southern Italy and Sicily had in the political sense, been completely eliminated from the empire. However, between this point and the time of Benjamin's visit about 1165 it may be assumed that the residue had increased to some extent.

The Spanish Jew's famous itinerary contains in Adler's text statistics for 25 communities, totaling 8691; he neglects to give the figures for three others which were visited (182). These statistics present a twofold problem, because of the facts that the manuscripts vary, and that it is not specified whether the writer intended his figures to denote individuals, families, or possibly taxpayers. In opposition to the usual view, it was the opinion of Andréadès that the figures for the empire, at all events, can scarcely denote families. He emphasized especially the fact that less than a century before Benjamin's visit to Chios, fifteen families lived there whereas his figure for the local community is 400. Taking this as a general total, it represents a fourfold increase, in itself rather unusual, and the rise becomes absolutely incredible if the number be taken to denote families (182). Hence, barring a textual or other irregularity we must view Benjamin's figures as estimates of the entire number of Jewish souls.

The largest Byzantine-Jewish community visited by Benjamin was that of Constantinople, where he found 2000 Rabbinite and 500 Karaite Jews, out of a total population estimated at half a million (140 n.). In Thebes he reported 2000 Jews, in Thessalonica 500, and in the other cities small groups ranging from 20 to 400 (182).

Although the value of Benjamin's statistics is problematic, they are practically our sole guide, and we must use them for what they are worth. At the same time it must be borne in mind that he says nothing regarding the inland communities of the European division, and likewise makes no reference to those in Asia Minor. There are several localities where we have reason to believe there were Jews at that time (Exc. E), and we must allow for these as well as for the three which he names without giving the figures. If then to the previously mentioned total of 8691 we add 2500 as a conservative allowance for those, we obtain approximately 12,000. This falls below Andréadès' estimate of 15,000, but it may be useful to keep the latter as a maximum. This should then be compared with the same scholar's opinion that the total population of the Empire at that time was fifteen million at the most (182n.). It may be objected that the foregoing computation has produced an unduly conservative result. It seems preferable, however, to stay close to the known facts pending further progress in investigation, which will undoubtedly add to our information; for future research may be trusted to discover additional communities and perhaps even to clarify the peculiar statistical problem presented by Benjamin's notes.

CHAPTER V

COMMUNAL AND SOCIAL LIFE

It is only in southern Italy that we are enabled to observe in any detail the forms which corporate Jewish life assumed on Byzantine territory. In Oria it is clear that both Shefatiah and his son were the recognized leaders in their community, by reason of wealth as well as personality and cultural attainments (80). Amittai, the former's father, had apparently occupied the local leadership before them (49). In the time of his grandson and namesake a committee of « elders » is also seen functioning, in the communal duty of burying a deceased stranger, but this did not deter their leader from exercising arbitrary power. It was in the same connection that a local pedagogue took occasion to murmur a parody on the dirge recited by Amittai, by way of voicing a protest against his administration. In consequence, as judge in a case that late arose, Amittai seized on a pretext and ordered a subordinate official, the *hazzan,* to pronounce the ban on his critic. The latter now had no recourse but to leave Oria (81). Amittai's position was apparently that of « head of the community », as the presiding officer of Bari is designated in the following generation (95).

It appears to have been the rule for the communal leadership to be vested in one whose learning had earned for him the title and prerogatives of rabbi, but it is too much to assume that the office was a paid one at this time. In the account of how Silano of Venosa assisted a guest-preacher from Palestine by rendering his Hebrew sermons into the vernacular, we have apparently a concrete example of rabbinical activity (22). Among the twenty-one tombstone inscriptions discovered from time to time at this

place, one refers to a man bearing that title (29), while otherwise merely the name is found (24, 26, 27, 30-35, 37, 40, 41, 43, 46).
At Brindisi an apparently contemporary epitaph celebrates the
memory of a local rabbi (37 n.). In Amittai's community (Oria) his
cousin Hasadiah was the senior rabbi, since Donnolo, who must
have known him as a child, terms him *ha-rab ha-gadol* (87). One
of his local colleagues also appears in Bari, but only after he had
resided there almost twenty years, following the sack of Oria
in 925 (88). The groups living in this region must each, of
course, have included a member who could be called upon when
the rite of circumcision had to be performed. A certain Menahem
Qorési, who performed this function in Otranto, is named among
the prominent men there. His father, judging from the title
parnas, which he bore, participated in the communal leadership,
presumably in the same city (89).

Like the vast majority of Jews in other lands, those of Byzantine Italy must have preferred to have the law-suits in which no
Christians were involved, tried by their own judges. Such, at any
rate, is the situation reflected in the story of the dispute between
one of Amittai's descendants and the rabbis of Bari over the
latter's family possessions, which ended in amicable compromise
(116). The local court is also known to have been consulted on a
question of Talmudic law, and the responsum which has been
preserved, is, as far as the present work is concerned, a unique
document. Its form is rather peculiar in that it is signed by seven
men, then countersigned as approved by six others, and then submitted to him who consulted the court, apparently a local
resident (120).

In principle the Jewish court of the Middle Ages had waived
jurisdiction over capital cases in order to avert a conflict with the
state. Yet in (Christian) Spain the latter is known to have permitted the Jewish authorities to try such cases and to execute the
death-sentence in the ninth century, and, if one may put any
stock in Eldad ha-Danī, the same privilege was exercised in

certain parts of contemporary Africa and Persia. Accordingly, the related material touching southern Italy, to be presented here, cannot be said to be *a priori* devoid of historical reality.

The local traditions included a miniature cycle of tales concerning a remarkable foreign scholar who visited Oria in the ninth century. This individual, Aaron of Bagdad, came fresh from the great centers of Jewish learning in Mesopotamia and Palestine, and during his Italian sojourn gave the impetus to a revival of a number of Jewish activities. For the present purpose let it suffice to note that he is depicted as sitting as judge at the trials of several criminals in Oria, who were sentenced to death in accordance with Jewish law, and who were duly executed by the Jewish community. Now, apart from the problems raised by the content of this story, its form is quite unhistorical, due to the fact that the narrator, Aḥīma'as, explicitly intended, by way of exaggerating Aaron's beneficial influence, to make of Oria a latter-day successor to Jerusalem as the seat of the Sanhedrin. Thus, the cases in the story are four in number, each punished by a different method of execution, in reminiscence of the traditional procedures, the *'arba' mitot bet-din*. (The fact that each offense was of a sexual kind is certainly only incidental to the main point.) The story becomes even more perplexing when we consider that the exercise of such powers in Aaron's homeland was never desired. The fact that two of the cases overlook the other criminal involved, in addition to the one tried, is understandable as the omission of elements not essential to the writer's theme (51). It is necessary to point out also that one of the condemned men escaped punishment through the intervention of the governor, who, however, is depicted as assuming that the community was acting within its rights (52).

Such material, it might be argued, cannot be said to have any historical value unless corroborated by more reliable data. But in its light, it is perhaps no mere coincidence that in a case cited in another connection, in which the proxy of a Jew's murderer was turned over to the Jewish authorities of Bisignano for execution, the scene is laid in the same Byzantine province. It is true that this Christian tale also contains a tendencious motif, and we cannot, for example, believe that the Jews intended to crucify the individual involved (105). But despite these various considerations, is it likely that such stories would have developed in regions where the Jews never possessed the power of trying and punishing capital offenders in their own ranks? On the contrary, we have reason to maintain that since the Spanish Jews exercised this unusual right, the available evidence indicates that their contemporaries in Byzantine Italy did likewise.

For the eleventh and twelfth centuries the signs of communal activity are comparatively sparse. As earlier in the western province, rabbinical leaders are mentioned here and there, e. g., Elijah b. Shabbetai, apparently in the capital (125), and Eliezer *ha-gadol,* presumably in Thessalonica (153). The latter title is also found in Benjamin of Tudela's remarks on Thebes. But the most important of this traveler's relevant data is the fact that Samuel, the leader of the Thessalonica community, presided by virtue of *imperial* appointment (182). Some two generations earlier Alexios I is said to have extended his protection to the local Jews (153), but neither situation explains the other. One may, however, conjecture that imperial intervention was needed on account of the strong anti-Jewish sentiment in that city, as both sources attest.

It is to be assumed that the men named by Benjamin with regard to the localities he visited, were the communal leaders even when he does not specify that. The number which he gives varies: in about half the instances (12 out of 23), three names are given and one or two for the remainder, with the exception of the three greatest cities (Constantinople, Thebes, and Thessalonica), in which more than three occur. The note on Harmilos is interesting in that each of the three leaders bears a different title, viz., rabbi, *parnas,* and head. The last is not used again with reference to the empire in this itinerary, and the second one recurs only in the capital. Both of them are common in other countries, but no scholar has yet succeeded in differentiating between their functions.

Communal activities east of Italy are represented in this period only in limited variety. One interesting instance allows us to see how the Rabbinite majority attempted to deal with the heretical Karaite sect, when because of their different calendrical systems the latter saw fit to celebrate the New Year a month later than the former. The antagonism thus engendered expressed itself verbally even before the later date, and a foreign scholar was consulted on the question. His reply was given in letters sent to two brothers, apparently both leaders in this unnamed city, which may be the capital. A meeting was called, and during the festival week of Tabernacles the orthodox congregation assembled in its synagogue to hear the letters which upheld its stand. But this did not deter the Karaites, who retaliated against certain unspecified acts by slandering their opponents to the civil authorities who, in consequence, imposed a heavy fine on the Rabbinites (125). This incident makes one wonder whether the fence which divided the residential quarters of the two camps in Constantinople, was put up as the result of a similar row (182).

In such internal squabbles the orthodox majority must have had occasional recourse to the ban, which when pronounced against an entire group was naturally much more serious an event than when applied to an individual, such as the schoolmaster in Oria (81). In the year of the first Crusade the classic weapon was invoked by the Constantinople community as well as another one nearby against the Messianic enthusiasts who were at that time migrating to Palestine via Abydos (153). In the following century Benjamin reports a sect in Cyprus set apart by the same means because of its non-conformist tendencies. Our only clue to the identification of this group is the fact that its adherents ignored the Sabbath Eve and observed the weekly rest through Saturday night. In this they concurred, perhaps only accidentally, with the heresy initiated by Meswī al-Okbarī in the tenth century, as Poznanski pointed out. The possibility of the connection is strengthened by the testimony of Benjamin's contemporary, Hadassī of Constantinople, that these sectarians had not yet become extinct at this period (182).

In certain situations there arose a need for correspondence between one community and another. The communications which passed between Hasdai in Cordova and the Jews of Bari, after they had weathered a crisis, are illustrations of this (94, 95). We have also just seen the role played by a letter of public interest from a foreign scholar. A similar matter is known from another source to have been the subject of letters between the Karaites of Constantinople and those of Jerusalem in the middle of the eleventh century (125 n.). Still another time of stress, the Messianic excitement, brought letters to the capital from Thessalonica, Tripolis in Syria, and from France (153). In addition to the appeal from Egypt to the community of Mastaura (139), we have another type of petition from a fallen state official in Egypt, which he addressed to the community in Constantinople. However, the present condition of the document does not enable us to determine the specific kind of assistance he hoped to procure (163).

In the litigation instituted by the convert of Attaleia, one has an opportunity to witness the community actively defending its interests. It seems that one of its members died, leaving a dwelling combined with a private synagogue, which normally should have been inherited by his four sons. The latter, however, all adopted Christianity and this prompted certain of the Jews to take possession of the inheritance. They were, as has been seen, compelled to relinquish the building, but succeeded in withholding certain objects, presumably constituting the synagogal equipment (167, 171).

The Jews of the Empire, one would suppose, had as much occasion to succor captives as those of Egypt are known to have had. The archives, however, have, unlike the latter's, not survived, and the few casual references to ransoming involve only private funds (87, 112). Hence, it is likely that, although the Mastaura community as a whole was solicited from Alexandria, it was the relatives of the captives who responded with the necessary money (139). Similarly with regard to the known instances of general philanthropy, whether for the support of needy scholars (80), or of the poor at large, (68, 121, 125) no organized system seems to have functioned.

One of the most common characteristics of Jewish life in the diaspora for the past two thousand years, is the occupation of a special quarter of a given town, for which the Venetians coined the term ghetto. This is applied in current usage to instances of both obligatory and voluntary segregation, and it is, indeed, difficult to discriminate in Roman and early medieval times between the two categories. In the background of our period we note the existence of such situations in Alexandria, in Antioch (and its suburb Daphne), and in the capital (the Chalkoprateia). But, as might be expected, the data falling within our proper scope are scantier by far than those available for contemporary Islam or for western Christendom. Since about the tenth or eleventh century, the Jewish quarter of Constantinople was located across the Golden Horn, in the suburb known as Pera or Stenon, and with the aid of a random note in the itinerary of Anthony of Novgorod, it is possible to fix it more precisely as adjoining the Pégai, the modern Cassim Pacha (191). It is this which Benjamin terms the Jews' *migrash* (182), herein stood the wooden dwelling-houses mentioned earlier (150), and nearby lay their cemetery (190). It was a stroke of good fortune that the soldiers of the Fourth Crusade established their headquarters in that region in the winter of 1203-4, for otherwise it might not have escaped the sorry fate of the city proper. We learn also that at this time the « juerie » was not devoid of that beauty and wealth which made « Mikelgard » a glamorous dream to western Europe (196).

In view of the strong hostility toward the Jew prevalent in Thessalonica, one would expect the local community to have kept to its own quarter in self-defense, if for no other reason. Up to some time in the twelfth century that does seem to have been the situation, but then for unknown reasons the Jews began to spread into other parts of the city. They even moved into houses partially occupied by Christians, in violation of an ancient canon (8) and to the dismay of the patriarch Eustathios. We do not know whether he ever took any action against this movement, but it is significant to note that rather than act on his own responsibility he first consulted his superior in Constantinople (184). In the west Bari also had its *Iudea,* which in the course of a conflict between an imperial official and some local leaders in 1051, was destroyed by fire (144). Perhaps the Jewish quarter of Attaleia, mentioned in the early fourteenth century, also harbored the Jewish inhabitants known to have lived in that city during our period (128 n.).

Within any Jewish group there were, naturally, differences of wealth and social standing. In Oria the class distinctions are seen to have been rather sharp; thus, in the vocabulary of Ahīma῾as, a member of the upper stratum is qualified as *hashub* (literally, « eminent »), as contrasted with ῾*alub* which he also uses synonymously with the common word meaning « poor » (68). In one of his stories a certain individual shows a decided reluctance to accept the hand of a girl offered to him by her father, for fear that the other members of her family would violently oppose the mésalliance (53). Again, Shefatiah's brother and associate in communal leadership, Hananel, was considered by the former's wife socially inferior, and for this reason she rejected his offer of a match between his son and her daughter. She was, however, forced to waive her objections by her husband (58). Another aspect of this inequality is given by a Christian writer who had apparently witnessed certain holiday observances. The fast of the Day of Atonement, he tells us, was broken by the richer Jews by feasting on fowl, while the others contented themselves with fish. But during the feasts of the week of Tabernacles, the latter would be the guests of the former (121).

The traditional emphasis laid on marriage is not ignored by our sources (**58**), including one which echoes Tacitus' remark on the Jewish *generandi amor* (**54**), and they afford us occasional glimpses into the procedure involved. It was, of course, customary for the match to be arranged by the parents (**53, 58**), or, in the case of orphans, by relatives serving as guardians (**54**). With regard to the wedding-festivities which took place in Synnada, the hagiographer who describes them was undoubtedly dependent on monastic tradition, and his description is, accordingly, not entirely reliable. He does, at any rate, pique one's curiosity with the scene of the guests becoming merry and demanding to be entertained by the bridegroom's dancing (**54**). Elsewhere about the same time the marriage of Shefatiah's daughter to her cousin was apparently celebrated with great simplicity : at the close of the morning-service in the synagogue the worshippers were invited to the bride's home, and the ceremony was performed there. The only other feature recorded is the recitation of an original liturgical poem by Amittai, the bride's brother, who dedicated the composition to his sister. The text of this has but recently been made available in Schirmann's new Italian anthology, and we know that in general such hymns were very popular. Davidson has published a longer work written by the same poet, which he recited as part of synagogue service on the Sabbath following the wedding of some friends of his (**58, 62 n.**)

The record of a marriage which took place in Mastaura in 1022 has been preserved in the contract drawn up on the occasion. This Aramaic document conforms in its scheme and style to the standard form, but its specific contents are of special interest. The wedding was held on Friday, and four witnesses affixed their signatures to the marriage-contract. As prescribed by Jewish law, the document includes an itemized list of both the bride's dowry, and of the *donatio propter nuptias* presented to her by the bridegroom. All of these articles have their valuation, or weight, or both, noted in nomismata and « shekels », respectively. Greek is in the main employed to designate the gifts, which are of three kinds: jewelry, wearing apparel, and household equipment. In addition the bride received from her mother the lower story of the family-dwelling and half-ownership of its well. The total value of the bride's possessions, apart from the real property, is given as 35 $\frac{1}{4}$ nomismata, a sum which probably represents more than the annual earnings of the average local artisan. It seems clear that both of the persons concerned came from families of some wealth (**130**).

The mass of the population of the empire was of a rather turbulent disposition, and its Jewish element shared this quality to a degree. The riot which broke out in the capital shortly after the death of Heraclius attracted some Jews as participants, very much as had happened some sixty years before (**2**). However, an alleged recurrence of this in the eleventh century is of questionable reliability (**140**). That the Jews should have ventured into open conflict with their neighbors with any frequency, is very improbable, although they did so once under unknown circumstances in Amorion (**38**). Their internal squabbles may have been more common, but could scarcely be as serious. Venosa once witnessed a lively scene of a Sabbath eve. The villagers who had driven in to spend the rest-day there, fell out among themselves, but were not allowed to settle their own affair, for the local housewives sallied forth brandishing their oven-poles, and with these they proceeded to beat the disturbers. The next day a Palestinian guest-preacher, whose visit was apparently the occasion of the villagers' trip to town, arose and delivered his sermon in the synagogue. In the meanwhile, Silano, the local rabbi or cantor, had inserted into his homiletic text a roguish reference to the incident, and when the guest read it out, sensing all the while that something was wrong, the former added insult to injury by openly deriding him. The slight was sufficiently serious to be reported to the scholars at Jerusalem, who punished Silano by excommunication (**22**). Finally, the reader will recall the conflict between the Rabbinites and Karaites related above (125), as a result of which the civil authorities imposed a fine on the orthodox group.

The social relations of Jews and Christians were for the most part either inimical or marked ¦by indifference. In the legend of Abraham and Theodore mentioned above we find not only that the Christian had rejected the business offers of the Jew, but that his friends refused even to act as his surety for a loan partly because of their aversion to the Jew as such (3 n.). Manifestations of hostility in Constantinople and Thessalonica in the Middle Ages were very likely as frequent as they are today. With regard to the former city Benjamin tells of the Jewish tanners spilling their stinking liquids out into the Pera as a specific cause of trouble, and of the beating of Jews in the streets. Another local manifestation of the anti-Jewish feeling seems to be embodied in the rule that no Jew, except the emperor's physician, was permitted to ride a horse. Although we have no legal text for this, it may have been more than a social restriction, as is true of a similar prohibition in certain Islamic states. Thus it is readily seen that there probably was considerable need for the intercession of the Jewish physician to the emperor Manuel I, as Benjamin hints (182).

It is possible that the situation was less acute in the earlier centuries, considering that the council of 692 showed a certain concern for the souls of some Christians because they maintained intimate relations with Jews. Yet, despite that, it is doubtful whether at that date there still were Christians who ate the Passover *massot*, or who frequented the baths in company with Jews (8).

Was it easier for Jews to associate with heretics than with orthodox Christians? The question is particularly vital in connection with their alleged intimacy with the Athinganoi of ninth-century Phrygia. Although this sect is usually coupled with the Paulicians, who also lived in that region, nothing is known of their doctrines, and there is insufficient ground to warrant the assumption often made that they constituted a subdivision of the better-known heresy. Their chief religious characteristic definitely known to us is the observance of the seventh day as the Sabbath. There are also certain indications that they shared the iconoclast viewpoint. The emperor Michael II, who was unsympathetic to icon-worship, is said to have been nurtured within this sect in his birthplace Amorion, and the chronicler on whom we are dependent goes into some detail to describe what purports to be his background. According to his account, every such household arranged for a Jew or Jewess to take over the management of both its worldly and its spiritual concerns, and though the members of the sect practiced baptism and were uncircumcized, they otherwise adhered to the Mosaic law (20). The hostility of our source to this emperor shines through every line, and it is not difficult to recognize the old sensational cry that it is the Jews who have injected the poison of iconoclasm among the heretics. Indeed, he asserts that after Michael ascended the throne he made a privileged class of the Jews (28), and decreed that Saturday be a fast-day, presumably another manifestation of Jewish influence in his mind! The material is thus highly suspicious, and its specific inspiration may perhaps be traced to the fact that the chronicler found the Jews mentioned in some source as residing in Michael's native town (38).

The long-standing acquaintance of Donnolo with the monk Nilos is an interesting item (106), as is the former's presence at a ceremony of consecration (107). In order to see the famous stylite Lazaros, Jews in Ephesus are also said to have climbed up the neighboring mountain to the monastery there (141).

Religious disputations, naturally, also involved a certain form of social contact. This activity seems in the seventh century to have retained some of the intensity shown in the preceding period, as manifested by Leontios, bishop of Neapolis (1), by the Damascus instance (7), and by the work of the itinerant monk, Anastasios the Sinaite (6). Thereafter a slackening becomes evident, attributable in part to the effect of the subsequent persecutions. The particular use to which Basil I put the disputation will be recalled, but the contemporary incident related of Hananel of Oria and the local bishop is somewhat peculiar, although it is undoubtedly to be understood in the light of the emperor's program. It is related there that the two men had a friendly difference of opinion as to the exact time of the birth of the new moon. The bishop risked only a sum of money on the correctness of his opinion, while the Jew staked his faith against it (68). The loss of appeal on the part of the oral polemic is shown by the manner in which Nilos declined a Jew's challenge, remarking in substance that there was little hope of converting him (107). Nevertheless, the archbishop of Thessalonica in the early eleventh century is said to have held frequent discussions with a certain Jewish scholar. The monk, who was his guest, would on the other hand have preferred to avoid the encounter which his host prevailed upon him to undertake with the Jew, before an audience containing others of that faith. At another time, a second Jewish scholar is said to have challenged this monk on his own initiative. One cannot, however, trust the statements that these disputants openly abused the Christian religion, since such indiscretion was bound to have painful consequences (118).

CHAPTER VI

INTELLECTUAL INTERESTS AND
LITERARY PRODUCTIONS

The contribution of Byzantine Jewry to the culture of their people appears to have been on the whole rather mediocre. That, however, should not prevent us from finding among them interesting developments representative of the various pursuits to which the medieval Jewish mind was attracted. It is unfortunate that practically no light is shed on the subject of education, although one gathers indirectly that the training of the young in traditional Jewish subject-matter was not neglected. We have a random allusion to a schoolmaster in Oria (81), and to the study of Hebrew literature by a Jewish boy in Synnada, later converted. In the latter instance, according to the Christian biographer, the boy's schooling was supposedly limited to the Bible, but this is probably not accurate (54). In the eleventh century a captive, who apparently came from the Empire, is described as a well-educated youth (129).

There has been preserved a page of a Greek Mishnaic glossary, which may have been intended for some kind of educational use. The fragment represents a work prepared in the tenth or eleventh century, and is thus far the only one of its kind published, although references to such material among Arabic-speaking Jews have been found. It is, moreover, the sole instance of the writing of Greek characters by a Jew in this period, and while the situation with respect to the Byzantine Karaites differs, it is the only indication that the Rabbinites of the Empire could use the written language to any degree. However, the vocabulary and orthography of this glossary are quite dependent on colloquial usage and reveal no literary background. On the side of Jewish scholarship it is more diffIcult to assess the author's equipment, for the material happens to be of much more than average difficulty and a considerable number of the terms involved are either illegible or otherwise indeterminable. According to the present writer's computation, the glossary contains seventy-five correct equivalents as against twenty incorrect ones (86).

In the secular sphere there can be no doubt that the most important works in our period were produced by Shabbetai Donnolo, an eminent intellectual figure among both the Jews and Gentiles of southern Italy. His high standing as a physician has already been adequately noticed, and in addition to medicine, he had a strong interest in astronomy, although he acquired no profound knowledge of that field. Unfortunately, he leaves us completely in ignorance of how he acquired his professional training, and though he describes, after a fashion, how he quenched his thirst for his avocation, his literary mannerisms effectively prevent the reader from gleaning any concrete details. He states that, despite the existence of certain Hebrew writings on that subject, the scholars whom he consulted were in no position to appreciate that literature. He thereupon turned to the non-Jewish works and made extensive researches in the Greek and Oriental treatises, claiming to have studied them in their original tongues and to have made copies of them for himself. We have no difficulty in crediting him with a knowledge of Greek and, to a lesser degree, of Arabic also, since Sicily and Kairwan were readily accessible to his native province. But instead of naming these or other localities, he vaguely writes that he traveled around « in many lands », where he studied under Gentile masters. In particular he names an astrologer from « Babylonia » who, in return for a generous fee, instructed the ardent student. The career of Constantinus Africanus in the following century offers some interesting parallels to that of our physician (100).

The extant fragment of Donnolo's medical treatise, which Steinschneider has placed at the disposal of scholars, is a source of prime importance for the history of European medicine, especially as part of the background of the Salerno school, the beginnings of which are so obscure. The work, styled « The Precious Book », was written in the author's latter years, and as is invariably the case in medieval Europe up to the Pyrenees, its language is Hebrew. In content it is an antidotarium and the chief *constituens* of the remedies discussed is honey. The terms involved are given frequently in Arabic, Greek, and Latin (110).

There undoubtedly were certain Jews in this region in every generation who dabbled in astronomy and astrology, a field which enjoyed time-honored approbation. Hananel of Oria seems to have been one of these (68), and Paltïel, a descendant of his, who rose to fame in the Fātimid court, was noted for this knowledge (103). It should also be pointed out that a lost treatise by a foreign scholar, Dunash b. Tamīm of Kairwan, on astronomy, was composed in response to questions received via Constantinople (?), from Cordova, although one cannot prove therefrom that the interest in the matter was shared by the Jews of the former city (98). Time has not been kind to Donnolo's « Book of the Planets », which is known only from a few scanty citations in works that are rarely read today even by specialists. The significance of these fragments lies chiefly in their indication of the study in southern Italy of a certain anonymous work on astronomy, entitled the « *Baraita* of R. Samuel », for Donnolo's work was written as a commentary thereon. Nevertheless, the author insists here that Israel has lost the astronomic knowledge with which it was once endowed, in the trite vein of the idealization of « the good old times ». We also note with interest the several glosses in Greek, Latin, and Arabic, and the fact that the book was equipped with illustrations which are mentioned in a twelfth-century source (101).

The third of Donnolo's interests falls under the head of mystic speculation. His outlook was governed by « The Book of

Creation », a peculiar work of unknown authorship. It claims to contain the plan followed by God in the *creatio ex nihilo,* which was transmitted to Abraham and written down by him. For our purpose its outstanding characteristics are the microcosm theory of the relation of man to the universe, which was the accepted view among Jews and most Christians everywhere, and the cosmic significance attributed to the letters of the alphabet, a feature likewise common to the general culture of the Empire. Donnolo, like Saadia and others, composed a work as a commentary on this revered text, which is in actuality for the most part irrelevant to it, yet contains a store of interesting material. Inasmuch as the text of this *Hakmoni* has survived in entirety, and reveals the writer's *Weltanschauung,* it is appropriate to review it here in detail.

The Introduction opens with a rhymed prose section containing an acrostic which identifies the writer. This is followed by the biographical details (**87, 100**), which have been cited in other connections, including his career as a student of astronomy mentioned in an earlier part of the present chapter. At this point another rhymed piece is given with the acrostic « Shabbetai bar Abraham *qoneh hokmah* ». The author then proceeds to discuss the duty incumbent on Israel to study God's world, particularly as revealed by astronomy, in the course of which he gives 982 as the year of writing, the seventieth year of his life. In the unique manuscript which preserves the lengthy section in question, the Introduction has an addition which apologizes for entering into the delicate and sacred subject of creation, and closes with a prayer for assistance. (There seems to be something suspicious about this latter passage, and it may in fact be spurious.) (**113**).

The author's ostensible aim is not reached until he has devoted a chapter to the verse, « And God said, Let us make man in our image, after our likeness ». The difficulty felt is the fact that God has no corporeal form, no celestial or earthly being having ever perceived it, and any Biblical evidence to the contrary being

explained away. Furthermore, the absolute lack of similarity between Him and physical man is emphasized by means of a
detailed catalogue of the latter's anatomical parts and their respective functions, even to beard and finger-nails. This strengthens
the *reductio ad absurdum* involved in any argument in favor of an
anthropomorphic conception of God, for He could scarcely be in
need of any such anatomical equipment. On the other hand, these
organs are common to the animal kingdom as well, from which
however, man is distinguished by three qualities: knowledge,
understanding, and speech. Yet rather than point out in the traditional manner that herein lies the resemblance between God and
man implied in the Biblical verse, the author applies his microcosm
theory and interprets the divine statement as though addressed
to the universe. That is, God must be understood as saying to His
handiwork, Now that the universe is finished, let us make man
at once in My form and in yours. The non-corporeal resemblance
to the Author of life lies in the power, which man possesses,
relatively speaking, to rule the world, in his building and planting,
in the invisibility of his soul(literally, « breath »), in the knowledge
of future time and unseen places which his dreams reveal, and in
the inscrutability of his inner consciousness to all but God. As for
the other aspect of the resemblance, the physical universe, this
consists of an analogy drawn between the four cosmic elements
and the four humors. Air corresponds to blood, water to phlegm,
fire to the red (instead of yellow) bile, and earth to the black bile.

Thus, at length, our author announces that he is about to
begin his commentary on « The Book of Creation », which God
presented to Abraham at the time that the covenant was made.
As was taken to be implied in the Bible (Prov. 8: 30), He had
given a great deal of loving attention to the problem of creation,
and for two thousand years before He executed it, had toyed with
the letters of the alphabet, the constituent elements of everything
on earth. Then He turned to the celestial part of the work, in the
course of which He assigned to each man to be born on earth

his star and planet, — somewhat tentatively, however, for this predetermined fate is subject to revision. The subject of the commentary begins with the « 32 mysterious ways of wisdom », i. e., the ten spheres and the twenty-two letters. The former group appears in that text as « the spheres of *blimah*» (a Biblical ἅπαξ λεγόμενον, usually rendered « nothing » [Job 26:7]), interpreted there as enjoining the pious man from saying or thinking aught with regard to them. To this exegesis Donnolo adds a second explanation, deriving from the expression an indication of the *creatio ex nihilo*, the reasonability of which he proceeds to prove in a most remarkable though unconvincing fashion, by means of the analogy of the glass-worker's blowing into a mold from which a new product emerges. As for the « spheres » themselves, the commentary preserves the enumeration, which is lost in the extant form of the text, thus: the divine spirit, the three elements (omitting earth), the dimensions of height and depth, and the four points of the compass.

The remarks on the letters of the alphabet are the most tedious part of this work, but are relieved by certain more interesting items interspersed among them. Following his text, the commentator discusses the five phonetic groups of sounds, and goes into such subjects as the 231 possible bi-literal permutations, a classification of the letters in three groups, and *aleph, mem, shin*, as the « mothers » of the three elements. At this point we find an excursus on the problem of heterosexuality, which, we note with interest, applied to the stars also. Then the seven « double » letters are treated, and their suitability as instruments in the process of creation is shown by the enormous possibility of permutation, which is illustrated *in extenso* with the letters composing six selected words. Each of these letters served to create a planet, a day of the week, an organ, a physical condition and its opposite (e. g., life and death). These factors are connected one with the other through horoscopes. Thus, Saturn is cold and dry, hence, an individual born on Saturday is slow to anger, and difficult to appease. The connection of each planet with its day is then shown to depend on the order of creation. Finally, the last point which needs to be mentioned in this connection is the twelve « simple » letters, on which depend the signs of the zodiac, as well as the months, and the organs governing the moods.

Toward the end of the commentary, the author discusses a certain cosmic factor termed the *Teli,* which also figures in his « Book of the Planets ». This is the common term for the imaginary line or « dragon » connecting the lunar nodes, or points of intersection of the orbits of the sun and moon. The significance attributed to it by medieval astronomers is due to the fact that eclipses were known to take place only at these nodes, the « dragon's head and tail », which bring good and bad luck, respectively (**101**). Donnolo claims to have read on the subject in Arabic works, some of which mention two « dragons », the second apparently referring to the constellation. He locates it strategically in the fourth of the seven heavens, whence it controls planetary movements, functioning like the heart in man. Finally, one of the very last passages in the work strikes a note of praise for astronomy, the science from which the greatness of God is perceivable to best advantage (**114**).

The works of Donnolo constitute a valuable proof of the kind of intellectual ferment which was taking place among the better educated Jews of his province, which is noteworthy for other cultural activities as well. The most important manifestation of the latter is the very valuable chronicle of Ahīma'as. This was written at the close of the Byzantine regime in southern Italy, and is thus far the only historical writing that can be definitely credited to that section of Jewry. For although it is now known explicitly that *Yosippon,* the Hebrew version of Josephus, was available there before the middle of the tenth century, there is as yet no proof that it was composed in the same region rather than in northern Italy (**95**); and with regard to such writings as the *Yerahmeel* chronicle and the Alexander-romance, these seem to belong to a later period. Elsewhere in the Empire we know only of a lost work on general Byzantine history, which is cited in the early twelfth century for its information on the wars with the Khazars (112).

Ahīmaʿas is an historical source of the highest importance for our purpose, and its contents are by no means exhausted by the numerous extracts from it included in Part Two of the present work, for it bears as well on the contemporary history of several extra-Byzantine localities in Italy, Egypt, and Palestine. Its chronological scope, as the reader has undoubtedly gathered, extends from about 800 to 1054, the year of its composition, but a sense of modesty seems to have inhibited the author from giving more than a few sketchy details regarding himself and his contemporaries. Its purpose was to present the story of a family of Jewish leaders, from whom the writer was descended, and he undoubtedly had written as well as oral materials to draw upon. Its contents are by no means free of legendary embellishment and a pronounced romantic tendency, yet even where the critical reader must reject certain items as impossible or improbable, there is always an atmosphere of local color in the tale, so that the historical investigator need not leave it empty-handed. In one instance, important for the light it seems to shed on Ahīmaʿas' method, we are enabled to check one of his stories with the aid of a parallel in another Hebrew work. The former relates that the rise of Paltīel to high office in Kairwan began while he was still in his native town of Oria, where the Moslem general who invaded the region sought him out, having heard of the illustrious family of Shefatiah (103). The parallel, to which Marx has called attention, occurs in a later work, but is probably more reliable in narrating instead that the individual in question was transported across the sea along with other captives (104), a procedure which was quite common at the time.

While emphasizing the unusual value of this source, one must not overlook its literary quality. For the work is written in rhymed prose, the *saj'* borrowed from Arabic literature, and in a highly ornate style. Undoubtedly neither of these features will please the modern taste, and for that reason it is perhaps no serious loss that the translator cannot hope to reproduce its flavor; yet from the standpoint of the medieval canons of literary art, it is a composition of distinction (145).

Considering the literary background of the Jewish environment which produced Ahīma῾as, it is not entirely surprising that he composed his chronicle in a style of well-known genre, viz., that of the contemporary liturgical poetry or *piyut*. To the taste of that age there was no incongruity between the form and substance of his work, because of the fact that secular poetry was apparently unknown, and that the writing of unrhymed prose was not considered an art. The latter is illustrated by the text of the letter which some communal representative of Bari sent to Hasdai Ibn Shaprūt, in response to an inquiry which, on the analogy of the latter's letter to the Khazar ruler, was most likely also written in rhymed prose (94, 95). It is this consideration which makes it appropriate to bring in the liturgical poets at this point, rather than in close connection with general question of the Byzantine-Jewish religious service.

The earliest known manifestations of this art in Europe appear in southern Italy in the early ninth century, the poets of which had inherited the compositions of their Palestinian predecessors of the sixth and seventh centuries, probably to a greater extent than modern scholarship has thus far been able to ascertain. The family from which Ahīma῾as sprung, included a number of poets, who held a distinguished place in the history of the *piyut*, prior to the attainment of its highest expression in the Spanish school. Both Amittai (49) and his sons Shefatiah (51) and Hananel (76) are signalized for their compositions by the chronicler, who evidently possessed more of them than are extant now. A contemporary of the father, Silano of Venosa, wrote one which, when recited in a Jerusalem synagogue by a visitor from Apulia, is said to have effected the revocation of the ban under which its author had been laid. The recent discovery of its text by Marcus is a welcome addition to the available materials (22). The Brindisi epitaph of 832 has also attracted some attention because of its poetic style (36).

Later in the same century we have Amittai II, whose occasional poems have been mentioned in the foregoing pages. Davidson now lists twenty-one to his credit, and points out that Ahīma'as alludes to certain others now lost (80). It is thought also that Zebadiah *Hazzan* is to be assigned to the same period and provenance (80 n.). In the following generation we are now able to cite Menahem Qorésī of Otranto, whose affinities with the contemporary poets of northern Italy furnished Sonne with the clue to a new dating, considerably earlier than all previous ones (89). A minor figure in this field is Shabbetai Donnolo, from whose pen also there are a few verses (113). Elijah b. Shemaiah of Bari, whose extant compositions are comparatively voluminous, is believed to have lived about the beginning of the eleventh century (121 n.). Finally, there is Ahīma'as himself, who includes a eulogy on his illustrious relative Paltīel in his chronicle, and was also author of several other poems preserved in liturgical collections (145).

The remaining evidence for the cultivation of this art, — that is, in the other parts of the Empire, is extremely meagre. The Corinth epitaph is of some interest because of its structure, which is obviously that of a brief *piyut*. The initial letters form an acrostic of the name of the deceased, and the final syllables of the lines are identical, as are those of the second and fourth words within each line (85). The two famous Karaites of Constantinople, Tobiah b. Moses and Judah Hadassī, contributed poems to the liturgy of their sect (**App. A**), but among the Rabbinites, we have only a conjectural assignment to the Empire of a few obscure writers (80 n., 121 n., **Exc. B**). For the sake of completeness one may be pardoned for noting the uninspired « poem »

by Tobiah b. Eliezer of Castoria, which he included in the introduction to his Pentateuchal commentary (164). When Harīzī
visited Thebes *ca.* 1218, he was somewhat impressed by the
relatively high quality of the compositions of a local poet, Michael
b. Caleb, who had the advantage of literary training as a student
in Spain (182 n.). It is not improbable that this part of his life
falls in the closing years of the present study, but such instances
were presumably extremely few.

The cultivation of the staple rabbinic studies in the European
part of the Empire, at least, is amply attested. In Apulia the center
was at first in Oria, where a group of scholars sat under the
patronage of Shefatiah and his son after him (80). It would seem
that the ten learned Jews named by Donnolo as slain in the sack
of the city in 925, comprised the local college (87). Thereafter
we must look to Bari and Otranto for the continuation of this
activity. In connection with the calamity that descended on
the Jews there *ca.* 930, a contemporary resident of the former
town refers to its body of scholars, six of whom he names,
as *talmidé haburah,* which, as Mann correctly notes, is a
quasi-technical expression denoting a rabbinic college, such as
existed in contemporary Palestine. The names of several of
the learned men of Otranto are also given in the same connection (94). Although none of these communities is represented
by any extant contribution to this field of study, there is no
dearth of indirect evidence of its status, notably in the phraseology of the liturgical poems mentioned above, in the responsum
of the court at Bari (120), and in the oft-quoted parody: « From
Bari shall go forth the Law, and the word of the Lord from
Otranto ». The latter occurs as a popular saying in a twelfth-century source, but the foundation for the reputation it reflects was
laid as early as the tenth (116).

It is entirely true that at no time did Jewish scholarship in the
Empire approach the level achieved at the seats of the *Geonim* in
Mesopotamia or in contemporary Palestine, and one would, accord-

ingly, expect the latter centers to have exerted some influence here. The suggestion is strengthened by the fact that students from Constantinople are known to have studied under the celebrated Hai at Pumbeditha (122), yet other evidence, to be cited later, indicates a greater degree of indebtedness to the west. At any rate, the remarks of Benjamin on the Jewish scholars whom he met in the communities of Constantinople, Thebes, and Thessalonica, can be supplemented to a considerable extent (182). In the last-named, it is a hagiographic source which attests their existence early in the preceding century (118). The long letter written there, probably about the same time, likewise reveals the hand of a learned man (119). The name of a Moses of Cyprus has been preserved because of circumstances which brought him international fame. For he was summoned by the Emperor as consultant in the great controversy over the date of Easter in 1007, which raged both in Byzantium and the rest of eastern Christendom (127). In the following century, the « Greek » whom Abraham Ibn Ezra attacked, was apparently an immigrant from the Empire to Italy (175). The experience of a certain Elijah b. Caleb in a number of Egyptian communities, caused him to criticize very severely the appreciation of a scholar's worth in those places, apparently because he was accustomed to a different attitude on the part of the Jews in his native country (169). The same situation is reflected in the case of a better-known figure in Alexandria, Pinhas b. Meshullam, whom Maimonides seems to have dissuaded from returning to «Romania», because of his dissatisfaction with matters in Egypt (194).

In addition to the general indications contained in the foregoing material, there are yet to be considered the more important scholars, those who wrote learned works which have either survived to some extent, or are otherwise known. The greatest of these is Hillel b. Eliaqim, whose lifetime falls at the close of our period, having been born in the otherwise unknown community of Selymbria. He wrote commentaries on two ancient sources of Jewish law, the *Sifra* and the *Sifré*, both of which are extant in full, but are still for the most part in manuscript. The former is the earlier of the two, and under the circumstances one is dependent for his information as to its contents chiefly on the brief description by Rabbinowicz, and on the few pages from it which were printed by Jellinek and others. Rabbinowicz commends it as employing the celebrated pithy and lucid exegetical style associated with the writings of Rashi, and states that it cites the works of Hai, Nissim of Kairwan, Nathan b. Yehīel of Rome, and Baruch b. Samuel of southern Italy. Its Greek glosses have been treated by the late Felix Perles, and one of its passages is said by a scholar of the thirteenth century to have influenced Byzantine Jewry toward laxity in a certain religious observance, as will be seen later.

The commentary on the *Sifré* has come down in several manuscripts, and its value for scholarship is indicated by the long list of writers who have cited it, extending from the thirteenth century to our own times, when we find it praised highly by Meir Friedmann, who made use of it in his edition of the *midrash*. A very full description of the copy in the Sassoon collection has recently been published, enabling us to see that Hillel worked with a large equipment of ancient and medieval Hebrew writings. It is, for example, interesting to note so early a reference to an older contemporary in western Europe, the well-known Samuel b. Meir of France (179).

One of Hillel's contemporaries, Abraham *Zutra* of Thebes, in his writings is known to have criticized certain views expressed by the former. His commentaries are, so far as is known, not extant, but may be judged from the citations to have been quite extensive. He wrote one on *Sifra,* another on the Talmudic tractate of *Sabbath*, and a third on the entire order of *Tohorot* (178). An unknown Shabbetai is also cited as one of Hillel's critics within our period, but it is not certain that he lived in the Empire (180). Somewhat earlier is the date to be assigned to Moses Dābā of Greece, but, as was observed in another connection, *Yavan* need not necessarily denote Byzantium (161).

The remaining field of interest is Biblical study, to which several Byzantine-Jewish writers contributed in the twelfth century. A certain Joseph of Constantinople wrote a treatise on the text of the Bible, which has been preserved in a copy made by a Karaite, as yet unpublished (193). However, the more usual form for works dealing with the Scriptures was that of the commentary. At the time that Ibn Ezra briefly reviewed the contemporary exegetical schools, he observed that in the Byzantine works the homiletical method prevailed, as opposed to the rationalistic and grammatical one for which he stood. He had particular reference to the commentaries of Tobiah b. Eliezer and his pupil Meir, both of Castoria in the province of Bulgaria, where no definite sign of Jewish life is found before this time. The former's work on the Pentateuch and the « Five Scrolls » is relatively well known, and was widely quoted in the centuries following its composition. It must have been a popular commentary with the average Jew for whom it seems to have been intended. Even today it may be said to retain a certain degree of pedagogic value, because of its selection of material from the classic Jewish sources bearing on the Biblical text. Here and there the author also adds incidental notes of some special interest for the contemporary Jewish scene. His several strictures on the Karaites are also noteworthy, in view of the fact that none of the other orthodox writers pays any attention to these sectarians (164). The commentary of his pupil Meir is completely lost except for its name (166). Ibn Ezra also cites the interesting identification of Nineveh with Troy as current among Byzantine-Jewish scholars, an idea that undoubtedly would not have occurred in another land where Homer was not so important; but if he had seen it in some commentary, it is not known which that was (174).

The only other commentator whose works are extant is the obscure Meyuhas b. Elijah. The determination of both his date and provenance is dependent on internal evidence, the former being the more problematic. His commentary may have encompassed the entire Old Testament, since there are extant the portions dealing with the Pentateuch, Chronicles, and Job. Only the parts on Genesis and Exodus have been published (by Greenup), and these, while enabling us to assign the time and place of writing, also reveal the author's woeful lack of originality, even as as a compiler, for he is slavishly dependent on Rashi, whom he reproduces *in extenso,* although he hardly ever names him. In addition he intersperses his exegesis with lengthy excursuses on one or another point in Jewish law, consisting merely of catenae of Talmudic quotations. He manifests a penchant also for grammar, but on an utterly elementary level. Besides Rashi he cites Nathan b. Yehīel, Ibn Ezra, and his own *Sefer ha-Middot* of which, however, nothing is known (117).

Mosconi, a native of Bulgaria of the fourteenth century, informs us of a certain Caleb Korsinos of Constantinople, who was renowned for his knowledge of Hebrew grammar, as manifested in his super-commentary on Ibn Ezra. This work is lost and we have no way of determining whether he lived in the late twelfth or in the thirteenth century (183), unless we may be guided by the fact that he is mentioned together with the author of a similar writing whose date is given, viz., Abishai of Bulgaria. The latter is said to have written his super-commentary in 1170, but it has survived only in a few citations in Mosconi. However, enough is known of these lost works to indicate that a new direction in Biblical study had been taken by these two writers, as compared with the homiletical commentaries which preceded them.

To judge from the authorities on whom the foregoing Byzantine-Jewish writers drew, it is seen that they were not affected by the Karaite scholars of Constantinople, such as Tobiah b. Moses, Judah Hadassī, and Jacob b. Reuben (**App. A**), nor by those of Mesopotamia and Palestine, to any great extent. Instead we find them using for the most part the works of several famous western scholars. This accords well with the random fact that a legal work by Judah b. Barzillai of Barcelona was also available in the Empire, whence it was brought to Worms (195).

CHAPTER VII

ASPECTS OF RELIGION AND CULTURE

It is appropriate for the limited purpose of the present study to enter into the religious life of this section of Jewry not in any comprehensive fashion, but only insofar as the sources yield material specifically bearing upon it. The liturgy constitutes one of its main factors, functioning as it did in both synagogue and home. Like certain other geographical divisions of medieval Jewry, that of Byzantium evolved in the course of time its peculiar set of prayers, comparable to the *Euchologion* and termed the *Mahzor Romaniah.* However, the present form of that collection is no more than four hundred years old, and the manuscripts and editions of it have not yet been adequately studied. It is clear, however, that the text of the prayers and order of service varied in a large number of details from those prevailing elsewhere in Europe and Asia, as has remained the case with respect to the different systems in use in the various parts of the world to the present day. Especially noteworthy is the extensive use of the vernacular in the service, in which Greek-speaking Jews anticipated the modern Reform movement perhaps as early as the third century, when in the Caesarea synagogue one could hear a prayer of fundamental importance (the *Shema'*) recited in that language. At a later time the passage containing the announcement of the New Moon is known to have been repeated in translation, the latter being extant in Hebrew transcription in two of the manuscripts of the *Mahzor*. In addition, the book of Jonah, the reading of which was prescribed for the Day of Atonement, was read before the congregation in both languages. The text in the Bodleian manuscript shows that the Hebrew and Greek were given alter-

ö

nately, verse by verse, although in sixteenth-century Candia, Meir Katzenellenbogen of Padua was informed that the custom was to read first the opening three verses of the Hebrew, and then the entire book in translation. Besides this, certain hymns were probably recited in Greek, although the earliest known example is somewhat later than the period to which this study is devoted (**Exc. B**).

A few other liturgical notes may be gleaned from sources of a different type. Reverting to the scene in the Venosa synagogue we find the preacher from Jerusalem using the text of a *midrash* in his sermon, but it is not known that this custom took root in southern Italy (**22**). A western writer on liturgical procedure criticizes the custom followed in the Empire with respect to the benediction introducing the *Hallel,* which was recited there only by the cantor, as the Greek-speaking congregations still do today (**158**). Another commends the procedure followed in reading the scriptural lesson (**188**). In the commentary of Tobiah b. Eliezer, there is a reference to a difference in the procedure governing the sounding of the *Shofar* during the New Year service, which has also survived to the present time (**164**).

The text of the formula of abjuration, which was published by Beneshevich, contains a list of Jewish holidays (in the course of the prescribed anathemas), and an Appendix on the observances, for the information of the priest charged with the responsibility of admitting the convert. With the exception of the Feast of Weeks and Hanukkah there are interesting notes on the several important days of the Jewish calendar. The New Year is archaistically termed the « Feast of Trumpets », and one of its features is the wrapping of candles in silks of various hues. In addition to this unique custom, we are informed that the holiday service had a magical function in protecting the worshipper against the demons of illness.

The Day of Atonement is represented as a fast not only for adults but apparently for children as well, unless one adopts the alternative rendering of παιδίον, « servant ». However, since the fast is said to have been enforced even on domestic animals, it should perhaps be inferred that these observations refer to the Karaites, some of whom are known to have been capable of this kind of severity. The ultra-pious Jews remained standing while they recited the prayers, which lasted from early morning to sunset, by way of emphasizing the penitential significance of the day, a procedure which may occasionally still be seen among Jews anywhere. The author of the Appendix uses the expression Μεγάλη Ἡμέρα, which is still current in Greek-speaking communities as the designation for that day, but at the same time he states that it was called by the anomalous name μονοποδαρέα. The etymology of this compound involves something in the sense of « one-legged », but that only increases the obscurity. Indeed, the formula proper indicates that the name was applied to another and minor day, the invention of which was attributed to an ancient « arch-rabbi » called Lazaros. That fact, while not solving the difficulty involved in the term, shows that the scholiast is not to be trusted in this particular. Finally it should be noted that the fast is said to be broken at its close by a special meal of fowl or of fish.

By a slight inaccuracy Tabernacles is placed seven instead of five days after the Day of Atonement. During that week the Jews took their meals in the usual holiday fashion in specially constructed « booths ». However, each family did not build its own as the law required, but a common hut was set up in the court of each synagogue, just as was done, for example, in contemporary Baghdad. Our source calls such huts καρ-αγλυβαι, which is quite unintelligible, being apparently a mistake for the common καλύβαι. The latter renders the Hebrew *sukkah* in the medieval translation of Jonah mentioned above, and is the word used today in this connection. The rich extended hospitality to the poor at these symbolic repasts, and the climax came on the eve of the last day in the form of a communal feast.

The description of the Passover states that the Jews are prevented from using the lamb as food for the holiday out of fear of the Christian objection to the custom. It is, indeed, said by Procopius that Justinian had forbidden it, and thus this situation seems to have continued long after him. The meal which ushers in the festive week is said to be eaten while holding a staff, in literal fulfillment of the Biblical regulation. One of the special dishes, described as consisting of a mixture of raisins, walnuts, and crumbs of *massah*, is readily recognizable as the *haroset*. Our informant also attests the eating of meat together with the «bitter herbs» at this initial meal. Finally, another custom mentioned by him, the eating of ordinary bread with chickpeas on the evening after the termination of Passover, is otherwise unknown.

The anathema hurled at the Purim effigy-burning, in which both Haman and Christianity were supposed to have been combined, seems but to echo the fifth-century law which suppressed the custom. The fast of the Ninth of Ab is said to be styled Λυπηρά, i. e., Sorrow. In addition to the customary recital of appropiate prayers, the Jews are said to have sprinkled ashes on their heads. It is difficult, however, to accept the statement that the fast commenced in the evening, instead of at dawn. We note, finally, the survival of the ancient observance of the New Moon as a special female rest-day (121).

There was a considerable degree of popular veneration of the memory of Ezra the Scribe among the contemporary Jews in the Near East. There is no reason to doubt that those of the Empire also shared in it, although the information is from a distant Moslem writer, who mentions it *à propos* of the Koranic claim that the Jews believed Ezra to be the son of God (48).

It is curious to note that the Byzantine Jews were surprisingly lax in the observance of one ritual requirement, viz., the purification-bath prescribed for all married women after each menstrual period. A learned visitor from Italy, Isaiah of Trani, observed in the early thirteenth century that the Jewish wives of the Empire were content to bathe in the water supplied in the bath-houses, although it was considered to be disqualified for their purpose in rabbinic law. He attributed the situation to the opinion expressed by Hillel b. Eliaqim to the effect that the stringent requirement of well- or spring-water was optional, since it had been introduced by post-Mosaic legislators. However, it seems hardly likely that a change took place in this observance due to such a statement in a learned work. One should rather infer that the laxity antedated it and the situation may, as Maimonides noted with respect to Egypt, have been due to Karaite influence (179).

Medieval Jewish life was surcharged with mysticism and superstition just as was the surrounding environment, although the respective backgrounds may have been quite dissimilar. With respect to the Empire, the Christian sources occasionally attribute such interests to individual Jews, but only in the form of anti-Christian connivance. Thus, Jewish soothsayers are said to have foretold the accession to the throne of the humble youth Konon as Leo III, having induced him also to change his name, and, above all, to abolish image-worship, a matter to be considered somewhat further on (10). In contemporary Catania a Christian magician is seen consulting a Hebrew colleague in a certain impious undertaking (17). The famous patriarch Photios was so outstanding as an intellectual that an inimical chronicler could account for his achievement only by describing how he had, like Faust, sold his soul in order to gain his great knowledge. Young Photios was supposed to have received a charm from a Jewish magician, which endowed him both with worldly riches and with the knowledge for which he strove, but only in return for betraying his religious faith (25). In Cyprus, on the threshhold of our period, a local story told of the punishment of a Jewish sorcerer by burning (3 n.). It is curious also to see that the formula of abjuration anathematizes in one breath all the traditional post-Mosaic observances and « all their witchcraft, incantations, sorcery, soothsaying, amulets, and phylacteries ».The last-named, however, had long before lost their magical significance (121).

From what is known in general of this aspect of Jewish culture, and with special reference to the Empire as well, it is clear that even if such material as the foregoing does contain some historical kernel, it is of extremely limited importance. The main lines of the magical activities and supernatural interests of the Jews are of an entirely different bearing. At the outset it must be noted that in southern Italy, whence comes most of our material, a learned Jew apparently sensed no incongruity between his sober pursuits and those of a less rational quality. Ahīmaʿas was undoubtedly not alone in honoring the memory of the sons of Amittai for their mystical interests (*sodīm, razzīm*) as much as for anything else (**49**). They were, however, preceded by a foreign wonderworker and scholar, Aaron of Baghdad, of whom some interesting feats are related. Almost immediately after landing at the port of Gaeta, he restored to his normal form a boy who had been changed into an ass. Then at Benevento he detected that the cantor was really a *golem* who was being kept alive indefinitely by magical means. In view of the fact that the same individual is credited in another source with having served as the medium for the spread of Oriental Jewish mysticism to northern Italy, it is reasonable to suppose that his visit had a similar effect on Oria and the rest of Apulia (**50**). At any rate, the *Sefer ha-Yashar,* which Amittai's sons are said to have studied earnestly, may be identical with a work of the same title, containing amulets and other magical formulae, which was known in Aaron's homeland. This same country may also have been the source of the esoteric study of the *Merkabah* (**49**). That term refers to the speculations regarding the divine court, which took as their point of departure the first chapter of Ezekiel and the sixth of Isaiah. A work bearing that name is said to have been used by Shefatiah, and handed down as a revered heirloom for three generations before it was lost (**102**).

Among the magical themes involved in Ahīmaʿasʾ tales, is that in which a corpse is given a new lease of life by the use of the ineffable name of God, a motif familiar from the later *golem*-stories. The instance of the cantor of Benevento differs somewhat in that the magical Tetragrammaton was inserted in the individual's arm while he was still alive, because his preordained death would have prevented his guardian from returning him safely to his mother, as he had promised (21). Hananel of Oria in like manner revived a young relative, who had died prematurely, in order not to have to bury him before the return of his absent brothers. Here, however, a reaction is expressed against this device, in the form of a dream which the latter had before their return home (57). Another aspect of the efficacy of this magical name appears in the manner in which Shefatiah was once saved from the desecration of the Sabbath. He set out from Bari late one Friday afternoon, but managed to reach Oria before sundown by inscribing the four sacred letters on his horse's hoofs, thus enabling them to travel at a supernatural speed. Here we have the well-known « shrinking of the ground », so familiar to Jewish folklore. (It should be observed also that instances of this are found in Byzantine literature as well, minus the element of the magical name, as in the speedy trip across Greece to Corinth related of Nikon the *Metanoeite*) (57 n.).

The control of demons was another factor in this atmosphere. Thus, Shefatiah is shown curing the daughter of Basil by exorcism, indicating the persistence of the same outlook involved in the Talmudic model of this story, some six hundred years earlier (64). There is more distinctive material in the tale of how the same individual foiled a couple of female demons. They had stolen a young child from his grave for the purpose of eating him, after he had been interred there by his parents, who believed him to be dead. These female demons were *Lilits,* as is implied in their appetite, and in their description as hairy (female) demons of the night. The similarity between this conception and Byzantine Γελλώ is, if a coincidence and no more, at least, a noteworthy one (59). In the story of the plague in which the descendants of Shefatiah perished, no demonic forces are invoked by the narrator, since it came as divine retribution for a sin. Nevertheless, the manner in which the epidemic was stopped, viz., by casting into the sea the book the defilement of which had caused the calamity, suspiciously resembles the sinking of the demon in the exorcism story (102).

As other instances of the current conception of supernatural affairs, one may note the disappearance of Teofilo of Oria (53), the rescue of Hananel from baptism by divine interference with the economy of nature (68), and the clairvoyance of Shefatiah on his death-bed. In the latter, the popular imagination seems to have capitalized the fact that the Jewish leader died shortly after the death of the emperor Basil, and too soon, apparently, for the news to have reached Oria. Shefatiah is depicted as having a vision in which the enemy of the Jews received his due (76). In the light of such material as the foregoing, one can understand why a pseudepigraphic responsum attributed to Hai, should allude to a correspondence on a mystic subject between him and the communities of this region, although it is quite certain that nothing of the sort ever took place (124).

For the rest of the Empire the related phenomena are extremely sparse. An instance of the bibliomantic use of the Torah appears in the case of a woman who contemplated a trip across the Mediterranean, but decided against it after opening the scroll at random to an unfavorable passage (161). It is peculiar that Petahiah, who is supposed to have visited the Empire toward the close of this period, should in the very brief space which he devotes to it, emphasize the expert exorcists whom he found there; for by this time mystic and magical interests had undergone considerable development in western and central Europe, so that it would be erroneous to view Byzantine Jewry as in any sense outstanding in this respect (186). Nevertheless, Maimonides did suppose that a certain ancient writing containing some anthropomorphic speculations on God, was of Byzantine authorship (185).

The Jewish nostalgia for Palestine expressed itself in this period in the form of pilgrimages to Jerusalem, similar to those made by the Christians. Pilgrims were attracted thither not only by the historic appeal of that city but apparently also by the fact that the scholars resident there before the Seljuq conquest, were religious authorities who commanded the esteem and financial support of world Jewry. Thus in the early ninth century a certain Ahīmaʿas, whose home was in southern Italy, is said to have made the pilgrimage three times, apparently in fulfillment of successive vows, each time bringing his donation to the scholars (**21, 22**). At a later time we find a Jew from Thessalonica, who upon his return influenced a relative from Russia to make the pilgrimage (**119**). Another one from Attaleia, who was among the captives ransomed at Alexandria, preferred to travel on to Palestine rather than to return home directly (**133**). In 1047 a Persian traveler also saw these pilgrims in the holy city (**142**). Finally, the contemporary Karaite scholars in the Empire are likewise known to have made this journey for various purposes (**App. A**).

The latent Messianic expectations are another well-known characteristic of the Jewish spirit (**30, 35**). One Christian chronicler had the bizarre notion that the Jews awaited Antichrist, who was to be born of a nun, a curious projection of his own belief in the virgin-birth (**25**). Theophanes makes a brief reference to the appearance of a Syrian pseudo-Messiah on the eve of Leo III's edict, in which a related misconception of the Jewish hope manifests itself, for the individual in question is said to have posed before the Jews as Christ, the son of God(!). It has been generally assumed that although the impostor himself remained in Mesopotamia, he acquired supporters both in the Empire and in distant Spain. However, a fresh study based on additional, as well as better, texts has convinced the present writer that there is no valid basis for supposing that the movement spread beyond Asia Minor (**11 n.**).

Byzantine Jewry did, however, definitely experience an upheaval due to such yearnings, at a later date. In the summer of 1096 one of the advance parties of the First Crusade, made up of Franks, reached Thessalonica, and since the group included women, we infer that it pertained to the « People's Crusade », a group known to have journeyed πανοικί. The news of the massacres perpetrated in central Europe had not yet reached the Empire, and despite a dubious notice of a similar event in that region (157), there is no reason to believe that the Crusaders ever committed such excesses there. There was nothing then to oppose the suggestion that these Westerners were the harbingers of a glorious climax to Israel's sufferings. Nothing is known of the particular person on whom the Messianic hopes were pinned, but no one doubted that he had already made his appearance. The huge Gentile migration to Palestine was viewed as one of the preliminaries of the new era, and, in accordance with tradition, it was understood that neither the Christian nor the Moslem combatants realized the true import of their divinely governed movements. They were to meet at Jerusalem where they would battle to their mutual destruction, and clear the way for the triumphant arrival of the Messiah leading the former exiles to their ancestral home. Moreover, his precursor, the prophet Elijah, had appeared in visions in Thessalonica and elsewhere, to both Jews and Christians. At first the groups of enthusiasts who left their homes and assembled at Abydos were excommunicated by the Constantinople community, but this cool-headed opposition could not withstand such a palpable sign as the restoration of sight to a blind man of prominence. The attitude of the emperor and of the local authorities, including the archbishop of Thessalonica, normally an anti-Jewish city, was entirely sympathetic, and not a few non-Jews were swept into the current. Whole Jewish communities were uprooted and were *en route* for the grand gathering to take place in that port. Here the imminence of the Messiah's advent had so distracted the Jews that their economic life was brought to a standstill. The days were filled with discussions of the latest exciting news, with the doing of penance by almsgiving, fasting, stripes, and confession, and with watchful waiting, while garbed in prayer-shawls. At this point, however, the curtain is drawn on the scene, for the remarkable document which relates these details closes, and we are left to supply for ourselves the heart-breaking anti-climax which inevitably followed it (153).

The excitement in Thessalonica during this abnormal season reveals incidentally certain phases of the Jewish reaction to the alien religious world about them. It seems clear from this, as from numerous other indications that, despite the *modus vivendi* arrived at between the orthodox majority and the adherents of the minority faith in daily life, their respective outlooks remained as irreconcilable as ever. Although a foreign observer like Benjamin of Tudela was carried away by the splendor of Christendom's greatest city, it is significant that to certain native Jews and Karaites the name Constantinople was anathema (63, 146). But since our period produced polemic literature of Christian authorship only, we are seriously handicapped in any effort to recover in concrete terms the attitude of the Jews to the Christian religion. Nevertheless, the sources in question are worthy of study because they may reflect in some degree the Jewish criticism of the dominant faith.

More common than any other polemic theme is the refutation of the Jewish argument that the veneration of images was idolatry. Bishop Leontios of Neapolis at the opening of our period bitterly protests against the Jews' stigmatizing good Christians as out and out idolaters (1), and his arguments are echoed in a number of later works within the Empire and elsewhere (1 n., 7, 82). On the eve of the execution of the iconoclastic policy by Leo III, Patriarch Germanos pens a statement to the same effect (9). Certain historians, including the late Prof. Uspenski, have held that the edict was motivated by a desire to silence such criticism on the part of Jews as well as Moslems and heretics, and it is true that the orthodox spokesmen accused both Leo III and Michael

II of yielding to Jewish influence. The most recent studies, however, tend toward the view that iconoclasm was essentially an inner development within orthodoxy itself, and that even such a sect as the Paulicians played no great role in its genesis. What room is left then for the alleged Jewish factor? Specifically with respect to Leo III there is available only a legend, which aims to show that the same Jews who persuaded a caliph to order the destruction of Christian images, caused the Emperor to do likewise in his own realm. Apart from the conflict between this tale and Leo's policy toward the Jews, there are certain elements here which suggest that this tale grew out of an historical personality, namely, Bésér, who was reputedly a convert from Islam, and the emperor's lieutenant in the iconoclastic program. But whether this theory be acceptable or not, the legend in question proves nothing with respect to Jewish influence (10). The case of Michael II has been discussed in detail in an earlier chapter, where on independent grounds it was seen that the sources in question are likewise not to be trusted (20, 28). The conclusion is inescapable that for a critical understanding of the iconoclastic movement, it is of little avail to look for a Jewish factor.

The polemic of Leontios indicates also that the Jews scoffed at the miracles of their own day which Christians pointed out to them (1). Finally, as might have been expected, the latter criticized the doctrine of the Trinity (6), and the eating of pork in violation of the explicit words of the Old Testament (7 n.).

CHAPTER VIII

CONCLUSION

The pursuit of research in medieval Jewish history is dependent in no slight measure on the status attained by the studies of
specialists in the contemporary Jewish literature. The dating of
the late *midrashim*, for example, constitutes one of the unsolved
problems relating to our subject. While there is no doubt that the
task of assigning each of these works to its probable time and
place has been proceeding with a certain amount of success, there
is still wide disagreement among scholars in this field. A concrete illustration of the ambiguous nature of the problem is the
controversy over the *Seder Eliyahu*. This *midrash* has been dated
variously from the fifth to the tenth century, and its author assigned to regions ranging from southern Italy to Mesopotamia.
Most recently the problem was reopened by Aptowitzer, and his
arguments seem to have disposed of the suggested European provenance quite effectively. He would place the work in the age
and realm of Hārūn ar-Rashīd, but believes that its author was an
immigrant from the Byzantine Empire (23 n.)! Such complications
may be rather discouraging, yet they do indicate that there is a
trend toward the development of a number of definite criteria
which will some day aid in distinguishing among the late
midrashim with respect to dating and place of composition.

A certain amount of progress could be achieved by access to
unpublished writings, For example, the publication of Mosconi's
super-commentary on Ibn Ezra in full would perhaps shed further
light on Byzantine-Jewish literature of the twelfth to fourteenth
centuries. As for the rabbinic commentaries of Hillel of Selymbria, an edition of these is long overdue. On the other hand, such

minor writings as the Biblical commentaries of Meyuhas b. Elijah need hardly be printed in entirety; it would be more useful for a competent student of medieval exegesis to examine the manuscript in detail and to furnish an adequate description of its content, citing the text wherever needed.

The historical Genizah material in Hebrew, which is relevant for our purpose, has apparently been fairly well exploited, and until the unpublished documents have been catalogued, it will be difficult to proceed with this task. There is no doubt, however, that there are hundreds of private letters in Arabic of this period, located in several European and American libraries, which may incidentally allude to aspects of Byzantine-Jewish life, and it is unfortunate that the limited attention which this material has received to date shows no signs of increasing. On the other hand, the liturgical poetry is under intensive study and, barring a cessation of this activity in the future, this branch of Jewish culture will unquestionably be better known as time goes on.

There are undoubtedly Christian and Islamic sources still in manuscript which have reference to Byzantine Jewry. Specific investigation of this literature for our purpose prior to its publication is naturally not feasible, except in the few instances where the material involving the Jews is relatively full. It is to be hoped that the scholars to whom such unpublished material is accessible will undertake source-extracts of that type. Thus, the process of collecting scattered references must continue as new sources are published, and along with it the finding of such references in a certain number of printed works which the present author has failed to obtain.

In view of their favorable situation, both economically and culturally, the mediocre achievements of the Jews of the Empire constitute a serious historical problem. We search in vain among them for at least one of those towering figures who once or twice each century arose in Israel and stimulated Jewish life in one or another aspect. The handful of writers and scholars to whom

Jewish history has awarded a place on the contemporary roll of honor, such as Donnolo, Ahīma'as, and Hillel b. Eliaqim, are but isolated phenomena and their scope extremely limited. It is true that neither was the preceding period in Byzantine history a particularly glorious one for the Jews, yet it was marked by a greater aggressiveness and participation in the contemporary political and cultural life. Were it not for the Apulian communities, one would be constrained to conclude that the visible continuity of Byzantine-Jewish life had been utterly disrupted by the Moslem conquests and the contemporary policy of Heraclius. The cultural atmosphere of that region, moreover, is sufficient answer to those whose ready solution of our problem is to point to the persecutions of the eighth to tenth centuries, as having stunted the development of Byzantine Jewry.

Students of medieval Jewish literature and history are accustomed to finding reflections of and reactions to the contemporary Islamic or Latin Christian environment. In the present study where the scene is laid in a large state certainly not inferior to its neighbors in commerce and in cultural activity, such materials are conspicuously absent. No doubt we are most seriously handicapped not only by the meagreness of the data from the Greek sources but also by the lack of such common records as Responsa, Genizah documents and archival materials, which illumine the situation in other parts of the world. There is, however, considerable encouragement in the fact that our store of data has increased in recent years to a remarkable extent, and there is reason to expect the accumulation to continue. It is not too much to expect that in the not too distant future research will uncover the causes which have interfered with the growth of Byzantine Jewry, as well as gain a better idea as to how Judaism was affected by its interaction with that environment.

PART TWO

SOURCE-MATERIALS AND NOTES

SYMBOLS AND ABBREVIATIONS

[ ] = enclosing the entire excerpt denotes a legendary or pseudepigraphic source of indirect interest only.

* = indicates that the source is reproduced partly in resume and and partly in quotation, as marked.

* * = description of a learned or literary work.

⟨ ⟩ = textual restorations.

Acta Sanct. = *Acta Sanctorum*, published by the Bollandists.
b. = son or daughter of.
Byz.-neugr. Jahr. = *Byzantinisch-neugriechische Jahrbücher.*
BZ = *Byzantinische Zeitschrift.*
CMH = *Cambridge Mediaeval History.*
Cod Iust. = *Codex Iustiniani.*
Cp. = Constantinople.
CSHB = *Corpus Scriptorum Historiae Byzantinorum*, published at Bonn.
Echos d'O. = *Echos d'Orient.*
EJ = *Encyclopedia Judaica.*
EL = Ἐγκυκλοπαιδικὸν Λεξικὸν Ἐλευθερουδάκη.
En. Is. = *Encyclopedia of Islam.*
Hasofeh = *Hasofeh le-hokmat Yisrael.*
HB = *Hebraeische Bibliographie.*
HUC An. = *Hebrew Union College Annual.*
JA = *Journal Asiatique.*
JE = *Jewish Encyclopedia.*
JHS = *Journal of Hellenic Studies.*
JQR = *Jewish Quarterly Review.*
Magazin = *Magazin für die Wissenschaft des Judentums.*
MGH = *Monumenta Germaniae Historica.*
Monats. = *Monatsschrift für die Geschichte und Wissenschaft des Judentums.*
Or. chr. = *Oriens Christianus.*
PG = *Patrologiae Graecae Cursus Completus*, published by Migne.
PO = *Patrologia Orientalis.*
ps. = pseudo.
R. = Rabbi.
REJ = *Revue des Études Juives.*
Rivista = *Rivista degli studi orientali.*
Sem. Kon. = *Seminarium Kondakovianum.*
Viertel. = *Vierteljahrschrift für Sozial-und Wirtschaftsgeschichte.*
VV = *Vizantiiski Vremennik.*
ZDMG = *Zeitschrift des deutschen morgenländischen Gesellschaft.*
ZfhB = *Zeitschrift für hebräische Bibliographie.*

a. Christian: The use of images is, despite Ex. 20: 4, ordained in Ex. 25: 18 and Ezek. 41: 18. Solomon also had them.

Jew: The various concrete representations used in the Israelites' worship served « solely to commemorate » (ὑπομνήσεως μόνης χάριν) certain events.

Christian: Well spoken. It would be equally repugnant to my faith to worship inanimate objects. Of course their symbolic function is their justification. « If you condemn me for bowing down to the wood of the cross as to God, why not condemn Jacob who 'bowed down at the point of Joseph's staff' (Septuagint, Gen. 47: 31; Heb. 11: 21)? »..... Yet no sooner do you see me adore the icon of Christ or of His Immaculate Mother,.... than you flare up. Straightway you turn aside with your calumny, and «stigmatize us as idolaters» (εἰδωλάτρας ἡμᾶς ἀποκαλεῖς)....

« How grievous is the obstinacy of these sinful Jews! How many shadow-appearances (ἐπισκιάσεις) and miracles of gushing (ἀναβλύσεις) have taken place, how many times has blood flown from the icons and the martyrs' relics! Yet these witless fellows, rather than being converted by such sights, held them to be imaginary and foolish » (μύθους καὶ λήρους).

Jew: Scripture forbids the worship of any created thing.

Christian: The earth and the hills were created by God, yet the Psalmist bids us worship them.

Jew: Not as deities, but for their Maker's sake.

Christian: Know then that I do likewise. In view of the variety of anti-idolatrous activities which we carry on, how can Jews stigmatize us as idolaters?

Leontios, bishop of Neapolis (Cyprus), Polemic against the Jews, extant portion from Bk. v; *PG*, XCIII, 1597 - 1609. Cf. variant text

84

cited by John of Damascus, *l. c.*, XCIV, 1272-6, 1381-8; tr. M. H. Allies. *St John Damascene on Holy Images.* London, 1898. pp. 43-8, 128-35. Read as appropriate to the signalizing of the triumph of orthodoxy at the Council of Nicaea, 787; J. D. Mansi. *Sacrorum conciliorum nova et amplissima collectio.* Florence, 1767. XIII, 44. Cf. O. Bardenhewer. *Geschichte der altkirchlichen Literatur.* Freiburg, 1932. V, 139.

Cf. Stephen of Bostra (*ca.* 700), *PG,* XCIV, 1376 (tr. Allies, *op. cit.,* 126-8), and I. M. Mercati, *Theologische Quartalschrift,* LXXVII, 1895, 663-8. Cf. the introductory section grafted on to later polemic: A. C. McGiffert. *Dialogue between a Christian and a Jew.* Marburg, 1889. pp. 51 f.; cf. 37 f., 85 f. Note also the refutation of the argument based on Gen. 47:31 given by a Byzantine Karaite, Judah Hadassī (12 th c.); ed. W. Bacher, *JQR,* VIII, 1897, 432.

« *b.* Show me the portent of the coming of Christ in the light of [the predictions regarding the millennium made in (quoting) Mic. 4: 3, Jer. 31:34 [Septuagint], Is. 11:6, 9.' This is the Jews' well-known challenge (τὸ πολυθρύλλητον ζήτημα). Now then, let them know these things have actually occurred......»

Leontios; citation apparently from the same work as the foregoing, preserved by Euthymios Zigabenos (12 th c.), *PG,* CXXX, 292-6. See no. **160.**

661 **2**

The vilest and wildest element of the populace [of Cp.] took up arms against [Patriarch] Pyrrhos, and proceeded to the church [St. Sophia], where, however, they failed to find him. They entered it about the time of the Lamplight Service [Vespers], drawing along with them a mob of Hebrews and other misbelievers, and penetrated as far as the altar-section. They ripped up the altar-cloth and shamefully defiled the sacred precincts. Then, seizing the gate-keys, they hung them on a pole, and thus marched in disorder around the city.

Nikephoros (9 th c.). Ἱστορία Σύντομος, ed. K. de Boor, *Opuscula historica.* Leipzig, 1880. pp. 30 f. "No Jewish issue is known to have been involved in this uprising, on the circumstances of which see J. B. Bury. *History of the later Roman Empire.* London, 1889. II, 285.

Cf. J. Starr. «Byzantine Jewry on the eve of the Arab conquest», *Journal of the Palestine Oriental Society*, XV, 1935, 289; A. Andréadès. «The Jews in the Byzantine empire», *Economic History*, III, 1934, 14. On the supposed prohibition of residence within the city proper since *ca.* 435, see J. Juster. *Les juifs dans l'empire romain.* Paris, 1914. I, 470, n. 2. Yet the author of the legend of Theodore and Abraham depicts the latter as living inside the city under Heraclius. See M. Hoferer. *Ioannis monachi Liber de miraculis.* Würzburg, 1884. pp. 7-41. Cf. E. Caspar, *Zeitschrift für Kirchengeschichte,* LII, 1933, 49-53.

(For a late fabrication relating to this period, see I. Loeb, *REJ,* VI, 1882, 115; XV, 1887, 262-70).

648-9   **3**

A certain seventeen-year-old youth, who had been rescued from captivity in the east [Asia Minor], approached Bishop John of Amathos [Cyprus], and urgently requested him to deem his petitioner worthy of the sacred baptism and to aid him to become a Christian. Christmas was at hand and the youth importuned the holy bishop to consider him worthy of the sacred rite of baptism on that feast. The godly prelate, trusting in the grace of the Holy Spirit abiding within him, said to the youth, « Hearken unto me, my son, and bide your time until Easter. Put your hope in God that you become worthy to receive manifestly the grace of the Holy Spirit, so that the Christian faith may be glorified thereby. »

The lad heeded the words of the saint and through the glory of the Lord was deemed worthy of events, revelations, and visions, such as, I dare say, none of the ancient converts to Christ had ever experienced. He was baptized on the Holy Sabbath....

Anastasios (the Sinaite?; late 7 th c.), ed. F. Nau. «Le texte grec des récits utiles à l'âme d'Anastase (le Sinaïte)». *Or. chr.,* III, 1903, 71; abstract, *idem, Revue de l'institut catholique de Paris,* VII, 1902, 142. For the author to whom Nau would assign this work, see no. **6**. On the Arab incursions in 'Ανατολὴ and in Cyprus, the latter being likewise mentioned in the context, see L. Caetani. *Annali dell'Islam.* Milan, 1914. VII, 178, 222-31. This *exemplum* is immediately preceded by another narrating the fate of one Daniel, a Jewish sorcerer of Salamis, who *ca.* 637 was burnt at the stake for plying his craft.

On the encouragement of an extended catechumenate, cf. no. **76**. Justinian had prescribed a two-year period for the Samaritans, and his successor renewed the law in 572; see F. Dölger. *Regesten der Kaiserurkunden des oströmischen Reiches.* Munich - Berlin, 1924. I, pt. l, p. 4, no. 28. Cf. also a canon of 506 in the Visigothic kingdom which requires 8 months; Juster, I, 114, n. 2.

ca. 655 **4**

The bishop Zosimus had the church at Syracuse [Sicily] restored and re-decorated in extraordinary fashion in the eighty-second year of his life, which was the fifth of his episcopate. The event was celebrated by all with great rejoicing and exultation. When certain Hebrew immigrants observed this, they desired to build a synagogue of their own; however, they greatly feared.... Zosimus. Knowing that it was in his power to stop them, they vainly hoped to achieve their aim by paying a hireling and by means of corrupt individuals. For a certain Syracusan official, who had previously been corrupted by gifts and bribery, approached the bishop with regard to this matter. « Father », he said, « what I ask of your Holiness is not to contemn me, your son, for I come not with a profitless request.»

« I will by no means contemn you, my son, » replied Zosimus, « if what you ask be worthwhile without being difficult of performance.» The request was then laid before him: that he should permit the Hebrew strangers in that city to build themselves a synagogue, the previous one having been destroyed by the Vandals some time ago. The bishop, greatly perturbed, responded, «'Do I not hate them, 0 Lord, that hate thee?'... [Ps. 139: 21f.]» After a brief silence he turned to the man, and continued, « Why was it necessary for you to accommodate yourself to those from whom Christ now suffers insult? This Zosimus will never allow».

Seeing this reaction, great fear and astonishment came over the official, because the man whom he had always found gentle and affable, had become angry with him and because he had so rendered his decision. Wherefore did the former from then on turn his mind away from the synagogue and the Hebrews, although he had been their fautor and champion up to this time.

Anon. contemp. life of Zosimus, ed. O. Gaetano. *Acta Sanct.*, Mar., III. Paris, 1865. p. 839 (tr. of a lost Greek text). The bishop's legal support is *Cod. Iust.* 1.9.18. The destruction of the synagogue probably occurred during one of Gaiseric's raids on the island, *ca.* 457 or later; the *terminus ad quem*, if not within his lifetime, is 536-7. See Procopius (6th c.). *History of the wars of Justinian*, ed. and tr. H. B. Dewing. London-New York, 1916. Bk. III, v, 22 f.; xiv, 4 (vol. II, pp. 52, 326). See the local Greek synagogue inscription in J. B. Frey. *Corpus inscriptionum iudaicarum.* Rome, 1936. I, 468 f.

The foregoing interpretation of *Vandali* is opposed to that of Lancia di Brolo. *Storia della chiesa in Sicilia nei primi dieci secoli del cristianesimo.* Palermo, 1884. II, 25, n. 1, 32, 356. That scholar took the term as paronomasia for the Arab raiders some years before, on the basis of a parallel usage in the *9 th c.* life of St. Leo Luke, *Acta Sanct.*, Mar., I, 98. But since the Arabs in 652 failed to enter the city proper, he was forced to assume that the synagogue stood outside the walls. Cf. B. Pace, *Archivio storico siciliano,* XXXVI, 1911, 24. This view fails to account for the fact that the Jewish petitioners were all *advenae* or *peregrini*, and that there was no community in Syracuse at this time.

The title *Princeps* is too grandiose if it designates a local *(Syracusanus)* official. Perhaps it refers to the strategos (or patrikios) of Sicily, regularly stationed in this city.

ca. 660   **5**

About this time many Jews believed and became Christians.

Michael «the Syrian» (12th c.). *Makhtebhānūth zabhne (Chronique),* ed. and tr. J. B. Chabot. Paris, 1899-1924. IV, 435, col. 3; tr. II, 453. One of a series of disparate notices in the division devoted to the eastern patriarchates.

ca. 665-700   **6**

... However, when we cited this word [Ποιήσωμεν, Gen. 1: 26] on a certain occasion to one of the Hebrews, — for many disputations and conflicts have again and again (quite extemporaneously) arisen between members of that people and ourselves — the impious fellow countered, « Any king may say either 'Let us make', or 'We command' even though he is is but a single individual. »

(Cum nos autem aliquando hanc vocem proferremus apud quendam ex Hebraeis, multa enim et saepenumero cum eorum genere ortae nobis sunt controversiae ac contradictiones [plane extemporales]...).

To this we replied as follows, « And why did not God choose to employ this expression, 'Let us make', with reference to any other creature whatsoever, prior to the creation of man? He chose to limit it to the case of man alone, as well as to that of woman...» At this the Jew's voice failed, and there was no further attempt at refutation....

Note then that in the countless multitude of men there is one nature. This has been discussed in the second book of our *Against the Jews.....*

Anastasios the Sinaite, *PG,* LXXXIX, 931, 933 (Latin version only); closing words quoted in Greek from the ms. in I. B. Pitra. *Iuris ecclesiastici graecorum historia et monumenta.* Rome, 1868. II, 244, n. 2. See K. Krumbacher. *Geschichte der byzantinischen Litteratur.* 2 nd ed., Munich, 1897. pp. 64 f. Bardenhewer, *op. cit.,* V, 43. J. Parkes. *The conflict of the church and synagogue.* London, 1934. pp. 288 f.

For the great antiquity of the controversy over Gen. 1 : 26, see A. H. Goldfahn, *Monats.,* XXII, 1873, 143 f. It reappears in an Arabic tract composed in 997, but purporting to recount an event which occurred on Byzantine territory in 622. See R. Griveau. «Histoire de la conversion des juifs habitant la ville de Tomai en Égypte d'après d'anciens manuscrits arabes». *Revue de l'Orient Chrétien,* XIII, 1908, 302 f.

680   **7**

The Jews who had met us previously came secretly, and having greeting us courteously said, « God knows, you have won gracefully and decisively. Nevertheless, we are still troubled in spirit, for there are among us here some Cappadocian (?) Jews of whom we are proud beyond all others (τινες ἐνταῦϑα καμπάδοκες ἰουδαῖοι εἰς οὓς καυχώμεθα πλείω πάντων). God will impel you to hold a public debate with them.»

We gladly acquiesced and on the morrow reassembled with the Jews, and as impudence was habitual with them, they assailed us with questions in this wise.....

Anon. dialogue, ed. and tr. G. Bardy. «Les trophées de Damas». *PO*, XV (1927), 234. From the prologue to the third of the four sessions, no further allusion being made to the provenance of the Jews in question. Among the issues discussed in the 3rd session occur those of image-worship (cf. no. **1**) and the Biblical prohibition of pork; with the latter cf. the undated fragment, *PG*, LXXXIX, 1272 f. See also F. Dvornik. *Les légendes de Constantin et de Méthode vues de Byzance.* Prag, 1933. pp. 198 - 203 ; Parkes, *op. cit.*, 287 - 9 ; A. L. Williams. *Adversus Judaeos.* Cambridge, 1935. pp. 162 - 6.

692
8

... Whatever remnant of pagan or Jewish perversity is mixed with the ripe fruit of the truth, must be uprooted like a weed.....

Canon 11. [a] Neither clergyman nor layman may partake of the unleavened bread of the Jews, [b] associate (προσοικειοῦσθω) with them, [c] accept medical treatment from them, [d] or bathe with them. Should anyone attempt to do it, he shall, if a clergyman, be defrocked, if a layman, excommunicated.

Acts of the Trullan (Quinisext) Council at Cp., ed. Mansi, XI, 933, 945. See also C. J. Hefele. *Histoire des conciles.* Tr. H. Leclerq. Paris, 1907. III, pt. 1, 564. The slightly fuller form of *c* which is given by Andréadès, *Econ. His.,* III, 12, n. 4, follows the variant text of G. A. Rhalles and M. Potles. Σύνταγμα τῶν Θείων καὶ ἱερῶν κανονῶν. Athens, 1854. II, 328 f.; *PG*, CXXXVII, 552. The canon was adopted by Latin Christendom and incorporated in less concise form in the *Corpus iuris canonici,* ed. A. L. Richter and A. Friedberg. Leipzig, 1879. I, 1087 (XXVIII, q. 1, c. 13). However, corresponding to our clause *b* the text reads: «aut cum eis habitet», which may be a mistranslation or may be due to the use of a Greek copy which read προσοικεῖσθω. Cf. the same mistake made by a modern translator; R. Janin. «Les juifs dans l'empire byzantin», *Echos d'O.,* XV, 1912, 130.

The immediate predecessor of *a* is canon 38 of the Laodicean Council (late 3 rd c.); Mansi, II, 571. With regard to *c*, John Chrysostom, speaking in Antioch three centuries earlier, had made it a clear-cut issue, saying in effect: Would you heal your body, even if you thereby lost your soul?; *PG*, XLVIII, 855. (Cf. Juster, II, 281, n. 2, 283, n. 4). The other two provisions appear here for the first time. For later Byzantine references, see Simeon Metaphrastes (10 th c.), *PG*, CXIV, 284, no. 10; Balsamon, *PG*, CXXXVII, 508, 552; Arsenios, (13 th c.) *PG*, CXXXIII, 57. The prohibition of praying together included in the canonical synopsis of Stephen of Ephesus, ed. M. Krasnojen, *VV*, XVII, 1910, 239, goes back to an earlier source; Juster, I, 279, n. 2.

715-25.   9

In the first place it is necessary to know this fact, that not once but many times have the Jews brought these things [icon-worship] up to us for shame.

Germanos, patriarch of Cp., to Thomas, bishop of Claudiopolis *PG*, XCVIII, 168. A copy seems to have been sent to the Pope; see E. Caspar. «Papst Gregor II und der Bilderstreit». *Zeitschrift für Kirchengeschichte*, LII, 1934, 33. Cf. nos. **1**, **7**.

[*ca.* 715-727   1C

The first man to give the inspiration to this heresy [icono-clasm] was named Konon, but adopted the name Leo. He acqui red that dark notion from the Hebrews. Before his accession while he was out for a walk, a Hebrew said to him, «You shall become emperor and if you will adhere to the advice which now give you, your reign and glory will be long-lasting. Dis card your present name and call yourself Leo, for during you reign, the images in which the Christians believe, will be over thrown. So give me your word to overthrow them durin; your reign.»

Taken in by this, «the dragon of the deep» promised accord ingly.... Ten years after his accession, upon going out, he me his guide to destruction, who handed him a paper, no doubt con

taining his request. The emperor recognized the Hebrew, immediately invited him into the palace, and accepted him from then on
as collaborator in his impious work.

John of Damascus. *PG*, XCV, 336 f. See Bardenhewer, V, 56. Cf.
H. Koretz, *EJ*, V, 472. The scene of the first encounter is probably
meant to be the province of Isauria; Bury, *op. cit.*, II, 374, 430. In
other versions this story is assimilated to a similar tale involving
one or two Jews who misled the caliph Yazīd II in the same way.
He died, however, contrary to their promise of a long reign, whereupon they were duly executed by his successor; Mansi, XIII, 197-200
(read before the Council of 787). But cf. the variant of this in a
spurious letter to Emperor Theophilos, *PG*, XCV, 356 f. For further
discussion and source-references see Starr, «An iconodulic legend and
its historical basis». *Speculum*, VIII, 1933, 500-3. For a western reflection, H. Loewe, *Monats.*, LVI, 1912, 262 f.

Of the vast literature on this subject, the most relevant studies
for the present purpose are: E. J. Martin. *A history of the Iconoclastic
movement.* London, 1932; W. Elliger. «Zur bilderfeindlichen Bewegung
des achten Jahrhunderts». *Forschungen zur Kirchengeschichte und zur
christlichen Kunst.* Leipzig, 1931. pp. 40-60; ct. F. I. Uspenski. *Istoria
Vizantiiskoi Imperii.* Leningrad, 1927. II, pt. 1, 23 f.]

721 - 2   **11**

a. In this year the emperor [Leo III] compelled the Jews
and the Montanists to undergo baptism. The Jews, though unwilling (ἀπροαιρέτως; or « without reflection »), accepted baptism
and then washed it off. They partook of the holy communion
after having eaten and thus polluted the faith.

Theophanes (9 th c.). *Chronographia,* ed. de Boor. Leipzig, 1883.
p. 401. Cf. Kedrenos, *PG*, CXXI, 869 (where it is shifted to the following year), and no. 12. See Martin, *op, cit.,* 26; P. de Labriolle. *Les
sources de l'histoire du montanisme.* Paris-Freiburg, 1913. pp. 250 f.

b. In that year [*ca.* 720] Leo, the emperor of Byzantium,
undertook to convert to Christianity the dissenting sects of his
empire, and the non-Christians. He began by christianizing the
Jewish people and the HR'S, and the converts were called
« New Christians. »

Agapius (Mahbūb, 10th c.). *Kitāb al-ʿUnwān = Histoire Universelle,* ed. and tr. A. A. Vasiliev. *PO,* VIII, 504.

c. At this time [723] Leo instituted a persecution of all those resident in his realm who were alien to his faith. Many thereupon fled to Arab territory... Some of the Jews accepted baptism and became Christians; these were called νέοι πολῖται, which is to say « New Citizens.»

Michael, IV, 457; II, 489 f. Cf. Bar Hebraeus (13th c.). *Makhte-ɉhānūth zabhnē,* ed. P. Bedjan. Paris, 1890. p. 118; tr. E. A. W. Budge. *The chronography of Gregory Abu'l Faraj.* London, 1932. p. 109. See also the *Anonymi auctoris chronicon ad A. C. 1234 pertinens,* ed. Chabot. Paris, 1920. I, 308. The following chronographers agree with Michael's date: Khwarizmī (9th c.) in Elīsha b. Shināyā. *Makhtebhā-nūth zabhnē* (Arabic-Syriac) = *Opus chronologicum,* ed. E. W. Brooks. Paris-Rome-Leipzig, 1910. p. 162, tr. 178. Ekkehard (12th c.). *Chronicon universale,* ed. G. H. Pertz. [*MGH:* Script., VI.] Hannover, 1844. p. 157. But cf. Dölger, *Regesten,* I, pt. 1, 35, no. 286.

J. Mann, *Journal of the American Oriental Society,* XLVII, 1927, 364, in a summary of an unpublished paper suggested that the edict was precipitated by the problematic Messianic excitement-discussed by H. Graetz. *Geschichte der Juden.* 4th ed., Leipzig, 1909. V, 169 f., 457-60. Cf. S. Krauss. *Studien zur byzantinisch-jüdischen Geschichte.* Leipzig, 1914. pp. 38-40. The present writer's study of the known facts regarding this pseudo-Messiah, «Le mouvement messianique du huitième siècle antérieur», will appear in *REJ* in 1937.

In the opinion of S. Vailhé, *Échos d'O.,* V, 1902, 386, there is an allusion to this persecution in a sermon by Andrew of Crete, *PG,* XCVII, 1905. The reference, however, appears to be irrelevant.

[721-2 **12**

He [Leo III] forcibly baptized the Jews and they were thenceforth called Montanists.

«Leo Grammatikos». (10th c.) *Chronographia,* ed. I. Bekker. Bonn, 1842. (*CSHB,* XLVII) p. 179. A confusion due to the juxtaposition of the two groups in no. 11, and to the fact that both terms were hurled as epithets against the iconoclasts; e. g., Mansi, XIV, 120 (Council of

814). For another manifestation of the confusion, no. **122**, end. The editor of the latter text, however, holds that the two notices constitute evidence of some relationship between the Jews and this Christian sect. See V. N. Beneshevich. «On the history of the Jews in Byzantium, 6-10th centuries.» (Russian) *Evreiskaya Mysl.* II, 1926, 216.]

ca. 722   **13**

The Jews began to come [to Khazaria] from Baghdad, from Khorasan, and from the land of Greece.

Anon. letter (12-13th c.?), ed. and tr. S. Schechter. «An unknown Khazar document.» *JQR,* III, 1912, 206, lines 36 f., tr., 215. The conversion of the Khazar nobility to Judaism is usually dated within the ensuing two decades: e. g., J. Brutzkus, *EJ,* V, 341. See also A.A. Vasiliev. *The Goths in the Crimea.* Cambridge, Mass., 1936. pp. 102 f. But cf. A. Brückner, *Zeitschrift für slavische Philologie,* X, 1933, 468. Even before the discovery of this source it was inferred that refugees from the Empire had a hand in the matter. See L. Zunz. *Gesammelte Schriften.* Berlin, 1875. I, 89; Graetz, *Gesch.,* V, 198. In this source, however, the influx of the Jews is placed immediately *after* the conversion.

There is now available an exhaustive treatise on the Hebrew sources relating to the Khazars: P. K. Kokovtzov. *Evreisko-Khazarskaya Perepiska v X Veke.* Leningrad, 1932. He recognizes the historical value of our source, but considers it a pseudepigraph, rather than of genuine Khazar authorship. He shows that its style has been influenced by *Yosippon* (no. **85**), and is inclined to assign it to a Byzantine provenance; pp. XXVI-XXXVI. In his notes to the tr. he gives a number of instances of the transcription of gentilic and geographical names which correspond to the Greek form as against the Arabic; pp. 119-23.

[731   **14**

He [Leo III] burdened the Calabrians and Sicilians with new taxes, decreeing that they should pay the capitation-tax like the Jews, and that they should register their male births.

Zonaras. *Epitoma historiarum,* ed. T. Büttner-Wobst. Bonn, 1897. III, 263 (*CSHB,* XLVI). Based on Theophanes, 410; cf. Kedrenos, 877, 880.

94

THEOPHANES	KEDRENOS	ZONARAS
κρατυνόμενος φόρους	φόρους κεφαλικῶς τῷ	τούς τε Καλαβρούς
κεφαλικούς τῷ τρίτῳ μέρει	τρίτῳ μέρει Σ. καὶ Κ.	καί τοὺς Σικελοὺς
Σικελίας καὶ Καλαβρίας	τοῦ λαοῦ ἐπέθηκε...	φόροις νέοις ἐβάρυνε,
τοῦ λαοῦ ἐπέθηκεν...		κεφαλητίωνα τελεῖν
ἐποπτεύειν τε καὶ	ἐποπτεύειν τε καὶ	κατὰ τοὺς Ἰουδαίους
ἀναγράφεσθαι τὰ	ἀναγράφεσθαι τὰ	δογματίσας αὐτοὺς
τικτόμενα κελεύσας	τικτόμενα βρέφη	καὶ τὰ ἐν αὐτοῖς
ἄρρενα βρέφη, ὡς Φαραώ	πρὸς τὸ ἀπαιτεῖσθαι	τικτόμενα ἄρρενα
ποτε τὰ τῶν Ἑβραίων.	τὸν λεγόμενον	ἀπογράφεσθαι.
	κεφαλητίωνα.	

The matter is registered in Dölger, *Regesten,* I, pt. 1, 36, no. 300. See also Brooks, *ZDMG,* LI, 1897, 584, n. 6. The *kephalétiôn* problem is discussed by Dölger, «Die Frage der Judensteuer in Byzanz.» *Viertel.*, XXVI, 1935, 1-24. A contrary viewpoint was maintained by A. Andréadès, «Les juifs et le fisc dans l'Empire byzantin.» *Mélanges Diehl.* Paris. 1930. I, 7-29; cf. *idem, BZ,* XXVIII, 1928, 312-5. The latter announced his agreement with the former's interpretation in *Economic History,* III, 18.

On the taxation of the Jews in the earlier period see Juster, II, 287 f. But his citation of *Basilika,* IX. 54. 30 is erroneous. As extant that code does not repeat the act regarding the *aurum coronarium;* no. 83].

[74] **15**

Manichees and Montanists shall suffer death by the sword.

Leo III and Constantine IV. «Eklogé», XVIII, 52, ed. J. and P. Zépos. *Jus graecoromanum (ex editione C. E. Zachariä a Lingenthal).* Athens, 1931. II, 61. Tr. E. H. Freshfield. *A manual of Roman law : the Ecloga.* Cambridge, 1926. p. 113. See K. E. Zachariä von Lingenthal. *Geschichte des griechischrömischen Rechts.* 2nd ed., Berlin, 1892. p. 338. On the date see Dölger, I, 1, p. 37, no. 304; V. Grumel. «La date de la promulgation de l'Écloge de Léon III». *Echos d' O.,* XXXVIII, 1933, 326-31.

On the preoccupation of the administration with internal revolts and external attacks, see Bury, *op. cit.,* II, 402-49. See F. Cumont. «La conversion des juifs byzantins au IXᵉ siècle». *Revue de l'instruction publique en Belgique,* XLVI, 1903, 9. There is no sound basis for Cumont's statement that aggressive Jewish propaganda was carried on during the ensuing period. The first to have expressed this notion of a contemporary «ardeur de prosélytisme» within the Empire, seems to have been A. Rambaud. *L'empire grec au 10ᵉ siècle.* Paris, 1870. pp. 248 f. Most recently even Charles Diehl has suscribed to this idea; *CMH,* IV, 7. See no. **23 n.**].

[768-75   **16**

Moreover, two Hebrews brought to the aforesaid emperor [Charlemagne] an official epistle written in the hand of the emperor Constantine [V], accompanied by extraordinary gifts. Their names are Ysaac and Samuel. The former is said to have been a man of truly great expertness and facility in his law, while Samuel was a priest in their midst, a devout man, versed in both languages [Greek and Latin].

«Exemplar epistole Iohannis patriarche» in the anon. «De sanctitate meritorum et gloria miraculorum beati Karoli magni ad honorem et laudem domini dei», ed. G. Rauschen. *Die Legende Karls des Grossen.* Leipzig, 1890. p. 48; cf. 147 f. Dölger, *Regesten,* I, 39, no. 329. See also M. Schwab. «Sur une lettre d'un empereur byzantin», *JA,* CXLIX, 1896, 498-509. The legendary character of this source taken in entirety is indubitable. No other mention of a Jewish messenger employed by a Byzantine emperor is extant, but the idea may have been suggested to the mind of this writer by the case of Isaac who served in the alleged embassy of Charlemagne to the caliph. See J. Aronius. *Regesten zur Geschichte der Juden im fränkischen und deutschen Reiche.* Berlin, 1902. p. 25, no. 68].

[*ca.* 780   **17**

That period brought forth during his [Leo's] saintly life, a certain demonic creature produced by Sicily, whose name was Heliodoros and who was full of all kinds of sorcery and jugglery.... Having found a certain Hebrew who was famed for his magic and witchcraft, Heliodoros invited him and associated with him on friendly terms, endeavoring to learn from him some device whereby to achieve his desire. The Hebrew being capable of evil and expert in such machinations, gave him a written sheet of paper, which looked like a letter, and directed him to go that very midnight to the heroic tombs and to stand upon a tall pillar. «From there» he said, «you will see him [the devil] coming through the air, fearful to behold and most frightful. When you see him, be not afraid but stand firm. When he orders you to descend, do not do so until he promises you to fulfill all your requests.»

Anon. life of Leo, bishop of Catania, ed. V. V. Latyshev. *Neizdannie gretcheskie agiografitcheski teksti.* *Zapiski* of the Akademiia Nauk (of Petrograd), historical-philological class, series 8, XII, no. 2. Petrograd, 1914. pp. 15 f. Hitherto known only from a somewhat free Latin tr., in O. Gaetano (Caietanus). *Vitae sanctorum Siculorum.* Palermo, 1657. II, 6. The latter notes that some other source makes Heliodoros a Jew also, and this though evidently a derivative notion is carelessly repeated by several scholars. Cf. di Brolo, *op. cit.,* 131; U. Cassuto, *EJ,* V, 96; C. Libertini. «Catania nell'età bizantina». *Archivio storico per la Sicilia orientale,* XXVIII, 1932, 251, 256. More accurately, M. Amari. *Storia dei Musulmani di Sicilia.* 2nd ed., Catania, 1933. I, 344.

For earlier and later references to the local community see Frey, *Corpus,* I, 466 f., and J. Mann. *Texts and studies in Jewish history and literature.* Cincinnati, 1931. I, 34-44.]

787

18

That Hebrews not be Accepted unless They Turn away with Willing Hearts

Certain deceitful adherents of the religion of the Hebrews, thinking to mock Christ our Lord, pretend to be Christians while secretly denying Him and stealthily observing the Sabbath and other Jewish customs. We prescribe that they be admitted neither to communion, nor to prayer, nor into the church, but that the Hebrews should live openly according to their own religion (φανερῶς εἶναι κατὰ τὴν ἑαυτῶν θρησκείαν), neither baptizing their children, nor purchasing slaves, nor possessing them. Should one of them voluntarily confess whole-heartedly, scorning their customs and pursuits, and in addition refuting and reforming others, then accept and baptize such an individual as well as his children. Moreover, guard him from apostasizing to the usages of the Hebrews. Never accept one who is not of this type.

Acts of the second Council of Nicaea, canon 8; ed. Mansi, XIII, 427, 430. See also Hefele-Leclerq, *op. cit.*, III, pt. 2, 282.

Zonaras and Balsamon take the canon to refer to Christian slaves; *PG,* CXXXVII, 916. The concluding lines are influenced by the text of the earlier formula of abjuration (ed. Beneshevich, *Fxr. Mysl,* 305, cf. 213 f.); ct. Juster, I, 119. Writing about 1150, Arsenios of Athos, remarked with respect to this canon that Jews and heretics must make their declarations in writing; *PG,* CXXXIII, 57.

797-802   **19**

a. A Jew cannot hold a post of honor, nor serve as magistrate, nor do military service. But he shall be subject to the lot of the decurionate and the disabilities thereof. And if one should by political influence attain any rank, he shall be expelled, and shall pay a fine of 30 lbs. of gold.

b. A Christian who becomes a Jew shall have his property confiscated.

c. Samaritans or Jews who tempt anyone to renounce the faith of Christians shall have their property confiscated and be decapitated.

d. A Jew shall not on any pretext possess a Christian slave or one belonging to any other sect. If he does and circumcizes him, the State shall emancipate the slave and the owner shall suffer capital punishment. A pagan, Jew, or Samaritan, and anyone who is not an orthodox Christian, cannot possess a Christian slave. If he does, he shall be freed and the owner must pay the fisc 30 lbs. of gold.

e. No Jew, pagan, or heretic, shall possess a Christian slave, and if any such should be found, the slave shall forthwith be taken and set free.

f. A slave who serves a pagan, Jew, Samaritan, or heretic, if he is not a Christian and wishes to become one, shall be set free at the same time as he receives the rite of baptism. And his master cannot take him back into slavery even though the former should afterwards become a Christian,

g. We impose confiscation of property and perpetual banishment on Jews who are found to have circumcized a Christian, or who command any other person to do so.

«Appendix to *Ekloge*», ed. A. G. Monferratus. *Ecloga Leonis et Constantini cum Appendice*. Athens, 1889. IV, 6, 16,24; VI, 26-8, 30 (pp. 64-6, 72 f.); tr. Freshfield, *Ecloga*, 130-2, 137 f. (requires occasional correction). The translator's inference that IV, 7, applies to Jews is false. An obscure private manual of selections from Justinian's *Corpus*; on the date see Zachariä, *op. cit.*, 18.

a. See no. **83**, n. *b*. The development of the theme-system had by this time caused the tax-burden once imposed on the decurionate to lapse into disuse. See F. Dölger. *Beiträge zur Geschichte der byzantinischen Finanzverwaltung*. Leipzig-Berlin, 1928. pp. 74 f. (Also pointed out by G. Caro. *Sozial- und Wirtschaftsgeschichte der Juden*. 2nd ed. Frankfort, 1924. I, 492.) Nevertheless, we find it again in a 12 th c. manual intended for use in Italy, the so-called «Ecloga ad Procheiron mutata», XXXVI, 13, ed. Zepos, *Jus graecor.*, VI, 297.

b. See no. **83**, n. *t*.

c. *Ib.*, n. *m*.

d., e. *Ib.*, nn. *o, w, x*.

f. Cf. *Cod. Iust.* 1.3.54 (56). s. 8; Juster, II, 76.

g. See no. **83**, n. 1.

ca. 800   **20**

He [Michael II] hailed from an upper Phrygian town called Amorion, in which a large number (πλῆθος) of Jews and Athinganoi had always lived together (ἀεὶ πως ἐγκατοικίζεται). Out of this constant intercourse of differing groups there sprung up a certain heresy........ in which he participated, following in the footsteps of his ancestors. This sect viewed the divine immersion [baptism] as a means of salvation, and permitted it to its initiates; as regards all else, they observed the Mosaic Law with the exception of circumcision.

Every initiate procured for himself as teacher and guide

(Διδάσκαλον δὲ καὶ οἷον ἔξαρχον) a Hebrew man or woman who had never been baptized, and entrusted to him or her the control of his household affairs, both the spiritual and the material ones being placed under him or her. Thus was he brought up within this sect.....

Anon. «Theophanes continuatus» (10 th c.). *PG,* CIX, 56; cf. Kedrenos, 954, Zonaras, III, 337. See J. B. Bury. *History of the Eastern Roman Empire.* London, 1912. p. 78; Martin, *op. cit.,* 170. Cf. Genesios, Βασιλεῖαι, *PG,* CIX, 1026, 1028, who, however, makes no reference either to the Jews or to the customs of the Athinganoi. See further, Starr, «An eastern Christian sect: the Athinganoi», *Harvard Theological Review,* XXIX, 1936, 93 - 106.

For a rather uncritical discussion see Caro, «Ein jüdischer Proselyt (?) auf dem Thron vom Byzanz». *Monats.,* LIII, 1909, 576 - 80; likewise, Krauss, *Studien,* 40.

Michael states that the emperor «was of Jewish extraction, . . . his grandfather having turned Christian»; *Chronique,* ed. Chabot, IV, 522, top, col. 2; tr. III, 72. Cf. Bar Hebraeus, 141; tr. Budge, 129.

800 - 850   **21**

In my time [ms. *be-yōmo*] there was a Jew named Rabbi Ahīma'as, who went up to Jerusalem the glorious three times to fulfill his vows. On each pilgrimage he took 100 gold pieces with him, as he had vowed......, in aid of those who were engaged in the study of the Torah, and of those who mourned for His majestic habitation. Before he set out for the third time he asked my mother for me, saying, « Let him go with me to be of service to me... » So we set out joyfully on our journey....

As we were sitting [in Jerusalem] around the dining-table with the head of the academy and the scholars, the former said to them, « Let the young man in our midst, who has come with our colleague R. A., cheer us and delight our hearts with the flow of his feelings... » Then I proceeded reverently to give praise to Him in psalm and song...

[One of the Jerusalemite scholars is moved to tears by the premonition that the youth is to die before reaching home. R. A., anxious above all to keep his promise to restore him to his mother, persuades the scholars to extend the boy's life indefinitely by incising the Tetragrammaton in his arm. They return to Italy, and the youth outlives R. A.].

Ahīmaʿas of Oria (11th c.). «Sefer Yuhasīn», ed A. Neubauer. *Medieval Jewish Chronicles. (Anecdota Oxoniensa :* Semitic Series, I, VI). Oxford, 1895. II, 113 f. Text reprinted in A. Kahana. *Sifrut ha-Historiah ha - Yisreelit.* Warsaw, 1922. I, 119 f. (The orthographic changes intoduced here rob this edition of its quality as a primary source, yet it has several features which render it indispensable. The introduction and annotations are quite good, considering their conciseness. The text is partially vocalized and divided into verses.) Another edition with an introduction and English translation, both very unsatisfactory, is given by M. Salzman. *The chronicle of Ahimaaz.* New York, 1924. pp. 2 f.; tr. 61 f.

On the theme of the *golem* in general, see G. Sholem, *EJ*, VII, 501-7. The date is uncertain but Mann is mistaken in making Ahīma ʿas a contemporary of Shefatiah, who died in 886 (no. **76**); *EJ*, I, 128 f. The sequel to this tale, after the lapse of at least a generation, occurs about the middle of the century; no. **50**.

For further discussion see J. Mann. *The Jews in Egypt and in Palestine under the Fatimid Caliphs.* London, 1920. I, 55; *id.. JQR*, XI, 1921, 450.

ca. 800-50 **22**

..... I will now relate an incident that occurred at Venosa. There was a man who had come from Palestine, who was well versed in the Torah....... He tarried there for some time [lit., « days and weeks »]. Every Sabbath day he would deliver a sermon in the synagogue... The sage would discourse, and R. Silano would interpret.

One day [Friday] the villagers who had come into the city in wagons, began to quarrel among themselves. Thereupon some women sallied forth from their houses, holding long poles, which had been charred by the fire in raking the oven. With these the men and women beat one another [?]. R. Silano then committed a grievous error in this wise. He took the Midrash of the Scriptural lection which the sage was to interpret that Sabbath, and erased two lines from it, replacing them with the account of the foregoing incident. This is the wording of his insertion: «When the men came in wagons, the women came forth out of their kitchens and beat them with their oven-poles».

On the Sabbath as the sage came upon these words, he stopped short. He looked at the letters, studied, examined, pondered, went over them again, and finally, suspecting nothing, read them aloud... Then R. Silano, in mocking laughter, cried to all assembled there, « Listen to the master's discourse on the quarrel that occurred among you yesterday, when the women beat the men with pokers and sent them scurrying in all directions!»

When the master realized what had been done, his face turned pale. He went back [to Jerusalem] to the scholars studying in the academy, and told them of the humiliation that he had suffered. All of them were deeply pained and distressed, and they excommunicated R. Silano *ha-nabon*. He remained under the ban a number of years until R. Ahīmaʿas arrived there on a pilgrimage with the contributions *(ha-nedarim),* and ingeniously brought about its revocation. Hearken now to the tale of his clever deed.

He arrived during the « ten days of penitence », and the scholars and dean of the academy prevailed upon him to act as cantor... After having recited a number of penitential hymns, he presented one composed by R. Silano.., which begins *'Aloh,* etc. But when he reached the words *Zakkū qadmonim,* he changed the latter to *rabbanim* (Rabbinites); as for *ve-garemū hammanim,* he made this *minim* («heretics», i. e., Karaites). When he concluded the service, they asked him whose was the... mouth which had composed such a prayer, wherein was expressed love and esteem for the Rabbinites and abhorrence of the heretics. He replied, «That mouth is R. Silano's, even he who is anathema among you.» Thereupon they all rose up and revoked the ban...

Ahima ʿas, ed. Neubauer, 114 f.; ed. Kahana, 120 f.; tr. Salzman, 67 f. (especially faulty here). Cf. Mann, *Jews in Egypt,* I, 55-7. As he infers, the preacher was a representative of the Jerusalem academy on a fund-raising tour; cf. no. **21**. Silano's position in the community may be alluded to in the term *nabon,* which in its common sense («wise») would be incongruous here. Instances of its use as a communal title are cited for the late Middle Ages by L. Zunz, *Zur Geschichte und Literatur.* Berlin, 1845. p. 518, n. *d.* He evidently translated the visiting scholar's sermons.

For the text of the poem, as well as another by the same Silano, see J. Marcus, «Studies in the chronicle of Ahimaaz». *Proceedings* of the American Academy for Jewish Research, V, 1933-4, 85-91. The former was part of an Atonement Day Service, and its tone of complaint is common in compositions of this type, so that it is gratuitous to see in it an allusion to the decree of Basil I, as in another poem (no. **62**). The words quoted in the chronicle appear in line 7. Cf. I. Davidson, *Osar ha-shirah ve-ha-piyut.* New York, 1924. I, 311, no. 6844.

The sectarian conflict, a burning issue in Palestine, was, of course, not experienced in contemporary Italy. Eppenstein, *Monats.,* LXIII, 172, n. 3, thought he found echoes of it in the *Seder Eliyahu,* which has been supposed to have been compiled in this region *ca.* 1000. See now V. Aptowitzer. « Seder Elia.» *Jewish Studies in memory of G. A. Kohut.* New York, 1935. pp. 5-39.

811 - 3 **23**

His [Nikephoros', patriarch of Cp.] zeal impelled him now to turn in another direction, against the unbelievers and the foreign heresies, which until then had (in their folly) shamelessly celebrated their filthy rites. I refer to the Jews, the Phrygians, and those who imbibe the lies of Mani... In a written work of some length he apprised the emperor [Michael I] of the absurdities of their religion, and indicated in his petition how they would poison the entire community, if they should be permitted to do as they pleased any longer. He struck at the Jewish deicides...., so that thereafter their blasphemies progressed no further than their lips. They [the non-orthodox] could do no more than mutter their misguided stupidities in some secret corner. For having been prohibited by the government from engaging in open activities (τὸ γὰρ παρρησιάζεσθαι ὑπὸ τῆς ἐξουσίας ἀφῃρημένοι), the

impious fellows subsided into inactivity, desisting even from
secret acts.

Ignatios (9 th c.). Life of Nikephoros, ed. de Boor, *Opuscula historica*, 158 f.; de Labriolle, *Les sources de l'histoire du montanisme*, 249 f.
On the dating, Martin, *op. cit.*, 156. The hagiographer seems to be
exaggerating his hero's success. Nikephoros' mention of «the Jews»
at the council of 814, refers to the iconoclasts; Mansi, XIX, 120.

(It was noted above, no. **15 n.**, that a false notion of the aggressiveness of Byzantine Jewry is exhibited among certain scholars. It is
the same groundless viewpoint which has led still another historian
to accept the present passage as proof of the intense propaganda then
carried on by the Jews. A. Vogt. *Basile Ier*. Paris, 1908. pp. 302-4.
Another proof cited by him is a passage in Photios' letter written in
865 to the convert King Boris of Bulgaria; *PG,* CII, 652. This,
however, is but another example of an orthodox writer stigmatizing
the iconoclasts as «Jews», as the context shows. And even if Photios
insinuates that these to him despicable persons are secret Jews, his
words must be taken with the same grain of salt.)

814   **24**

This tombstone *(siyun)* was set up on the grave of
/Sarah b. Jeremiah/, who died at the age of /five years/, in the
year seven/ hundred and forty-/ six after the destruction/ of the
holy Temple. /May it be rebuilt/ in our days and in the days
of/ Israel. Amen./

From Venosa, published by Cassuto, «Nuove iscrizioni ebraiche
di Venosa». *Archivio storico per la Calabria e la Lucania*, IV, 1934, 4 f.
Cf. the similar epitaph of Abigail b. Hebron (?) in the Museo Nazio-
nale, Naples, said to be of the same provenience; defective facsimile
in N. Ferorelli. *Gli Ebrei nell'Italia meridionale*. Turin, 1915. p. 28.
(Cf. the reading published by Chajes, *ZfhB,* XIV, 1910, 167 f. See also
Cassuto, *l. c.*, 2 f. The first word on the last line can only be *ha-qadosh,*
as the latter pointed out to me privately).

On the prefix in *mi-bat,* cf. D. Kaufmann. *Gesammelte Schriften*.
Frankfort, 1915. III, 405. On *siyun,* cf. Zunz, *Zur Gesch.,* 393. On the
era, E. Mahler. *Handbuch der jüdischen Chronologie*. Leipzig, 1916. pp.
149-59. On the earlier history of the local community, Juster, I,
182, n. 14; Frey, *Corpus,* pp. 420-43.

[*ca.* 815-40 **25**

... Sergios, his [Photios'] father, observing certain signs in him, exclaimed, « Is my wife perchance that nun who is expected by the Hebrews to give birth to the Antichrist..?»

He]Photios] once met a Hebrew magician who said to him, « What would you give me, young man, if I caused you to have a ready command of all of Greek literature, and to excel all men in wisdom?»

He replied, « My father would gladly pay you half of his wealth.»

Said the other, I have no need of money, nor do I wish your father to know of this matter. But come with me to this place, and deny the cross on which we nailed Jesus. Then I will give you a strange charm, and you will spend your whole life in prosperity and wealth, with great wisdom and joy.»

[ps.-] Symeon Magister (10th. c.). «Chronographia», *PG,* CIX, 732. Photios, patriarch of Cp. in the latter part of the century, was the leading intellectual of his time, and the extraordinary scope of his studies made him an object of popular suspicion. See J. Hergenröther. *Photius, Patriarch von Constantinopel.* Ratisbon, 1867.•I, 322. (Cf. the reputation of his contemporary, Leo of Thessalonica; Diehl, *CMH,* IV, 44). Although it must be recognized that Byzantine Jewry had its share of magical interests, there is no reason to be as gullible as is Krauss, *Studien,* 62, with regard to this calumniation of Photios. There is nothing definite known with regard to any of his teachers; Hergenröther, *op. cit.,* I, 324 f.].

818 **26**

.....forty-five years of age,/ who passed away to his eternal home [*bēt ʿolam,* Ex. 12: 5],/ in the seven hundred/ and fiftieth year after the destruction/ of the holy Temple./ May his soul be bound up in the bundle of/ life [I. Sam. 25: 29]. May he attain his/ resting-place in peace.

At Venosa; ed. and tr. G. I. Ascoli. «Iscrizioni inedite o mal note, greche, latine, ebraiche, di antichi sepolcri giudaici del Napolitano».

Atti of the 4 th International Congress of Orientalists. Florence, 1880,
pt. 1, p. 306, no. 29. Cf. H. Graetz. «Die alte jüdischen Katakombeninschriften in Süditalien . *Monats.*, XXIX, 1880, 447. On line 2 see
Zunz, *op. cit.*, 442, n. *m*, 444.

818-27   **27**

This tombstone was set up on' the grave of Ṣadoq b. ...../
who died in the month of ... / in the year seven hundred fifty/.....

At Venosa; Cassuto, *l.c.*, 9. For the photograph see *idem*, «Ancora
nuove iscrizioni ebraiche di Venosa», *l.c.*, V, facing p. 181.

820-9   **28**

Just as he [Michael II] oppressed the heritage of Christ, ...
he declared the Jews completely free of taxes (ἀνέτους φόρων
καὶ ἐλευθέρους ἐδείκνυεν), for he loved and cherished them, es-
teeming them above all other men.

«Theophanes cont.», 61; cf. Kedrenos, 957. Dölger, *Regesten*, I,
pt. 1, 50, no. 414. See also his remarks in *Viertel.*, XXVI, 11 f., stressing the omission of the article before φόρων. Cf. Andréadès, *Ec.
His.*, III, 15.

811   **29**

...... b./ Rabbi Abraham, who passed away/ at the age
of thirty-seven years, in the three hundred fifty-third year after
the destruction, etc./ May the Lord (*ha-Maqom*) allow his soul to
rest among/ the righteous in the Garden of Eden,/ until He lead
him to the Temple/ and make him one of those/ written down
for life in Jerusalem [Is. 4: 3]./

At Venosa; Cassuto, *l.c.*, 5. With the Messianic sentiment cf. no. **35**.

821-2   **30**

Here reposes Joseph b. Benjamin who died/ at the age of
thirty-five years in the four thousand/ five hundred eighty-
second year of the creation/ of the world, the seven hundred fifty-
third/ year after the destruction, etc./ May the Holy One blessed-

be-He cause his soul to be bound up/ in the bundle of life and his awakening to take place among the dead who are to be awakened,/ and his memory to be blessed in the company of the righteous and good./ Amen./

At Venosa; Cassuto, *l. c.*, V, 182 f., with photograph facing p. 180. Cf. no. **26**. For a Palestinian parallel to the use of both eras see T. Reinach, *REJ*, LXXXV, 1928, 3. The diffculty raised by Kaufmann, *op. cit.*, 407 (based on Ascoli's incomplete reading, *l. c.*, 302, no. 25; Graetz, *l. c.*, 447 f.), disappears when one considers that the two eras begin in the fall and midsummer, respectively. Hence, the arithmetical difference between the systems of dating is properly expressed in the form 3829-8.

822   31

Here was buried ..... b. Yaïm,/ who died at the age of thirty-six/ years in the seven hundred/ fifty-fourth year after the destruction, etc./

At Venosa; Ascoli, 305, no. 27; Graetz, *l. c.*, 448. The rare name recurs at Lavello; Ascoli, 309, no. 32.

824   32

This tombstone was set up/ on the grave of David b./ Daniel, who died at the age of/ sixty years in the/ seven hundred/ fifty-sixth year/ after the destruction, etc./

From Venosa; Cassuto, *l. c.*, V, 183. Practically identical in phrasing with no. **24**.

827   33

Verily it behooves all of you who pass to and fro [Lam. 1: 12],/ to read of the death of a youth: Here reposes Caleb [?] in his sleep [?]. Seek ye mercy for him from/ his Creator so that you may find mercy before your Creator. For he died at the age of/ twenty-three years, childless [?] in the year/ four thousand five hundred/ eighty-seven of the creation of the world,/ the seven hundred fifty-ninth year/ after the destruction, etc./

At Venosa; Ascoli, 307 f., no. 31; Graetz, *l. c.*, 448 f. (defectively copied).

829   **34**

This tombstone *(massebah)*/ was set up on the grave of/ Rebecca /b. Muktar/, who died' at the age of fifty-three years/ in the seven hundred sixty-first year/ after the destruction, etc./

At Venosa; Ascoli, 307, no. 30; Graetz, *l. c.*, 449. On *massebah* see Zunz, *Zur Gesch.*, 392.

829   **35**

This tombstone was set up on/ the grave of Parigori b./ Teodoro in the year four/ thousand five hundred/ eighty-nine [A. M.], the seven hundred/ sixty-first after the destruction, etc./ His age was sixty-three. May he be brought/ to the House of the Holy of Holies. Amen./

At Venosa; Cassuto, *l. c.*, IV, 6. Cf. no. **29**. On the name, E. L. Sukenik, *Jour. of Pal. Or. Soc.*, XV, 1935, 149.

829   **35 a**

This tombstone/ was set up on the grave of/ Rebecca b. Bono who died/ at the age of sixty-three years/ in the ⟨seven hundred⟩ sixty-first/ year after the destruction, etc.

At Venosa; Cassuto, *l. c.*, V, 180.

830   **35b**

....the grave of Dina b. Julia⟨no⟩/ who died at the age of thirty years / in the seven hundred sixty-/ second year after the destruction, etc./ May her soul be bound up/ in the bundle of life among those written unto life/ in Jerusalem [Is. 4: 3]./

At Venosa, *idem, l. c.*, with photograph.

832   **36**

Here lies Leah b. Yefeh-Mazzal/ (may her soul be bound in the bundle of life), / whose death occurred seven hundred/ sixty-four years after the destruction of the/ Temple, at the age of/ seventeen years. May the Holy-One-blessed-be-He deem/ her worthy of resurrection with the righteous,/ and may she attain [*sc.* her rest] in peace./ O guardians of the treasures of the garden of Eden,/ open its gates for her,/ and let Leah enter therein. Open for her the gates of/ the garden of Eden, [*sc.* that she may have] precious things to her right hand/ and sweet ones to her left. O respond/ and say to her: This is my beloved one, my companion [Song 5: 16]./

At Brindisi, now kept in the local museum. First published by Ascoli, *l. c.,* 298, no. 24. Cf. tr. by I. Broydé, *JE,* IX, 477. On the text, Kaufmann, *op. cit.,* 405. Ascoli's reading requires slight correction as may be seen from the photograph; see Frontispiece. The style is unusual and lines 9-11 have evoked comparisons with liturgical passages. (Cf. no. **130.**) See Assaf, *Ginzé Qedem,* IV, 1930, 111, who points to some lines published by B. M. Lewin, *l. c.,* 67. Another scholar asserts that he found almost the identical words of our inscription in a prayer in the Oxford ms. of the *Seder Rab 'Amram*; L. Ginzberg. *Geonica.* New York, 1909. I, 143, n. 3.

The name of the father corresponds to Εὐτυχής or Εὐτυχίος.

There are two other epitaphs from Brindisi which are undated but apparently belong to the same period as the one given above. Of these one consists of five lines and yields the name of Yokebed b. Sipporah, who died in the latter twenties; Ascoli, 296, no. 28, and Graetz, *l. c.,* 442. The other consists of nine lines, including the heading which reads: «The grave *(mishkab)* of R. Baruk b. R. Jonah.» In line 2 occurs the verb *hirgi'a,* as in nos. **30,** and **33.** In line 3 the name is followed by *noh nefesh,* which is not found elsewhere among this group. The succeeding lines give the age (with the usual *mi-ben*) as 68. Lines 6 f. are rhetorical and incorporate phrases from Is. 52: 7, and Job 25: 2; Ascoli, 297, no. 23; Kaufmann, *op. cit.,* 405. It seems hardly likely that these are earlier than the 9th c., as was suggested by D. Chwolson. *Corpus inscriptionum hebraicarum.* Petrograd, 1882. p. 164. See also H. P. Chajes «Appunti sulle iscrizioni giudaiche del Napolitano pubblicate dall'Ascoli». *Centenario della nascita di M. Amari.* Palermo, 1910. I, 238 f.

The other inscriptions which fall within the present scope are the three from Matera which are very badly preserved. In two of them the era of the Temple-destruction seems to be used, but the date is no longer legible; Ascoli, 311-3, nos. 34-6.

834 **37**

..... since the destruction of the Temple/ seven hundred sixty-six/ years. May He rebuild it in/ our time,/ etc.

At Venosa; Cassuto, *l. c.*, IV, 6.

ca. 835 **38**

The defense failed because of the connivance of one of the incompetent fellows. He had acquired a nickname derived from the diminutive form of βοῦς (ox), because of his unintelligent behavior at the time of a clash (στασιώτιδος) which had occurred between the Christians and the Jews.

Genesios, *PG,* CIX. 1072 f. From the account of the loss of Amorion to the Moslems in 838; see A. A. *Vasiliev. Byzance et les Arabes*. Brussels, 1935. I, 144-77, 188-90. For another reference to this community, see no. **20**. (Despite the abundance of source-material on the fall of this city, nothing is known with regard to the relationship of the local Jews to the event).

On this type of nickname see J. E. Kalitsunakis, *Mitteilungen* of the Seminar für Orientalische Sprache of the Königlichen Friedrich-Wilhelms Universität zu Berlin, XVI, pt. 2, 1913, 112.

837 **39**

When the barbarians took possession, they massacred both Jews and Christians mercilessly. Their ferocity went to such lengths that they violated and disembowelled the women. Then they destroyed the town by burning it.

Michael, IV, 531, col. 2; tr., III, 88 f. Cf. Bar Hebraeus, 148, tr. Budge, 135. With reference to the taking of the Armenian border-fortress Sozopetra (Zapetra), by the Khurramī troops allied with the emperor Theophilos against the caliph al-Muʿtasim. See Vasiliev, *op. cit.,* 137-43.

838 **40**

This tombstone is on the grave of Azriel b./ Levi, who died at the age of forty years./ May his soul be bound up, etc./

Since the destruction of/ the Temple seven hundred seventy/ years, etc.

At Venosa; Cassuto, *l.c.*, IV, 7; photograph, *l.c.*, V, facing p. 181.

838   **41**

This tombstone was set up on the grave of/ Samuel b. Joseph, who died at the age of/ fifty years in the seven/ hundred seventieth year after the destruction/ etc.

At Venosa; *id., l. c.*, IV, 7.

845   **42**

.... Now what was the reward of the inhabitants of Bari [for succoring Titus' captives]? The Holy-One-blessed-be-He bestowed more grace upon them than upon the remainder of Italy. There are none more beautiful in Italy than the inhabitants of Bari. It has been said: No man enters it without desiring to sin before leaving.

Anon. *Pesiqta Rabbati,* ed. M. Friedmann. Vienna, 1880. ·c. 28, pp. 135b-6a. For the tradition of the time of the settlement of Apulia, see no. **49**. For «Italy» the text has «Palestine», which urgently demands emendation. It has been suggested by Bacher that the scribe misread an abbreviation as standing for *Eres Yisrael* instead of *Italiah,* which is the only word that the context admits; *REJ,* XXXIII, 1896, 41 f. With regard to the saying quoted, it is of course not intended to advertise the inhabitants' reputation for moral laxity. It is rather a quaint manner of stressing their unusual beauty; *idem, Monats..* XLI, 1897, 608.

The city had shortly before this fallen into the hands of the Arabs. See J. Gay. *L'Italie méridionale et l'empire byzantin.* Paris, 1904. p. 52. For local epigraphic fragments of contemporary dating and later, see Cassuto, *Rivista,* XV, 1934, 316-22.

(This passage is one of the arguments which used to be cited for the hypothesis of the s. Italian provenience of this midrash. More recently, however, it has been assigned to a writer residing in Jerusalem, who may indeed have previously visited Apulia or migrated therefrom. See Mann, *Jews in Egypt,* I, 48; cf. Aptowitzer, *HUC An.,* VIII-IX, 1931-2, 408 f.)

846 **43**

This tombstone was set up on the grave of Nathan b. Ephraim,/ a revered man and a sage, dean of the academy [?],/ and the leader of his generation,.../ He died at the age of seventy/-four years in the seven hundred/ seventy-eighth year after the destruction, etc./

At Venosa; Ascoli, 303 f., no. 26; Graetz, *l. c.,* 406. For lines 3 f., 6, cf. Kaufmann, *op. cit.,* 406. It would be rash to take for certain that this individual was the head of the local academy, the readings being not at all clear.

846-86 **44**

They [the Byzantine government] collect from the Jews and the Magians a *dīnar* annually.

Ibn Khurdādhbah. *Kitāb al-masālik wa'l-mamālik (Livre des Routes et des Royaumes),* ed. and tr. M. J. de Goeje *(Bibl. Geog. Arab.,* VI). Leyden, 1889. p. 111, line 5, tr. 83. Repeated by Ibn al-Faqīh al-Hamadhanī. *Kitāb al-buldān,* ed. de Goeje *(Bibl.,* V). Leyden, 1885. p. 147, lines 8 f. (The dates are determined by the two editions which the former work underwent at the hands of its author). On al-Jarmī as the probable source see J. Marquart. *Osteuropäische und ostasiatische Streifzüge.* Leipzig, 1903. pp. 28 f., and Brooks, *JHS,* XXI, 1901, 70; cf. V. Barthold, *En. Is.,* IV, 468.

See the remarks of Andréadès, *BZ,* XXVIII, 312-5, and *Mélanges Diehl,* I, 12, 17; Dölger, *Viertel.,* XXVI, 6 f.; G. Ostrogorsky, *Sem. Kon.,* V, 1932, 519 f. (Russian). On the *jizyah* see C. H. Becker, *En. Is.,* I, 1051. On the relation of the *dīnar* to the nomisma see Ostrogorsky, *BZ,* XXXII, 1932, 302 f. On the taxes in general see S. Runciman. *Byzantine Civilisation.* Cambridge, 1933. pp. 96-9.

Whom can *majūs* designate with respect to residents of the Empire? It is applied also to certain troops who fought in Sicily in 964-5 and whom Amari, *op. cit.,* II, 300, identified as Paulicians. For the text involved see M. G. Remiro, ed. and tr., *Historia de los Musulmanes de España y Africa por En-Nugairi.* Granada, 1919. II, 248, line 8 from below.

846-86 **45**

The Route of the Jewish Merchants, the *Rādanīya*

These merchants speak Arabic, Persian, Greek, French,

Spanish, and Slavic. They journey from east to west, and from
west to east... From China they carry musk, aloeswood, camphor,
cinnamon, and other oriental products, returning by way of
Qulzum [near Suez], and Farama [Pelusium]. Here they set sail
on the Mediterranean Sea, some of them heading for Constantinople with their merchandise to sell it to the Byzantines....

Ibn Khurdādhbah, 153 f.., tr., 115. Cf. Aronius, *Regesten,* 50, no.
113, whose confidence that these were western Jews derives from a
questionable etymology mentioned below. The silk which these traders carried on their eastward journey must have been purchased in
the Empire; W. Heyd. *Histoire du commerce du Levant au Moyen
Age.* Tr. F. Reynaud (Reprint). Leipzig, 1923. I, 126 f. Cf. B. Hahn.
*Die wirtschaftliche Tätigkeit der Juden im fränkischen und deutschen
Reich bis zum 2. Kreuzzug.* Freiburg, 1911. pp. 38 f. Cf. no. **108**.

The peculiar name given to these merchants has as yet not been
satisfactorily explained. The editor, de Goeje, suggested a Persian
etymology in the sense of «traders in linen», *Bibl. Geog. Arab.,* IV,
251. Another hypothesis which has gained some acceptance is the
derivation from *Rhodani,* i. e., traders who sailed up the Rhone;
D. Simonsen, *REJ,* LIV, 1907, 141 f. This was rejected by de Goeje,
«Internationaal handelsverkeer in de middeleuwen». Koninklijke Akademie van Wetenschappen: *Verslagen en mededeelingen, Afdeeling
Letterkunde.* Series 4, IX, 1909, 253. (See also, *l. c.,* 256, where he
states with regard to the next c. that Jewish merchants were active
in Trebizond, although the sources, which mention Greek, Armenian,
and Moslem traders, nowhere refer to the Jews. See J. H. Kramers,
En. Is., IV, 661).

848   **46**

..... at the age of thirty years./ ... Lowly in spirit before
all/ ..... May his death atone and gain forgiveness/ .... his
entire sleep. Sleep thou in peace./ Since the destruction of the
Temple seven hundred/ eighty years, etc.

At Venosa; Cassuto, *l. c.,* IV, 7 f. Indicating a violent death; cf.
Ascoli, 309, no. 32 and Zunz, *Zur Gesch.,* 333 f., 446. Three undatable
fragments (see *id., l. c.,* 8 f.), yield the following data: Samuel b. ...
si died in the year 7?7 of the same era. Donnola (?) b. Ayyo died at

the age of 21; cf. wording of line 2 with corresponding portion of no. 30; adorned with three menorahs. On the third fragment the name has been lost, but the same era appears, and the epitaph closes with a quotation from Job 19: 25.

848-57   **46a**

This tombstone was set up on the grave of/ ... b. Elisha who died at the age of .... years. The youth was .../... at school, refined. .../... and was quick in all things. .../ while still of tender years.../ He passed away in the seven hundred eighty- .... year after the destruction, etc.

At Venosa; Cassuto, « Hebrew Inscriptions in Southern Italy. (Hebrew).» Tel Aviv, Sefer Klausner, 1937, pp. 240 f.

ca. 850?   **47**

..... A certain Gaon responded that the law mentioned in *Halakot Gedolot* regarding mourning.... is not authoritative.... In spite of the fact that the responsum is attributed therein to R. Yehudai Gaon of blessed memory, you are not to abide by it, for a hundred different objections have been raised against it. For you should know that these *Halakot* of R. Y. ... were not seen in Babylonia in his lifetime, but only about a century later when captives [from the Empire] brought the work to Babylonia.....

Isaac b. Moses. (12th c.) *'Or Zar'ua*, ed. A. Lehren. Zhitomir, 1862. II, 177b, s. 431. Discussed in full by Aptowitzer, « Responsa wrongly attributed to R. Hai» (Hebrew), *Tarbiz*, 1/4, 1930, 75-80, 96-105. On Yehudai (*ca.* 760), Elbogen, *EJ*, VIII, 1057f. The assignment of this responsum by Aptowitzer to Natronai I would bring the arrival of the *H. G.* within the writer's personal experience.

Jewish captives of war from the Empire do not seem to be mentioned in the sources, with the possible exception that they may have been included among the *dhimmi* exchanged in 845-6. See Vasiliev, *Byz. et les Arabes* , I, 202.

ca. 850   **48**

As for their [the Christians'] contention that the Jews do not term Ezra the son of God, it is true that there are two opin-

8

ions on this among the Jews, who are divided into scholars
and common folk. Now when certain men among the scholars
saw that Ezra restored the Torah to them from memory, after it
had been lost and its contents scattered around, they spoke thus
in exaggeration of his feat, and he is famous because of their
statement. Successors of these men exist in Yemen, in Syria, and
within the land of Byzantium.

al-Jāḥiẓ of Baṣra, «*Risāla fī radd ʿalā an-Nasāra*», ed. J. Finkel.
Three essays of Abū ʿOthman ʿAmr ibn Baḥr al Jāḥiẓ (d. 869). Cairo,
1926. p. 35. Tr. [O. Rescher]. *Excerpte und Übersetzungen aus den
Schriften des Philologen und Dogmatikers Ġāḥiẓ aus Baçra. (150-250 H)*.
Stuttgart, 1931. I, 65.

The point at issue is the statement attributed to the Jews in
Koran 9: 30, in support of which the Islamic tradition is here cited;
cf. B. Heller, «ʿUzair», *En. Is.*, IV, 1062f. (1934). As for the contemporary reference, one can only take it to refer to the veneration of Ezra
in general, his traditional tomb being near Baṣra, and perhaps to its
embodiment in the association of synagogues and Torah-scrolls with
his name which was prevalent among Syrian and Egyptian Jews, and
very likely in the Empire as well. See E. N. Adler. *Jewish Travellers*.
London, 1930. pp. 67, 136.

ca. 850   **49**

Now with great care let me arrange in due order... ⟨the
history⟩ of my ancestors, who were transported on a ship
over the river PA....... among the captives whom Titus ex-
⟨iled from⟩ the city [Jerusalem].... They came to Oria, where
they settled and prospered. They grew in number and in strength.

Among their descendants there arose a man, eminent in learning,.... a liturgical poet and theologian, who was distinguished
for wisdom among his people, R. Amittai by name. Now he had
a number of gracious and worthy sons, intelligent and learned
men, liturgical poets *[payṭanim]* zealously engaged in teaching
their worthy disciples, princely figures..., adepts in the myste-
ries,... wisely and discerningly occupied in the study and recitation of the *Sefer ha-Yashar*, and in pondering the secret discipline

of the *Merkabah*. The first of these was R. Shefatiah, who was zealous in the pursuit of wisdom; the second, R. Hananel, engaged in the study of God's law...; and the third, Eleazar, who was devoted to the Torah.

Ahīma ʿas, ed. Neubauer, 112; ed. Kahana, 117 f.; tr. Salzman, 61 f. For textual notes see Marcus, *Proc.* of the Amer. Acad. for Jew Res., V. ,92. The parallel traditions regarding the antiquity of the Jewish settlement of Apulia are exhaustively collected by J. Schirmann. «Zur Geschichte der hebräischen Poesie in Apulien und Sizilien.» *Mitteilungen* of the Forschungsinstitut für hebräische Dichtung, 11, 1933, 96-100.
For a list of the seven liturgical pieces attributed to Amittai, see Davidson, *Osar*, IV, 368. Cf. H. Brody, *EJ*, II, 609, and *Eshkol*, II, 983. On the *Sefer ha-Yashar* and the *Merkabah*, see P. Bloch. «Die jüdische Mystik und Kabbalah,» in J. Winter and A. Wünsche. *Die jüdische Litteratur.* Trier, 1896. III, 224 f.; Scholem, *EJ*, IX, 631-44. Cf. the dubious hypothesis of M. Mieses, *REJ*, XCIV, 1933, 82-5. With regard to the Kalonymos family, which may have originated here, see B. Suler, *EJ*, IX, 836 f.; S. Eppenstein, *Monats.*, LXIII, 1919, 168-71, 175, 185, n. 1.
For a late legend which seems to combine this source with no. **111**, see the liturgical commentary of Samuel of Babenberg, cited by J. Perles, *Monats.*, XXV, 1876, 373. Cf. Neubauer, *JQR*, IV, 1892, 616-8. Excursus A: The Amittai Family (see p. 116).
Based chiefly on the chronicle of Ahīma ʿas, especially its conclusion; nos. **49, 57, 58, 66, 80, 87, 102, 116.** See also Mann, *Jews in Egypt,* I, 184 (on Yehoseph, generation VIII). The family-trees given heretofore are somewhat less complete than the present one. See, e. g., Kaufmann, *Ges. Schr.,* III, 53; Kahana, *op. cit.,* 114; Cassuto, *EJ*, I, 730.

ca. 850-60 **50**

In the days of these pious men [R. Amittai and his sons] there arrived from Baghdad... an esteemed man of illustrious lineage, Aaron by name....
After this event [a miracle in Gaeta wherein a boy who had been changed into an ass, was restored], he skillfully proceeded to perform feats of the utmost difficulty. Upon his arrival at Benevento the entire community came out as one man to wel-

Excursus A: The Amittai Family

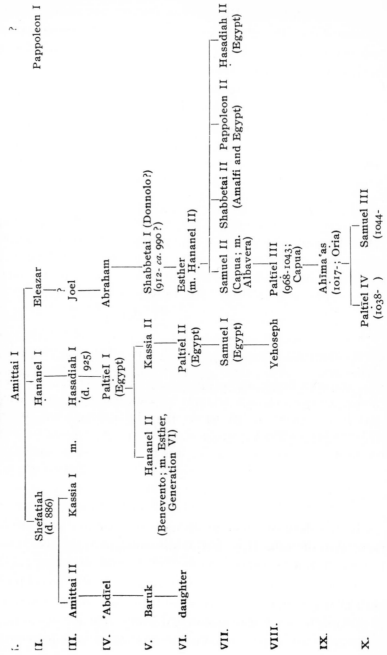

i.   ?
                                                                     Pappoleon I

II.   Amittai I
             _____|_____
             | | |
             Shefatiah   Hananel I   Eleazar
             (d. 886) | |
III. Amittai II   Kassia I   m.   Hasadiah I   ?
                                   (d. | 925)   Joel

IV. 'Abdiel   Paltiel I   Abraham
                                    (Egypt) |
                                    _____|_____
                                    | |
V.   Baruk   Hananel II   Kassia II   Shabbetai I (Donnolo?)
                    (Benevento; m. Esther,   (912- ca. 990?)
                    Generation VI)

VI. daughter   Paltiel II   Esther
                                    (Egypt)   (m. Hananel II)
                                                 |
VII.   Samuel I   Samuel II   Shabbetai II   Pappoleon II   Hasadiah II
                                    (Egypt)   (Capua; m.   (Amalfi and Egypt)   (Egypt)
                                                 Albavera)

VIII.   Yehoseph   Paltiel III
                                                 (968-1043;
                                                 Capua)
                                                 |
IX.   Ahima'as
                                                 (1017-; Oria)
                                                 _____|_____
                                                 | |
X.   Paltiel IV   Samuel III
                                                 (1038-)   (1044-

come him. On the Sabbath day a certain fine young man acted
as cantor.... He chanted with a pleasing voice, but when he
reached the words, « Bless the Lord Who is blessed », his voice
melodiously lingered without, however, reading the word «Lord».
The rabbi [Aaron] understood thereby that the worshipper was
actually a dead man, for « the dead will not praise the Lord »
[Ps. 115: 14]... Thereupon he loudly exclaimed, « Sit down and
do not glory thus, for you are not fit to give praise and recite
prayers unto God! »..., [The youth was made to confess, whereupon he related that a group of scholars in Jerusalem had once
inserted the Tetragrammaton into an incision made in his right
arm, thereby saving him from a premature death and giving him
an indefinite extension of life; no. 21.] When they brought the
shroud, he came forward and put it on. He then showed them
where the incision had been made. The rabbi [Aaron] tore the
Tetragrammaton out of it . His body now became lifeless...

Ahīmaʿas, ed. Neubauer, 112f.; ed. Kahana, 118-20; tr. Salzman,
65f. This Aaron was apparently the son of the Exilarch Samuel ha-
Nasī (773-816); Neubauer, *REJ*, XXIII, 1891, 230-7; M. Zobel,
EJ, I, 30-2.

Although Benevento was politically outside the Empire, the foregoing tale is nonetheless relevant for the cultural aspect of our subject. It is noteworthy that the chronicler indicates a close connection
between that community and those nearby within the Empire; nos. 51, 57.

ca. 850-60   **51**

From there [Benevento] he [Aaron] journeyed on until he
came to Oria. Here he found thriving homes [lit., «tents»]...
and well-established academies *[midrashot]*... Here lived my
ancestors, the sons of R. Amittai, R. Shefatiah and R. Hananel,
... given over to learned public debate and discourse *[doreshim
be-rabbim]*, ... and to piously extolling the God of Israel [in liturgical compositions]. .... Here among them did Aaron establish his
home. Here his wisdom bubbled forth, and his teaching was
planted. Here he revealed a competence in judicial decision remi-

niscent of the days of the Urim, the Sanhedrin, and the execution of the «law of the adulteress».. .

It happened that a certain Teofilo committed adultery with a married woman. Aaron before the assembled community condemned him to death by strangulation. Another man attacked a woman and killed her, and Aaron sentenced him to decapitation. A third one committed sodomy..., and he was sentenced to stoning. A fourth one had illicit relations with his mother-in-law..., and by order of the rabbi they [the community] assembled and executed him by burning.

Ahīma 'as, ed. Neubauer, 114; ed. Kahana, 120; tr. Salzman, 66 f.
For the modes of execution see S. Mendelsohn, *JE*, III, 557 f.
With regard to Spain, Mann, *Jews in Egypt*, I, 69; *JQR*, XI, 456 f.
Eldad ha-Danī's text on capital punishment is given in Kahana, *op. cit.*, I, 27, 29. On Mesopotamia see S. Assaf. *Ha-'onashin 'aharé hatimat ha-Talmud*. Jerusalem, 1922. pp. 59 f.

ca. 850 - 60   **52**

As he [Teofilo] went out to be executed by strangulation, all the people gathered about him at the sound of his bitter outcry. The governor of the town come upon them and drove off the crowd. Then he said to the man, «If you will abandon your religion and believe in mine, I will save you from a violent death.» He bowed his head [evasively], for he desired his life to be spared. Taking him at once to his mansion he [the governor] examined him, but found him firm in the Jewish faith. Thereupon the former declared, «I came to your aid and delivered you from death at the hands of the executioners, ..., yet you lied to me in mockery....» He then beat him in fiendish fashion. He cut off his hands and feet, cast him into prison, and kept him there in misery....

Ahīma 'as, ed. Neubauer, 121; ed. Kahana, 128; tr. Salzman, 80f. When read together with no. **53**, the point of the tale is seen to lie in the expiation of Teofilo's two sins (no. **51**) by these sufferings. Cf. no. **47 n.**

The rescue of the criminal in this fashion violates a civil law; no. **83**. With regard to the preliminaries before baptism, see nos. **3, 18, 74, 121.**

ca. 850-60   53

There was another Jew in prison with him [Teofilo], a God-fearing man, who brought him food and drink every day. When none had been set aside for him, he would give him some of his own, and thus he attended him faithfully for a full year. On the eve of the Day of Atonement... this Jew brought him food and drink and ate with him. Now he [Teofilo] had a young daughter, and he said to him [his companion], « Go and bring witnesses, for I wish to give her in marriage to you.»

He answered, « You, sir, are one of the upper class *[hashubim]*, and I belong to the poorer *['alubim]*. Should your family hear of this, they would rend me like a fish ».

He replied to him, « No one, including my relatives, has any authority over my daughter. She is subject to my authority alone.»

The other man went out, brought three witnesses, and married the daughter in their presence. Then he [Teofilo] said to him, « Go now from me in peace, for you shall never find me ». After the fast the man returned to seek him in prison, but failed to find him, either alive or dead, for God had taken him into His care. . . . . .

Ahīma 'as, ed. Neubauer, 121 f.; ed. Kahana, 128; tr. Salzman, 81, with regard to which see I. Elbogen, *Monats.*, LXIX, 1925, 331. The concluding sentence, omitted from the tr. above, expresses the idea mentioned in no. **52 n.**

ca. 850-60   54

His [the future monk Constantine's] birthplace was the town of Synnada [in Phrygia]. . . . By race he was derived from the Hebrews. . . . He showed promise in his education and progressed as rapidly as possible. He became expert in the Hebrew language, and studied the Old Testament diligently. . . . . His mother received many voices concerning the boy, informing her that he would become a Christian. Consequently she was highly perturbed.... She overwhelmed him with reproaches, and warned him that he would forsake his parents and their religion....

The summer harvest ended, and the markets groaned with the weight of the fruits brought for sale. As he came along the road admiring the articles on display, a certain fruit-dealer yawned ... and made the sign of the cross over his mouth.... When the saint saw this, he was seized by an impulse .... He too yawned and made the sign of the cross over his mouth, imitating that which he had seen....

The Hebrews, in accordance with their custom, were celebrating one of their holidays, which happened to coincide with the procession made by the godly people [Christians] in observance of the approaching festival [Easter?]. While on his way to the Jewish synagogue with his mother, he met the procession. Although he stood beside his mother, he paid no attention to her, but gave it to the precious cross on which he gazed, and besought God to teach him its power....

While walking with some young men, a Hebrew maiden shamelessly embraced him, being under the spell of some Satanic passion. Since she was raging mad,... he made the sign of the cross and immediately caused her to fall to earth, dead and speechless..., Then he made the sign of the cross over her, took her hand, and restored her to health and sanity....

The relatives who were taking care of the young man [after his mother's death], were anxious to bind him to a wife. (Such is the Hebrews' custom that they hold nothing more honorable and pious than to serve the flesh and become a father of children.)... They pressed the matter against his will, the betrothal was already under way, and the other details were expected to follow.... The wedding-feast arrived; as it went on, the guests became merry,.... and the young man was forced to entertain them with dancing.... As he stepped forward to dance, he saw a mighty hand grasp his thigh and restrain him.... Twice and thrice was he urged on by them, unwilling as he was, but the hand restrained him each time. The party marvelled at his inhibition.... But it made him burn the more, for he realized that it was the work of Christ. In this way the party broke up.

When night came on, his relatives urged him to obey the natural impulse and to go join his wife, but they found him adamant and most stubbornly opposed to this.... The nobleminded man looked around for his liberty, and left the house without a word. Trusting to a very speedy flight, he got away....

After he had told everything [in the monastery of the Φλου-βουτίνοι], the abbot, desiring the truth of the matter, ordered a cross to be brought, and requested the saint to kiss it. As he reverently kissed it at the base, it inclined... over him, and made the sign of the cross over his head.... They named him Constantine....

A certain Jew, who was related to him, devised a plot designed to force him to return to his ancestral error [while he was living in seclusion on Mt. Olympos]. (For many were the times when Hebrews attempted this on the saint). He sent some men to bring the hero back as a fugitive [from the Phlouboutinoi]. They went up Olympos, entered into the saint's retreat, and after dragging him out, brought him to the abbot....

Some Hebrews dwelt there [at Nicaea] for the sake of its trade and its other advantages, practising their religion and warring against Christ. When the saint observed them..., he strove... by word and deed to lead them to salvation. He paid them frequent visits and caught some of them in the net of spiritual wisdom... But the Evil One... stirred up some of them against him... They held a secret council... in order to make an attempt on Constantine's life, because he had brought disgrace on the religion of the Hebrews... The plotters met to carry out the murder... in a place well-hidden, ... a chapel of the Mother of God. But when they came forward, ... there appeared the distinct image of a woman... When the wretches saw this, they fled from there post-haste.

Anon. biography (early 10th c.), ed. H. Delehaye. *Acta Sanct.*, Nov., IV. Brussels, 1925. s. 2, p. 629; ss. 4-6, 8, p. 630; ss. 9, 11f., p. 631; s. 23, p. 634; s. 51, p. 642. The hagiographer had never known his hero, hence, his narrative is of ambiguous value. The oral monastic traditions on which he was dependent, had evidently nothing to say with regard to the hero's father, for example, or of the persecution of Basil I (no. **61**). On the chro1 ɔlogy see Dvornik, *Légendes de C. et M.*, 133.

With respect to Nicaea there is a source which asserts that it was inhabited by both Jews and pagans from the first century down to the author's own day, i. e., *ca.* 800. See Epiphanios' life of the apostle Andrew, *PG*, CXX, 229; cf. V. G. Vasilevski. *Trudy.* Petrograd, 1909. II, 264-82; J. Flamion. *Les actes apocryphes de l'apôtre André.* Louvain, 1911. pp. 70-8, 196-212.

On the commercial importance of Nicaea, J. Sölch, *Byz.-neugr. Jahr.*, I, 1920, 273ff.

For the church associated with this Constantine and located in the Jewish quarter of Cp. (no. **191**), see Anthony, archbp. of Novgorod, *Kniga Palomnik,* ed. in 3 recensions, C. M. Loparev. Petrograd, 1899 *(Pravoslavnyi Palestinskii Sbornik,* XVII, 3 = no. 51). pp. 34, 65, 91. Tr. M. Ehrhard. « Le Livre du Pèlerin d'Antoine de Novgorod. » *Romania,* LVIII, 1932, 63.

860-1   **55**

He [St. Cyril] set out and came to Cherson, where he learned the language and literature of the Hebrews. He translated the eight parts of the grammar....

Serbo-Slovene life of Constantine (St. Cyril), c. 8, tr. Dvornik, *Légendes de C. et M.,* p. 359. The language is supposed to have been learned together with Samaritan and Syriac. See A. Vaillant. « Les 'lettres russes' de la *Vie de Constantin.* » *Revue des Études Slaves,* XV, 1935, 75-7.

ca. 856   **56**

After this time the Arab soldiers began to march over the territory of the Christian kingdom. They wasted Calabria by upsetting their [the Byzantines'] cities, devastating their lands, and razing their villages [or «castles», *tirot*]. They advanced into

Apulia, where they waxed mighty. They shattered their strength and captured many cities, which they plundered and despoiled.

In those days there was in Bari Saudan, king of the Arabs, who controlled the whole region. He sent messengers to Oria to make a treaty of peace with its inhabitants, offering to refrain from laying their place waste, if they would but pay the tribute. (This, however, was but a ruse whereby he might take the city unawares and lay it utterly waste.)

So the governor of Oria sent R. Shefatiah to him to hear his offer... and to receive his sealed promise... King Saudan received him with honor [and detained him]... He refused to let him go, lest he inform his ruler of the enemy's plans... [R. S. pressed him, however.] So he permitted him to leave, and he departed [late one Sabbath eve]... He wrote the [magical] letters on his horse's hoofs, so that his journey might be quickly made. Forthwith he invoked the divine name and the ground shrunk before him.

When he reached the outskirts of his city, he called to the people on all the roads, «Hurry out, flee from the suburbs! For Saudan, king of the Arabs, is coming to take our possessions, to kill, rob, and plunder.» As he drew nearer, the governor of the town came out toward him. R. S. told him what had happened to him, and they took counsel with regard to the matter...

Then Saudan and all his host, arrogant and insolent, came by forced marches to attack them. He found the countryside deserted to the very gates of the town. On the Sabbath day... having found no satisfaction, he asked for R.S, saying, Give me the man who violated his Torah by desecrating his Sabbath...»

Ahīma'as, ed. Neubauer, 118; ed. Kahana, 124 f.; tr. Salzman, 74-6. The chronicler is only vaguely aware of the invasion of this region almost three decades earlier, Bari having been taken in 841. See Gay, *L'Italie méridionale*, 52, 66, 74-6, 96 f. «King Saudan» has been correctly identified as a genuine personal name belonging to a most important Arab military leader, who figures likewise in the parallel Latin and Arabic sources, and to whom justice has been done only recently; Amari, *op. cit.*, I, 513-25. On the likelihood that

Jews were among the captives transported in this generation to the sul-
tanate of Kairwan, see Mieses, *REJ*, XCIV, 83; Mann, *Tarbiz*, V, 1934, 292.
On the miracle of the speedy journey, see A. Marmorstein, *Jahrbuch für jüdische Volkskunde*, XXV, 1923, 319. Cf. the life of Nikôn,
ed. S. P. Lampros, Νέος Ἑλληνομνήμων, III, 1906, 158 f. = ed. M. E.
Galanopoulos. Athens, 1933. pp. 89 f.

In the sequel the chronicler tells of the entertainment of Aaron
of Baghdad by Saudan, just before the former's departure.

ca. 865   **57**

I will now proceed to tell of the wonderful feats performed
by R. Hananel. He had a young cousin [? lit., «brother»] named
Pappoleon, who died prematurely. On the day of his death the brothers [of R. H.] were away at Benevento on business. So he de-
ferred his burial in the tomb of his fathers until the arrival of
his brothers..... To prevent the body from decomposing and
becoming putrid, he wrote the name of God on a piece of parchment,... and placed it under his [the dead boy's] tongue. The
name revived him...

On the night before the day of the brothers' return, they
had a remarkable dream: an angel of God appeared to them in
a vision, and said..., «... Him whom God causes to die you restore to
life. You ought not to do so...» When they reached home, he [R.H.]
came out to greet them. They went in to see their cousin and
found him sitting up in bed... When they heard what had been
done, they wept bitterly..., As soon as the name was taken from
him, his body *(golem)* fell back upon the bed....

Ahīmaʿas, ed. Neubauer, 119 f.; ed. Kahana, 126; tr. Salzman,
77 f. Cf. no. **50.**

It is difficult to say just how this Pappoleon was related to the
family of Amittai (**Exc. A**), for elsewhere only three of his sons are
enumerated (no. **49**). But our chronicler is inconsistent with respect
to this matter; cf. nos. **51, 65.**

ca. 865   **58**

R. Shefatiah had a very beautiful daughter named Kassia.
Her father wished to marry her off, but her mother did not. When-

ever anyone sued for her hand, her mother would dissuade him, saying «My daughter is of high station *(hashubah)*, and her father is a distinguished man. If there appear not one like him, I shall not permit her to leave us. If there should appear a man comparable to her father in Mishnah and Torah, in legal erudition and reasoning, in *Sifré* and *Sifra,* in homiletics and Talmud, in the observance of major and minor precepts, in understanding and wisdom, ...in wealth and eminence, in courage and authority, ...in piety and humility, [in short,] he must be endowed with every good quality.

One night, as R. Shefatiah was about to recite his prayers, as was his wont, ...singing them sweetly, ...his daughter descended from her bed and, clad only in her night-gown, stood before him to render him the service of pouring out water for the washing of his hands. He observed that «the pomegranates had budded» [Cant. 7: 13], and that she had arrived at the marriageable age. He finished praying, and then turned to his wife whom he severely berated: « ...The time has come for her to be married, ...and yet when my brother asked for her hand on behalf of his son Hasadiah, I heeded you and did not find happiness for her... »

In the morning he left home, and on his way to the synagogue called for his brother R. Hananel, who promptly came running up. Then the former explained his mission to him: «It is my will and desire to give my daughter to your son Hasadiah, for it is best that I do so». R. H. bent his knees in deep humility.

After the service he [R. S.] invited the congregation and went with them to his home, where he gave *(qiddesh)* his daughter to R. Hasadiah... R. Amittai, the lovely bride's brother, composed and dedicated to her the hymn *(yoser)*, «The Lord Who from the Beginning Foretells the End».

Aḥīmaʿas, ed. Neubauer, 122 f.; ed. Kahana, 129 f.; tr. Salzman, 82-4. (The verb *qiddesh* is used here loosely, in the sense of the father giving away his *mature* daughter in marriage.) The text of the poem is given in J. Schirmann. *Mibḥar ha-shirah ha-ʿibrit be-Italiah.* Berlin,

1934. pp. 5-8. On marriage-hymns in general, see I. Abrahams. *Jewish Life in the Middle Ages.* 2nd ed., London, 1932. pp. 204 f.

ca. 865 **59**

Once R. Shefatiah was walking down the street of the city [Oria] at night, when he heard the sound of wailing in the home of a fellow-Jew. He also heard one woman speaking to another, the one above saying to her companion below, «O my sister, grasp the child and keep him, so that we may eat him together...»

Suddenly he went up to her and took the child out of her hands. (Those women were not human beings, but demons *[se'irim]* of the night)... He brought the boy to his [R. S.'s] home, ... and hid him in his bedchamber. All night long his father and mother wept and wailed most bitterly [for their supposedly dead son]... In the morning they carried him [as they believed] to the cemetery, where they buried him. When they had returned home from there, R. S. called on them, in accordance with the custom of comforting the bereaved... [After announcing that the boy was still alive], they went to the grave, but after a search they found only a broom... So R. S. returned to his home with them, recounted all that had happened, and restored the child to them...

Ahīma'as, ed. Neubauer, 122; ed. Kahana, 128 f.; tr. Salzman, 81 f. For *Lilit* in general see Horodetzky, *EJ*, X, 972-4. The synonym *se'irim* («hairy») appears in the Talmud; see *'Erubin* 100 b. Their appetite for children appears first about this time; Scholem, *Kirjath Sepher,* X, 1933, 70; Grünwald, *Monats.,* LXXVII, 1933, 245. Cf. the statement written in the middle of the 12th c. by a Karaite in Cp.: «*Lilit* eats human flesh and drinks human blood»; Judah Hadassī. *Eshkol ha-Kofer.* Eupatoria, 1836. s. 60, p. 30a. On the Γελλώ see H. A. Winkler. *Salomo und die Karina.* Stuttgart, 1931. pp. 136-40.

867-79 **60**

If a Jew buy a slave and circumcize him, he shall suffer capital punishment.

If a Jew dare to argue against the Christian religion, he shall suffer capital punishment.

Πρόχειρος Νόμος, XXXIX, 31 f.; ed. Zepos, *Jus graecor.*, II, 279. The laws are derived from *Cod. Iust.* 1. 10. 1 and 9.18 (19). 3, respectively, and, hence, probably do not reflect a contemporary situation, as was supposed by Andréadès, *Ec. His.*, III, 12, n. 2. Inasmuch as these provisions imply official toleration of the Jew, it might be argued that this manual was compiled before the inauguration of the contrary policy in 873-4 (no. **61**). It is not unlikely, however, that these abridgements of older laws were included without taking the prevailing conditions into consideration at all.

873 - 4   **61**

In the year 6382 the Jews were baptized. Seventh Indiction. (Ἔτους ϛ' T̄ Π̄ B̄ ἐβαπτίσθησαν οἱ ἑβραῖοι [ἰουδαῖοι] INΔ Z.)

Anon. s. Italian chronicle (*ca.* 1000), ed. G. Cozza - Luzi and B. Lagumina. *La cronaca siculo-saracena di Cambridge.* Palermo, 1890. *(Documenti per servire alla storia di Sicilia pubblicati a cura della Società Siciliana per la Storia Patria.* 4th s., II) pp. 32, 103; tr. 60 and 113. = Vasiliev, *Vizantiya i Arabi.* Petrograd, 1902. II, pt. 2, 69 f. Cf. ps.-Simeon Magister, 752 f. Dölger, *Regesten,* I, pt. 1, p. 58, no. 478; cf. no. **63**.

873 - 4   **62**

.... A sinful, brazen king, having succeeded to the rule over the virtuous ones [the Jews], ordered this discerning folk to be separated from the Truth, which is more precious than pearls. He was zealous for the defilement of the aged, as well as the uncircumcision of the young. He would have supplanted by the three deities the monotheism of the congregation of the faithful....

Amittai b. Shefatiah, in a liturgical poem *(Ahabtik)*, ed. Schirmann, *Mibhar,* 4. On the text, Sonne, *REJ,* XCVIII, 1934, 84. A longer composition by the same poet, written while «the evil decree» was still in force, has been published by Davidson, «A *qerobah* by R. Amittai b. Shefatiah». (Hebrew) *Abhandlungen zur Errinerung an H. P. Chajes.* Vienna, 1933. pp. 181-94. Cf. Sonne, «Notes sur une *Qerobah* publiée par Davidson», *l. c.,* 81-4.

873-4   **63**

In the eight-hundredth year after the destruction of the holy city... and Temple, [868 A. D.] ...there arose a king named Basil,

...who tried to turn them [the Jews] from the Torah, and to convert them to the worthless religion. He sent couriers and horsemen throughout his realm. ... to turn the Jews from their faith and to convert them to «the vanity». The messengers of the king went through the land as far as the harbor [? ma'abar] of Otranto. There they embarked on a ship and passed through the province of Apulia. Wherever the tidings came, the land quivered. They traversed the province from end to end, finally reaching the city of Oria. There they delivered a letter, sealed with the king's seal, a chrysobull (it was of gold), which the king had sent to R. Shefatiah.

Now these are the words of the letter inscribed therein: «I, King Basil, send this to you that you may be brought as my guest. Come and do not decline to do so, for having heard of your wisdom and your vast learning, I have a strong desire to see you. I swear by my life and the crown on my head that peace will attend your arrival and return homeward. I will receive you with honor as I would a kinsman, and any one request that you may make of me, I will most affectionately grant.»

Aḥīma'as, ed. Neubauer, 115 f.; ed. Kahana, 122; tr. Salzman, 69 f. Dölger, *Regesten,* I, pt. 1, 58, no. 479. At the end of the chronicle the same date is given in the form A. M. 4628. The passage gives the impression that compulsory conversion was decreed at the outset, which is thereafter contradicted by the implications of the succeeding narrative. Moreover, the announcement by the emperor's messengers is repeated below (no. **66**), where it suits the sequence of events; hence, it is proleptic in the present context. If messengers were sent at this time throughout the Empire, it was presumably for the purpose of summoning other representatives of the Jews to a disputation, in the same manner as was done to Shefatiah (no. **69**).

873-4   **64**

R. Shefatiah then embarked on board a ship and sailed to Constantinople, ... — may God break down its haughtiness and the whole multitude of its people! And God caused him to find favor with the king and all his court.

The king entered into a Scriptural discussion with him, raising the question of the comparative cost of the [Solomonic] Temple and the church called Sophia... [By referring to the Biblical text R. S. proved to the king's satisfaction that the former was the costlier.]

Then the king invited him to dine with him at his table... Golden dishes were set before him that he might eat in ritual purity...

Now Basil had a daughter, ...whom a demon tormented, and whom it had been impossible to cure. He privily appealed to him [R. S.], «Help me, Shefatiah, and cure my daughter of her affliction.»

He replied to him, «Surely will I do so, with the help of God Almighty.» ...He brought the maiden there [the garden of the Boukoleon or Great Palace], and proceeded to exorcise the demon...

But the demon screamed, «Why would you relieve the suffering of the daughter of a wicked man, ...seeing that she was delivered into my power by the Lord?...»

He replied to the demon, «...Come forth in the name of God...» He at once came out and was about to flee hastily, but he [R. S.] seized him, thrust him into a leaden vessel sealed with the name of his Maker, and sunk him in the sea. The maiden, restored to health and sanity, returned to the king and queen.

Ahīma'as, ed. Neubauer, 116 f.; ed. Kahana, 122 f.; tr. Salzman, 71 f. For the imprecation hurled at Cp., cf. no. **146**. Cf. the adaptation of the theme of the discussion to w. Europe; M. Brann, *Monats.*, LIII, 1909, 93, and *idem, Germania Judaica*. Breslau, 1934. I, 347, n. 21. With respect to the consideration shown to the guest's dietary requirements, it is relevant to note that care was taken not to serve pork to the Moslem prisoners of war in the capital, according to Hārūn ibn Yahyā (10th c.), cited by Ibn Rusta. *Kitāb al-a'laq an-nafisa*, ed. de Goeje. Leyden, 1891. *(Bibl. geog. arab., VII)* p. 123, lines 4 f.; tr. Vasiliev, *Sem. Kon.*, V, 157. The exorcism-story is closely modelled on that in *Me'ilah* 17 b (as is recognized by Krauss, *Studien*, 44, n. 3).

For similar material in the Christian sources see, e. g., F. Dvornik. *La vie de St. Grégoire le Décapolite.* Paris, 1926. p. 24; A. Delatte and C. Josserand. «Contribution à l'étude de la démonologie byzantine». *Mélanges Bidez (Annuaire* of the Institut de philologie et d'histoire orientales, II) Brussels, 1934. p. 229. For the motif of sinking the demon, F. M. Goebel. *Jüdische Motive in märchenhaften Erzählungsgut.* Gleiwitz, 1932. pp. 58-88.

873 - 4   **65**

He [Shefatiah] now went to the king to obtain permission [to return home]. The king came out toward him, placed his arm about his neck, and brought him into his chambers, where he began to tempt him to abandon his religion with a liberal offer. He walked out with him... When the master sensed the overbearing zeal, he exclaimed in a loud voice to the mighty man, «O mighty Sire, you overwhelm me by violence!» Thereupon the king arose from his throne, took him out from among the people, and gave him permission [to leave].

He sent him to the queen that she might give her gift and blessing. She inquired into his affairs, «Have you any daughters and sons?»

He replied, «Your servant has one son and two daughters.»

She then gave him the rings from her ears and the girdle from her hips, and adjured him thus, «By your Torah give them to your two daughters...»

Ahīma'as, ed. Neubauer, 117; ed. Kahana, 123; tr. Salzman, 72 f. The coherence of the passage is disturbed by the sudden shift of scene from a private dialogue to a setting in the throne-room, where an audience is gathered (?). In addition, as indicated in the third sentence, three obscure verses have had to be omitted from the tr. as unintelligible in context. In the last sentence, read *ve-hishbi'ato.* The false statement with respect to the number of Shefatiah's sons is probably to be attributed to the exigencies of the rhyme; no. **145 n.**

873 - 4   **66**

After he [Shefatiah] had received leave to go, the king himself called him and said, «Shefatiah, ask a gift of me and I will give you of my wealth. But if you do not desire money, I will make you the possessor of towns and cities, for in my letter I promised to grant your wish.»

Sorrowfully and with bitter weeping he replied, «If you, my lord, have any regard for Shefatiah, do not persecute the Jewish people, do not force them to abandon the divine Torah, and do not crush them in sorrow and affliction. However, if you refuse to fulfill my wish to that extent, then for my sake let my city be exempt from the compulsory conversion.»

The king indignantly exclaimed, «Had I not sent a letter with my seal and given my oath, I would this very instant myself punish you...» Then he prepared for him a precious chrysobull, so that the compulsory conversion should not be enforced in the city of Oria, and sent him off home with honor and in peace.

Then the wicked man sent out couriers to all the provinces, and despatched his agents to convert them by force... The sun and moon were darkened for twenty-five years until the day of his death. Cursed be his end!

Ahīma'as, ed. Neubauer, 117; ed. Kahana, 123 f.; tr. Salzman. 73 f. See Sonne, *REJ*, XCVIII, 81.

[873-4 **67**

An '*Ofan* by R. Amittai b. R. Shefatiah, both of whom were «masters of the (divine) Name». This R. Shefatiah is the one who saved five communities in the land of Greece from forced conversion. The king's daughter had become insane and he cured her by means of the Name. Previous to that the king had compelled more than one hundred communities to be converted, by crushing them in the olive-press. This is the basis of the line in the *Seliḥah* « '*Ani yom ira'*,» etc.

Kaufmann, «Aus Abraham b. Asriel's *Arugat ha-Bosem*». *Monats.*, XXXI, 1882, 421. Cf. a more developed form of this tradition, Neubauer, «The early settlement of the Jews in Italy». *JQR*, IV, 1892, 613 f., 616-18. The authorship ascribed to the *piyuṭ* is false; Davidson, *Osar*, II, 454, no. 4234. For the sole known composition of Shefatiah, *id.,* I, 304, no. 6696. Cf. Graetz, *Gesch.,* V, 257, written before Neubauer's discovery (no. **64**).]

873 - 4   **68**

I will now relate an event... in the city of Oria in the building... called *Hegemonia,* which befell R. Hananel, the brother of Shefatiah, who was on the point of [spiritual] destruction, but was rescued by Him who dwelleth on high...

One day the bishop questioned him with regard to certain matters recorded in Scripture, and passed on to the subject of New Moon calculations. Inasmuch as that day happened to be the New Moon, ...he asked him at what time it would appear. R. H. replied but gave the hour incorrectly. The bishop challenged his statement, saying, «If that be your calculation on the appearance of the New Moon, you are not competent in this matter.» (Now R. H. had not previously calculated the hour of the birth of the New Moon, whereas the bishop had done so for the purpose of casting a net and catching him).... He continued, «O wise H., if the birth be in accord with my calculation, you shall do my will and adopt my religion... But if it be in accordance with yours, I will comply with your desire. I shall give you my best steed, which is reserved for my use on the New Year [? *hakesseh*], and which is worth 300 gold-pieces. However, if you do not wish to take the steed, you may have its price instead.»

Both men accepted the terms and agreed to abide by them in the presence of judges and magistrates as well as of the governor... When R. H. returned home, he calculated the birth of the New Moon and found his error... He went to his brothers and the other members of his family, and told them of the plight that he was in, so that they should pour out their supplication before the Lord, in the hope that He would hear their cries and perform another of His miracles... When the darkness of night fell, he ascended his roof, looking to Him on high... When the time of waxing arrived, ...he cried mightily, ...and addressed the following prayer to God.....

And He... heard his prayer, so that the moon was not visible until the following night. In the morning he went to collect his due, and the bishop addressed him in the presence of all, saying, «You know as well as I that the birth of the New Moon took place as I had calculated it... But who can cause harm to one such as yourself, who cajoles his Maker like a son his father...?» He then gave him the three hundred gold-pieces, which the latter distributed among the poor and needy... Then his brothers and friends assembled and offered praise and thanks to the one God...

Ahīmaᶜas, ed. Neubauer, 120 f.; ed. Kahana, 127 f.; tr. Salzman, 78-80. Textual notes by Marcus, *Proc.* of Am. Ac. for Jew. Res., V, 93. For the sense in which the root ᶜ*gn* is used, cf. Ahīmaᶜas, p. 131, line 5 from below. It is doubtful whether Oria had a bishop at so early a period; E. Besta. «Aneddoti di storia pugliese medioevale». *Rassegna pugliese di scienze, lettere, ed arti,* XXIV, 1908, 222.

The word *Hegemonia* most likely designates the episcopal residence (ἐπισκοπεῖον) rather than a monastery (ἡγουμενεῖον), in accordance with the medieval Hebrew sense of the loan-word *hegmon;* ct. Krauss, *Studien,* 105, n. 4.

873 - 4   **69**

First, he [Basil I] drew into submission to Christ the Jewish nation... He summoned them to come to disputations prepared to justify their faith, and either to prove that it was firm and irrefutable, or, having been convinced that Christ is the head of the Law and the Prophets, ... to enter into the Lord's teaching and be baptized. To those who would come forward he made offers of appointment to office. He also promised to exempt them from the burden of the former taxes (τοῦ βάρους τῶν προτέρων ἀπαλλάξας φόρων), and to make honorable men of ignoble ones (ἀτίμων). He thus freed many of their cloak of stubbornness, and brought them to faith in Christ....

«Theophanes cont.», 357. On the assignment of the authorship to Basil's grandson, Constantine VII (*ca.* 930), see Krumbacher, *Gesch. der byz. Litt.,* 253. For other notices: Continuator of Georgios the

Monk, *PG,* CX, 1080; «Leo Grammatikos», *PG,* CVIII, 1088; Kedrenos, 1128; Zonaras, III, 435.

Cumont's emendation, περιτμήτον, in the first sentence is necessary, but his suggestion that Photios was influential in this matter is very doubtful, for it was not until 877 that he was restored as patriarch; *Revue de l'Instr. Publ.,* XLVI, 10. See also Dölger, *Viertel,* XXVI, 7 f.

Regarding the converts from Islam see the law cited from a work by Constantine VII by Rambaud, *L'empire grec,* 248 f.; Dölger, *Beiträge,* 51, alludes to it as dating from the reign of Leo VI. See also *id., BZ,* XXXIV, 1934, 372, n. On the Bogomiles see the act of Alexios I in 1115; *id., Regesten,* I, pt. 2, 55, no. 1268.

On the war with the Paulicians see Vasiliev, *CMH,* IV, 139.

873 - 4   **70**

But the godly emperor from whom we are descended, being more concerned than his predecessors for the salvation of the Jews, was not content to allow them, as the others did, simply to abide by their ancient laws. He won them over to the Christian religion both by the reading of the sacred Scriptures and by his admonitions, consummating these by means of the vivifying waters of baptism. He persuaded them, indeed, to reform and become new men, according to the doctrine of Christ, and induced them to renounce the old life and whatever belonged to the old dispensation, such as circumcision, Sabbath-observance, and all their other rites. Indeed, he thereby won them over from their Jewish way of thinking, yet he did not by explicit decree revoke the older laws which tolerated Jewish life.

Leo VI (886-912), Novel 55, ed. Zepos, *Jus graecor.,* I, 125; *PG,* CVII, 548. (Cf. the tr. made from the Latin by S. P. Scott. *The Civil Law.* Cincinnati, 1932. XVII, 255). For the rest of this passage see no. **76.** Cf. no. **69.** The προτέροις νόμοις are, of course, the relevant provisions of Justinian's *Corpus* and the ecclesiastical canons (nos. **8,18**).

873 - 4   **71**

.... Then God will set up... another king, and the symbol of his name will be two B's [*Basileus Basileios*]. Now he will begin to rebuild the community which was formerly the most despised of nations. He will greatly enrich his empire, will conquer many nations... Then he will turn against the Supreme One's holy people. He will baptize them against their will ruthlessly, and [cause them to be] in great trouble. Later he will sell them into slavery....

Anon. apocalyptist, ed. L. Ginzberg. *Ginzé Schechter*. New York, 1928. I, 318 f. This obscure composition, self-styled «a vision of Daniel», bristles with difficulties. Its author seems to have been a Byzantine Jew of the 13th c.; see Krauss, «Un nouveau texte pour l'histoire judéo-byzantin». *REJ*, LXXXVII, 1929, 1-27 = *Byz.-neugr. Jahr.*, VII, 1930, 57-86.

The immediately preceding lines refer to this emperor's predecessor, under the undecipherable symbol ARB, but say nothing with regard to the Jewish situation up to this point. In the second sentence the context opposes any reference to the Jews despite the suggestive phraseology. Cf. Krauss' rather imaginative tr., *REJ*, LXXXVII, 5. The precise meaning and historicity of the last clause present a more serious problem. Ginzberg suggested that being sold into slavery was an alternative to conversion, whereas Krauss (*l.c.*, 8 f) saw in it a punishment for apostasy after conversion. In view of the relative fullness of our sources for this matter, it seems safer to take this statement not as an addition to our earlier materials but as a later tradition which is not to be credited. However, the contemporary law did retain the *servus poenae* provision; see G. Ferrari. «Il diritto penale nelle Novelle di Leone il filosofo». *Rivista penale*, LXVII, 1908, 311 f., n. 3.

873-4   **72**

The emperor Basil caused many Jews to be baptized by force, and shortly afterwards at least a few of them manifested a spontaneous assent to Christ, and, in the customary fashion, willingly professed themselves adherents of the evangelic precepts and the apostolic writings as well. At any rate, none of them was ever re-baptized.

(Basilius siquidem imperator, ... multos Iudaeorum per vim baptizari fecit, ex quibus ammodum pauci parvo post tempore spontanei praebuerunt assensum credenti in Christum et evangelica mandata pariterque apostolica documenta, ut moris est, custodire libenter professi sunt, attamen nemo eorum iterum baptizatus est).

Auxilius (*ca.* 910). «De ordinationibus a Formoso papa factis», ed. E. Dümmler. *Auxilius und Vulgarius.* Leipzig, 1866. pp. 109 f. Cf. no. **69.** The passage gives a curious argument for the validity of baptism by *vis compulsiva,* and reveals that the mixed character of Basil's work was known to the writer but not understood.

878 **73**

.... Finally we were thrown into the common prison... And promiscuously with us there were confined in the same prison, as if to make stock of these afflictions, Ethiopians, Tarsians, Hebrews, Lombards and some of our own Christians, who had come from various parts, and among whom there was also the most holy bishop of Malta....

Theodosios to Leo the archdeacon, on the siege of Syracuse; Josaphat's Latin tr. (Greek lost) in L. A. Muratori. *Rerum Italicarum Scriptores.* Milan, 1725. I, pt. 2, p. 264. Cf. tr. in F. M. Crawford. *Southern Italy and Sicily and the rulers of the South.* New York, 1905. p. 96. On the basis of this notice it is frequently stated that the Jewish captives came from Syracuse, although that is entirely contrary to the context. See, e. g., Zunz, *Zur Gesch.,* 485 f. In general see Amari, *op. cit.,* I, 550.

ca. 878 **74**

.... It is necessary ... for us to recite the testimonies of God before emperors without timidity. One of the greatest of these is the principle that one should not hastily place his hands on Hebrews to baptize them. In conformance with the Gospel precepts and the apostolic and patristic canons, one should carefully consider an application for baptism and examine «the fruit» of the candidates lest we overlook [the teaching regarding] «the casting of holy things before dogs and pearls before swine» (Matt. 7:6), the ripe dogmas of our faith before shameless and undisciplined fellows, who after having learned that which they do not understand, will be thereby armed against us.

The first fruit of the candidates... is the renunciation of the world, the things therein, the flesh and the lusts of the soul [citing Matt. 16:24, Lk. 14:26, 33. Acts 4:32, 34 f.]... If then a Hebrew should abandon all of this world's goods...., and is prepared, ...then he should be deemed worthy of the eucharist....

As long as he remains within the Jewish deception, he is immersed in the tannery, hemmed in by dog-dung and a variety of filth, he is laden with heavy taxes, never dares to face a Christian, is exposed to all the abuses, and is even lacking in necessities... If while in this condition he should be invited by the highest authority, he would strike the best possible bargain, would receive assurance of relief from future mistreatment, from heavy taxation, and from whatever he had suffered until then. (ἀλλ᾽ ἔτι ταῖς Ἰουδαϊκαῖς καταιότησι κάτοχος ὤν, βυρσοδεψῶν τε καὶ κυνείᾳ κόπρῳ καὶ βρώμῳ παντοδαπῷ συμφερόμενος καὶ Χριστιανοῖς μὲν μηδ᾽ ἀντοφθαλμῶν, δημοσιακοῖς δὲ βάρεσιν ὑποκείμενος καὶ ταῖς ἐπηρεασταῖς ἐκκείμενος ἅπασι, καὶ τῶν ἀναγκαίων αὐτῶν σπανιζόμενος....)

Moreover, he would even lord it over (καταισταίη μὲν ἐπικρατὴς) the Christians, lead an idle and otiose existence, abundantly supplied with necessities throughout his life, attaining honors he had never dreamt of, and perhaps marrying the well-born daughter of the local governor. If ... he formally renounces Judaism and is baptized, all the while making sport of Christianity, I would not call him a Christian....

He came to turn Christian, not converted to Christ,.... but seeking the promised gold and worldly advantages. He puts up a pretense for the present, soon, however, to return like a swine to his own filth....

The baptism of certain Jews for gifts and promises of money... should be condemned not only as idolatry is, but as betrayal of Christ....

See how precise is the canon [*supra*, no. 18]! How it takes as proof of good faith that the Jew show contempt for his customs. This does not refer to the Mosaic precepts, as it seems to

some, nor to the Jewish sects...., but to the customs derived from
the sinful traditions and to the ceremonies observed outside and
secretly among them. Hence the canon adds, «refute and correct
others». This means only those who observe secretly, not those
who do it openly.

.... The toadies will prate that it suffices if a Hebrew merely
renounce his old precepts before the emperor. But we.... require
him to express his contempt for his peculiar customs and observances before the Church of God, the bishops and priests, not
with him reciting or writing these things, as some require, for
that is for us to formulate, rather than for him... Having done
so, we order him to anathematize those things, the Jewish sects,
and their founders. Then we make him a Christian. Once he is
a catechumen, we follow the proper order. We do not rush him
through the baptism like some of the careless bishops.... Rather,
in keeping with the divine canons of the second and sixth Coun-
cils, we detain him in the church, and make him study the writers....

Gregorios Asbestas. «A treatise maintaining that the Hebrews
ought not to be baptized with undue haste and without previous
careful examination», ed. and tr. E. de Stoop. «Het Antisemitisme en
te Byzantium onder Basilius den Macedonier». Koninklijke Vlaamsche
Academie voor Taal en Letterkunde: *Verslagen en mededeelingen.*
Ghent, 1913. pp. 474-80, 488-92; see also his introd., pp. 451-72. The
authorship was established by G. Mercati. «Un antisemita bizantino
del secolo IX, che era Siciliano». *Didaskaleion,* IV, 1915, 1-6. (The
epithet is quite gratuitous). For further details, Bury, *East. R. E.,*
184 f., 190 f., 432; Lancia di Brolo, *op. cit.,* II, 265-91.

Cf. Dölger, *Viertel.,* XVI, 10, where he interprets τοῦ δυσώδους
ἐπιτηδεύματος as «ihren übelriechenden Gewerbe», i.e. tanning. De
Stoop renders, «van het jammerlijk leven waarin was vervallen».
For the arguments on the jurisdiction of a bishop over his priest,
see the conclusion, p. 510.

ca. 879 ?   **75**

Pagans, Jews, and heretics shall not serve in the army nor
in a civil office, but shall be utterly without honors.

«Epanagôgé», ix, 13, ed. Zepos, *Jus Graecor.*, II, 255 = Constantine VII, Ἐκλογή, ix, 12, *PG,* CXIII, 488. Cf. no. **19** (iv, 6). This manual, xl, 33 f. (p. 362), also repeats two other provisions with respect to the Jews, which are derived from an earlier work, no. **60.** See Dölger, *Regesten,* I, pt. 1, p. 61, no. 500.

(Note also that the Νομοκάνων, supposed to have been compiled in 883, repeats the earlier laws which recognize the legal status of Jews and their religion. For the text, see ed. Pitra, *Iuris eccl.* v. II. Cf. Zachariä, *Gesch. d. gr.-röm. Rechts,* 22).

886   **76**

R. Shefatiah had grown old; God had blessed him with all the desirable personal qualities, and had endowed him with learning, great wealth and possessions of great value. He had also favored him with a worthy and upright son [Amittai]... R. Hananel was also eminent and upright. They were all pious, affectionately bound to one another, and unceasingly devoted to study and to religion... They proclaimed the might and glory of their King [in liturgical compositions]... They sorrowfully bewailed the exile and the destruction of the Temple, and lamented the forcible conversion throughout their lives... They begged the all-merciful One to nullify that decree. Thanks to their supplication... the decree did not cross over from the other side of the sea...

On the New Year's day R. S. alone was deemed worthy of sounding the ram's horn *[Shofar]* ... But on that [last] day he was prostrated with illness. Nevertheless, the whole congregation urged him insistently, saying, «O sir, blow the *Shofar* for us....,» so he arose to blow it. But being extremely weak, the blast was not as it should have been... He left the synagogue, and entering his home, lay down on his bed.

The entire congregation followed and entered his bedchamber.... He said, I am about to go to my resting-place..., and I wish to inform you that Basil... is dead.... There he passes before me bound in chains of fire and delivered into the power of the angels of destruction. My God... is sending for me to come

forth toward Basil and to face him at his trial for all the evil which
he has committed against His people....»

They wrote down the date and the hour. Some days later
the news reached them announcing the death of Basil...on a day
corresponding to the words of the righteous man. (Such was the
custom of the kings of Constantinople to convey the news of the
death of the king by an official dispatch to Bari, giving the date
and the hour of the event.)...

Ahīma'as, ed. Neubauer, 123 f.; ed. Kahana, 130 f.; tr. Salzman,
85 f. See also B. Halper, *Post Biblical Hebrew Literature*. Philadelphia,
1921. *Text,* pp. 66-68, 230-32; *English Translation,* pp. 96-99. As is
noted by Kaufmann, *Ges. Schr.,* III, 2, the emperor died on August
29, five days before the New Year.

886   **77**

After the death of the emperor [Basil I], most of them [the
converted Jews] returned like dogs to their own vomit. But even
if they, or rather, some of them remained as immutable as Ethiopians, nevertheless, the pious emperor must have received from
God full reward for his feat because of its difficulty.

«Theophanes cont.», 357 (continuing no. **69**). A number of other
sources confirm this information with respect to the lapse of the
decree, nos. **78, 79, 83,** and consequently, there are reasons for suspecting the one conflicting statement, no. **84.** Cf. Krauss, *Studien,* 44, n. 8.

The difficulty of converting Jews is apparent also from Photios'
contemporary letter to the archbishop of Kertch; *PG,* CII, 829.

For a contemporary parallel to the harsh epithet applied to the
Jews see Grégoire, *Revue des études grecques,* XLVI, 1933, 62.

886 - 912   **78**

He [Basil I] was succeeded by his son Leo [VI]. The Lord
God chose him, may his memory be blessed. He annulled the
decree that had been issued in his father's time, and permitted
the Jews to return to their faith....

Ahīma'as, ed. Neubauer, 117 f.; ed. Kahana, 124; tr. Salzman, 74.
Cf. no. **77** and ct. no. **84.** For the contrary interpretation, Krauss,
EJ, IV, 1240.

886-912   **79**

He [Basil I] will bequeath his sceptre to his son.... Leo, who
will grant relief and freedom *(hanaha ve-herut)* to the holy people
of the Supreme One.... In his days the lowly people will live
undisturbed....

Anon. apocalyptist (see no. **71**), ed. Ginzberg, *Ginzé Schechter,* I,
319. Cf. Krauss, *REJ*, LXXXVII, 9, who would distinguish between
the synonymous Hebrew terms, making the former refer to exemption from taxation!

ca. 886-910   **80**

After him [Shefatiah] there arose R. Amittai, his gentle son,
who followed in his father's footsteps. He strengthened the academy with the help of his circle of scholars... For on the day
before his death his father had made his will, stipulating that the
circle be properly sustained, lest the scholars become separated.
He held the band together and promoted learning with the aid
of the rabbis and scholars....

His soul grieved over the destruction of the Temple, and he
bewailed the forcible baptism throughout his life....

Aḥīmaʿas, ed. Neubauer, 124; ed. Kahana, 131; tr. Salzman, 86.
See no. **62**, and Brody, *EJ*, II, 609f. Davidson, *Osar*, IV, 368, lists 20
of his liturgical poems; see also no. **58**. Apparently the same writer
is cited in a ms. work abstracted by Marmorstein, *REJ*, LXXVI, 1923,
123, no. **13**; a reference to the angel *Bakya* involving a calculation
of the sum of its letters in *gimatria;* cf. the poem published by
Schirmann, *Mibhar*, 10.

On Zebadiah *Hazzan,* a poet believed to be of the same period
and provenience, see Davidson *Osar*, IV, 379; Zunz, *Literatur-
geschichte der synagogalen Poesie.* Berlin, 1865. p. 186; H. Brody and
M. Wiener. *Mibhar ha-shirah ha-'ibrit.* Leipzig, 1922. p. 49. For
another possible contemporary, Yudan b. Mesatiah ha-Kohen, see
Schirmann, *EJ,* IX, 525.

ca. 886-910   **81**

It happened that he [Amittai] went out one day to his vineyard, his estate outside the town, and on that day a learned and

pious stranger died. Thereupon the elders of the community summoned him [Amittai], to join them in the burial of the deceased stranger and the mourning for him, in accordance with the honor due him. He sent back word to them, «Come out of the town, where I shall await your arrival, and I shall accompany you to the cemetery and officiate at the burial». Then the whole community came out to attend the funeral...

R. A. eulogized him, in the dirge which he had composed for the occasion. The opening words were as follows:

« Alas, O alienage! Alack, O exile!

« He who has not experienced you, may mock you,

« But he who has, laments with bitter cries. »

A certain R. Moses, the teacher of the children, who was standing there,.... whispered to the bystanders, « Those who know you well are crushed with affliction ».

R. A. overheard it and held the pedagogue's offense against him for a considerable time. Years later a certain man's wife fell under suspicion of adultery... But when the community convened to try the woman, the only witness found against her was R. Moses .... R. A. asked him..., «Have you a fellow - witness as required by the Torah? » And inasmuch as no other witness could be found, he directed the *hazzan* to lay him under the ban .... He thus expelled him from Oria,... whence he went first to the city of Capua, and thence he traveled to Pavia.

Ahima'as, ed. Neubauer, 124 f.; ed. Kahana, 131 f.; tr. Salzman, 86 f. Cf. no **80**. The text has *'ahiv* before the first mention of R. Moses. but this is in conflict with the connotation of the phrase *met ha-miṣvah,* which the passage has in connection with the deceased stranger. Read perhaps *'ehad.* For some other details see Brody, *ŻfhB,* II, 1897, 163; Elbogen, *Monats.,* LXlX, 330, n. 1; Davidson, *Abhandl. Chajes,* 183, n. 1; Sonne, *l. c., ib.*

On the penalty of the ban see J. H. Greenstone, *JE,* V, 285 - 7. On the communal office of *hazzan,* see A. Z. Idelsohn, *EJ,* IX, 890.

(It is relevant to note here that an epitaph from Oria of uncertain date, which has been dated 898 by Chwolson, *Corpus,* 166, and Cassuto, *Eshkol,* II, 3, but which differs radically from the phraseology employed during the same century [no. **25**, etc.], belongs probably to a considerably later time. The year 1320, which is calculated for it by J. Derenbourg, *REJ*, II, 1881, 133, would seem more likely.)

ca. 890 **82**

... You refuse to heed all the various predictions which the prophets have made regarding him [Jesus]. Should you ask, «Why did they not speak more clearly?,» then we will put you to shame by means of the words of your own prophets..... [Ps. 17:10, Is. 7:14, Baruch 3:36-8, Dt. 18:15, Is. 68:9, Hos. 1:9, Ps. 46:9, 85:9.]

Are you not ashamed, O Jews, to call us idolatrous sacrificers and idol-worshippers? However, this is not so strange, for every harlot will call a pure woman by her own name. Moreover, if you had us in your power as we today have you, you would not allow one of us to live among you, as we permit you....

The Jew might say, «Inasmuch as God has forbidden the worship of wood, stone, or any human handiwork, how do you Christians venerate these things, with your crosses and images?» Then reply to him, «Tell me, O Jew, why do you venerate the scroll of the Law, etc.?...»

They have burned your Temple,... and led you away captive, so that you have been scattered throughout the world to this day.... More than eight hundred years have now passed, during which you have had neither altar, nor ark, nor a place in which to observe the Passover....

Ps.-Anastasios the Sinaite, *PG*, LXXXIX, 1228-38. Cf. nos. **1, 7**. There are some other polemic fragments which are likewise spuriously assigned to the same author, but these afford no definite clue as to date or provenance. See Williams, *op. cit.*, 175-80. The text from which the foregoing selections are taken, is derived almost verbatim from the Ἀντιβολή, ed. Mc Giffert, p. 65, line 4 to p. 80, line 19 (cf. pp. 35-7), and ultimately goes back perhaps to Jerome of Jerusalem; see *PG*, XL, 848-60, XCIV, 1409 (*apud* John of Damascus), and P. Batiffol. «Jérôme de Jérusalem d'après un document inédit.» *Revue des ques-*

tions historiques, XXXIX, 1886, 248-55. Cf. Bardenhewer, V, 43, 47. The changes consist chiefly in the weakening of the dialogue-form, and the downward shifting of the date. The last sentence of the second paragraph, which enables us to assign the adaptation to a Byzantine provenance, and to fix the *terminus a quo* as the death of Basil I, is not found elsewhere. See further E. J. Goodspeed, «Pappiscus and Philo.» *American Journal of Theology*, IV, 1900, 796-802; E. Bratke in *Texte und Untersuchungen zur Geschichte der altchristlichen Literatur*, XIX, 3, (1899), pp. 106-9. For a contemporary fragment, A. Ehrhard, *BZ*, VI, 1897, 415.

ca.* 890   **83

Laws concerning Jews in the *Basilika*

a. I. 1.16. Christians must not disturb unoffending Jews. A Christian guilty of violence or theft is liable to a Jewish plantiff for the object involved, plus double its value.

b. 30. Jews are excluded from all civil and military service.

c. 34. Jews may not testify in cases involving orthodox Christians on either side.

d. 37. Synagogues may not be used for the quartering of soldiers.

e. 38. Intermarriage between Jews and Christians is subject to the same penalty as adultery, and entails the loss of power of litigation.

f. 39. Jews must not be guided simply by their own laws in contracting marriages, nor may they practice polygamy.

g. 40. Cases between Jewish litigants involving religious matters, are to be adjudicated according to Roman law in Roman courts. But if a civil case involves only Jewish litigants, they may have it decided by judges of their own choosing, the ruling to be upheld by the civil official.

h. 41. No non-Jew may be an overseer (ἔφορος) over Jews.

i. 43. Jews may not be required by law officers to desecrate their Sabbath or holidays.

j. 44. Violence to the persons of Jews, to their synagogues, or to their homes is forbidden.

k. 45. If there be a quarrel between a Christian and a Jew, it must be judged by a magistrate, and not by the Jewish priests.

l. 46. The Jew who circumcizes a Christian, or who caused one to be circumcized, will have his property confiscated and will be permanently exiled.

m. 47. The holding of public office is forbidden to Jews. Although synagogues may be repaired, new ones may not be built. Violations are punishable by a fine of 50 lbs. of gold. Attempting to convert a Christian is punishable by confiscation of property and death.

n. 48. A Jew seeking conversion with the ulterior motive of escaping some obligation thereby, is not to be received into the church.

o. 51. No Jew may possess a Christian slave. Neither may he circumcize a catechumen.

p. 53. If a Christian transfers to a Jew the ownership of a plot on which a church is located, or bequeaths it to him, or appoints him administrator over it, both parties forfeit their rights to the local church. A newly built synagogue is also subject to seizure by the Church.

q. 57. The Scriptures are to be read in the synagogue in the vernacular, preferably the Septuagint version. Interference on the part of Jewish leaders is forbidden. The study of the post-Biblical literature (δευτέρωσις) is prohibited.

r. XXXVIII. 1. 15. s. 6. Jews may serve as guardians of non-Jews, and are subject to the other duties also, except those which are forbidden by their religion.

s. XXXIX. 29. 7. It is permitted to the Jews to circumcize their own children. But if they circumcize another's, they will be punished by decapitation and confiscation of property.

t. 54. 22. The Christian who turns Jew will have his property confiscated.

u. 23. If a deceased Christian is accused of having turned Jew or pagan within five years after his death, his will is invalidated.

v. 18. A Jew who throws stones at, or in any other manner disturbs a convert to Christianity, will be burned.

w. 31. A Jew may not purchase a Christian slave. If a Jew circumcizes a slave who is a Christian or an adherent of some other non-Jewish group, he will punished by decapitation.

x. 32. A non-Christian found in possession of a slave must lose that slave and pay a fine of 30 lbs. of gold.

G. E. Heimbach. *Basilicorum libri LX.* Leipzig, 1833-97. vv. I, III, V; v. VII, ed. J. Mercati and F. C. Ferrini. These laws are all drawn from the *Corpus* of Justinian, as will be indicated below.

a. Cf. v. VII, p. 173, and see Νόμιμον (*ca.* 1200), I, 12, ed. Zepos, *Jus graecor.*, VI, 417. Cf. *Cod. Iust.*, 1.11.6. The Christian plaintiff would in such a case receive three or fourfold the value; Juster, II, 180.

b. Cf. *C. I.*, 1.5.12. s. 6; Juster, II, 245. Cf. also Εὐξημένη ᾿Επαναγωγή (*ca.* 1025), LII, 24, LIII, 7, ed. Zepos, VI, 202, 214. Cf. no. **75.**

c. Cf. v. VII, 177. Cf. *C.I.* 1.5.21; Juster, II, 123. See also Πεῖρα, (11th c.) XXX, 16, ed. Zepos, *Jus graecor.*, IV, 128.

d. Cf. *C.I.* 1.9.4.; Juster I, 460.

e. Cf. v. VII, *ib.* Cf. *C.I.* 1.9.6.; Juster, II, 48f. Cf. Νόμιμον, I, 2, ed. Zepos, *op. cit.*, VI, 416.

f. Cf. *C.I.*, *ib.*, 7; Juster, II, 49-54. Νόμιμον, I, 13, *l.c.*, 417.

g. Cf. *C.I.*, *ib.*, 8; Juster, II, 152, n. 2. The omission of the negative particle in the first sentence both here and in *C.I.* can scarcely be «une mésure vexatoire de l'époque» (of the *Basilika*), as Juster suggests. See also Νόμιμον, I, 14, *l.c.*

h. Cf. v. VII, *ib.* Cryptic abridgment of *C.I.*, *ib.*, 10., which deals explicitly with the regulation of market-prices (Juster, I, 362); in our period such autonomy had undoubtedly lapsed. Cf. Νόμιμον, I, 15, *l.c.*

Cf. v. VII, *ib.*; Αἱ ῾Ροπαί, III, 8, ed. Zepos, III, 279. Cf. *C.I.*, *ib.*, 13; Juster, II, 123.

i. Cf. v. VII, *ib.*

j. Cf. *C.I.*, *ib.*, 14; Juster, II, 179. Cf. Νόμιμον, I, 12, *l.c.*

k. Cf. *C.I.*, *ib.*, 15; Juster, II, 99. Cf. v. VII, *ib.*

l. Cf. *C.I.*, *ib.*, 16; Juster, I, 266. Cf. VII, *ib.*

m. Cf. *C.I.*, *ib.*. 18 (19); ct. *supra, l.*

n. Cf. *C.I.*, *ib.*, 12.1; Juster, *ib.* See nos **18, 74.**

o. Cf. *C.I., ib.* 10. lf., Novel 37; Juster, II, 76. Cf. 'Επιτομή, (*ca.* 920), xiv, 43 f., ed. Zepos, IV, 576, 579.

p. Cf. Novel 131; Juster, II, 69 f.

q. Cf. Novel 146; Juster, I, 369-77; Krauss, *Studien,* 57-62; tr. Parkes, *op. cit.,* 392 f.

r. Cf. *Digesta,* 27. I. 15. s. 6; Juster, II, 64.

s. Cf. *ib.* 48.8.11 pr.; Juster, I, 266.

t. Cf. *C.I.,* 1.7.1; Juster, I, 260 ff. Ct. no **84n.**

u. Cf. *C.I. ib.,* 2; Juster, I, 261. Cf. 'Επιτομή, xxx, 44, *l.c.,* 465.

v. Cf. *C.I., ib.,* 9.3; Juster, II, 159.

w.x. See above, *l.* and *m.*

ca. 894   **84**

The preceding emperors promulgated various laws with reference to the Hebrew people... Those who undertook to regulate their mode of life, ordained that they should read the sacred Scriptures, and that they should not be prevented from observing their religious ceremonies. They also provided that their children should adhere to their religion, as much by the tie of blood as by the rite of circumcision. These are the laws which, as we have stated, were formerly enforced throughout the Empire...

Therefore, we, desiring to supply that which our father omitted, do hereby annul all the old laws enacted with reference to the Hebrews, and we command that they shall not dare to live in any other manner than in accordance with the pure and salutary Christian faith. And if any of them should be found disregarding the ceremonies of the Christian religion, and to have returned to his Jewish practices and beliefs, he shall suffer the penalties prescribed for apostates.

Leo VI, Novel 55; see no. 71 for the reference and forthe portion of the text which follows the end of our first paragraph. Regarding the date see Monnier, *Novelles de Léon,* 3. There is an indubitable contradiction between this document and the *Basilika* (no. 83), and the problem is further complicated by the lack of any precise dating for the publication of either one. Cf. Monnier, *op. cit.,* 56f., who suggests that the Novel may have been enforced for some brief period.

148

For the penalty under Justinian see reference in no. **83**, n. *t.*; repeated by Balsamon, Συλλογή, VII, 1, *PG,* CXXXVIII, 1205; Νόμιμον, I, 5, ed. Zepos, *Jus graecor.*, VI, 416; «Ecloga privata aucta», XVII, 35, *ib.*, 44; and Harmenopoulos (14th c.), ed. G. Heimbach. *Manuale legum sive Hexabiblos.* Leipzig, 1851. p. 102. Theodoros is cited in *Basilika,* ed. Heimbach, I, 29, n. *uu.* On the law affecting the Samaritans, see Dölger, *Regesten,* I, pt. 1, 4, no. 28. Leo VI's Novel 65 reads: τὴν ἐσχατὴν εἰσπραττέθω ποινὴν, τὴν τῶν ἀποστατῶν κόλασιν ὑφιστάμενος, ed. Zepos, *ib.*, I, 136 = *PG,* CXXVII, 568. Cf. Ferrari, *Rivista penale,* LXVII, 314. The tradition touching Constantine and the secret Jews occurs in Eutychius (10th c.). *Kitāb at-tā'rīkh al-majmūʿ,* ed. L. Cheikho, *et al.* Beyrut-Paris, 1906. I, 133 f.; tr. Pococke, *PG,* CXI, 1012 f.

ca. 900 - 50 ? **85**

E 1. I do weep. . . . .

L 2. For the good youth, whom the Good One had taken (?)...

Ia 3. My gold is become dim, my beloved one has been cut off. My son, ⟨my son,⟩ Eliaqim!

Q 4. His cedar - like stature has become as naught, and he has been mourned in the market- places.

I 5. His days were but few, his years so youthful. Praise him, O righteous men!

M 6. He Who comforts. . . . .

Eliaqim b. Eliaqim.

7. Here lies Eliaqim, surnamed Caleb

8. the dyer, who was cut off in his twenty-

9. fourth year.

Found at Corinth and first published through the courtesy of Dr. E. L. Sukenik by the present writer, «The epitaph of a dyer in Corinth.» *B. Ng. Jb.* XII, 1936, 42-49. See that article for a facsimile, for the relation of this inscription to the known facts with regard to dyeing as a Jewish pursuit during our period, and for the basis of the dating proposed. Detailed annotations on the text are also given there.

Another tombstone has survived to the extent of the beginnings of its five lines. Complete words can be made out only on lines 2f., viz., *he-hasid, ve-ha-sadiq.*

ca. 900 - 1000 **86**

A fragment of a Greek Mishnaic glossary.

First published by A. Papadopoulos-Kerameuv, in *Festschrift zu Ehren des Dr. A. Harkavy.* Petrograd, 1908. pp. 68-90, 177. Then treated again in a study accompanied by clearer photographs by Ph. Koukoulés, *BZ,* XIX, 1910, 422-29. Re-edited by Starr, «A fragment of a Greek Mishnaic Glossary». *Proc.* of the Am. Acad. for Jew. Res., VI, 1935, 353-67. The page originally contained 124 words selected from *Kilaim* I, 2-*Shebi'it* VII, 2. Prof. L.H. Gray was good enough to call my attention to the inclusion of nos. 64 and 77 in Brighenti, *Dizionario greco moderno-italiano.* For a similar fragment in Arabic, see B. Halper. *Descriptive Catalogue of Genizah Fragments in Philadelphia.* Philadelphia, 1924. no. 98, p. 55 = *JQR,* XIII, 1922, 22.

925 **87**

I, Shabbetai b. Abraham, known as Doctor Donnolo... was carried off into captivity from my birthplace, Oria, by the Arab army on Monday at the fourth hour, Tammuz 9 [July 4], in the year 4685 [A.M.] ... Ten learned and pious rabbis ... were slain: R. Hasadiah b. R. Hananel, the great and righteous man, ... who was related to us through my grandfather, R. Joel ..., R. Amnon my sainted teacher, R. Uriel, R. Menahem, R. Hiya, R. Ṣadoq, R. Moses, R. Hod, R. Jeremiah, and R. Nuriel...

As for myself, I, who was then twelve years of age, was ransomed at Taranto with my parents' money. My parents and relatives were carried off to the lands of Palermo and Africa. But I remained on Byzantine territory and turned to various pursuits...

Donnolo, introd. to *Hakmoni,* ed. D. Castelli. *Il commento di Sabbetai Donnolo sul libro della creazione.* Florence, 1880. pp. 3 f. Cf. the citation in corrupt form in the work referred to below, no. **104 n.** On the author see Cassuto, *EJ,* V, 1192. With regard to this sack of Oria, see Amari, *Storia dei Musulmani,* II, 171-73. In 927 it was sacked again and remained uninhabited until 968; Gay, *L'Italie méridionale,* 207.

A poem by a *Shabbetai ha-rofe* is included in the *Mahzor Romaniah*; Davidson, *Osar,* III, 410, no. 169.

For earlier evidence of a Jewish community in Taranto see Frey, *Corpus,* I, 444-49. For the 11th c. see no. **137,**

925   **88**

... In our community [Bari] there survives R. Abraham b. Jehoshaphat, who formerly served as rabbi for the [now] dispersed community of Oria. ...

Anon. letter, ed. Mann, *Texts*,I, 24f., cf. p. 14. For the context see no. **94**.

ca. 925 - (?) 945   **89**

Menaḥem Qoresī b. R. Mordecai the *parnas*, liturgical poet and *mohel* (performer of circumcision), of Otranto.

I. Sonne. «Alcuni osservazioni sulla poesia religiosa in Puglia.» *Rivista*, XIV, 1933, 68-77. Four of his compositions are listed by Davidson, *Osar*, IV, 435 (note his correction, *JQR*, XXIV, 1934, 352) and a long *yoser* for the last two days of Passover has been added by Schirmann, *Mitteilungen* of the Forschungsinstitut für hebräische Dichtung. II, 101-20. (See the review by S. H. Kook, *Kirjath Sepher*, XI, 1934, 78.)

The information given above is derived from the signature-acrostics of our writer's poems. Sonne has shown that the surname is equivalent to the title *mohel*; for the father's position of *parnas*, see no. **180n**. Sonne established the case for the earlier dating by means of a comparative study of the text published by Schirmann. In addition he shows how, in common with the other followers of Eleazar ha-Kalīr (see S. Spiegel, *EJ*, IX, 816-20), Menaḥem employs an extremely enigmatic style, abounding in rabbinic allusions and neologisms.

Somewhat more problematic is Sonne's theory that our writer is identical with a local leader who died in prison during a religious persecution; see no. **94**. Of the latter Menaḥem it is said that he was learned and pious, following which we have an obscure reading: *ve-toreah bekol misvot hazharah*. See Mann, *Texts, I*, 24, line 7, and cf. n. 13, II, 1458, where he offers his emendation of the last two words: *misvah ve-'azharah*. Sonne, however, would emend only the last word and read *ha-gezerah*, in the sense of «circumcision». A third suggestion is Davidson's, *be-zehirah*.

For the traditions regarding the local community see Schirmann, *l. c.*, 96-100. For a Greek inscription of *ca.* the 3rd c., Frey, *Corpus*, I, 450 f.

ca. 930   **90**

Then the patriarch of Jerusalem despatched a letter through his messenger to Constantinople, addressed to the emperor Romanus [or, «Roman Emperor»], and informed him of all those things [the conversion of the Jews in Jerusalem] which God saw fit to exhibit. He exhorted him to convert to the faith of Christ all the Jews of his empire, just as they were all converted in Jerusalem. The emperor, did, indeed, order all the Jews to be baptized, but when the Hebrews heard of God's miracles, they voluntarily believed and were baptized...

(Inde vero Hierosolimitanus patriarcha suas literas et legatum suum Constantinopolim ad Romanum direxit imperatorem et omnia innotuit, quae Deus ostendere dignatus est, commonendo, ut sicut Hierosolima omnes Iudei Christiani facti sunt, ita et in suum imperium omnes Iudeos ad Christi fidem converteret. Quod vero ipse imperator ⟨audiens⟩ omnes Iudeos baptizari iussit, et ipsi Hebrei mirabilia Dei audientes spontanea voluntate crediderunt et baptizati sunt...)

Doge Peter II Candianus (Venice) and Patriarch Marinus (Grado) to Henry I of Germany and Archbishop Hildibert (Mayence), in a letter read at the Synod of Erfurt, 932. *MGH: Legum Sectio,* IV, ed. L. Weiland. Hannover, 1893. p. 7; cf. 4 f. Supersedes ed. cited by Aronius, *Regesten,* pp. 53 f., nos. 123 f.; cf. Dölger, *Regesten,* I, pt. 1, p. 76, no. 624. (Mann, *Texts,* I, 11, n. 15, gives the impression that these two works cite different sources.)

See J. Brutzkus. *Pis'mo khazarskogo evreya ot X veka.* Berlin, 1924. p. 25; cf. *id., Zeitschrift für die Geschichte der Juden in Deutschland,* III, 1931, 101. Mošin, Byzantion, VI, 1931, 320 f., develops a rash theory of two successive phases of this persecution, by a misunderstanding of no. **91.**

ca. 930   **91**

... Many Jews had migrated thither [Khazaria], having come from all the cities of the Moslems as well as from Byzantium. For it happened in our own time, which is the year 332 [A. H.], that the Byzantine emperor Romanos compelled all the Jews in his kingdom to become Christians....

al-Mas'ūdī. *Kitāb murūj adh-dhahab wa-ma'ādin al-jawahir (Les Prairies d' Or)*, ed. and tr. C. B. de Meynard and P. de Courteille. Paris, 1861. II, c. 17, pp. 8 f. Composed in 943-4. See Mošin, *Byzantion*, VI, 323. For the contemporary persecution of the Armenians, see S. Runciman. *The emperor Romanus Lecapenus*. Cambridge, 1929. p. 115. On the conversion of Moslem captives, Marquart, *Streifzüge* 62.

The passage immediately preceding this tells of the conversion of the Khazar ruling class to Judaism in the time of Hārūn ar-Rashīd (786-809), and a 14th c. historian telescopes both notices thus: «Ibn al-Athīr (!) relates that in the time of Hārūn ar-Rashīd the ruler of Constantinople expelled the Jews from his realm, and they migrated to the Khazar land»; ad-Dimashqī. *Nukhbat ad-dahr fi 'ajā'ib al-barr wa'l-bahr (Manuel de la cosmographie du Moyen Age)*, ed. A. F. Mehren. Petrograd, 1866, p. 263, lines 6-8; tr. *id.*, Copenhagen, 1874. p. 380. This is nowhere to be found in the source named, and, nevertheless, since it was quoted by Fraehn (1822), it has been repeated by various writers, e.g., Zunz, *Ges. Schr.*, I, 89. That it is a mis-citation of al-Mas'ūdī, was made clear by Marquart, *op. cit.*, 6; yet Dvornik, *Légendes de C. et de M.*, 168, cites ad-Dimashqī still.

ca. 930   **92**

... In the time of my lord King Joseph [of the Khazars], ... during the compulsory conversion of the days of the wicked Romanos ....

Anon. letter (see no. **13**), ed. Schechter, *JQR*, III, 206, lines 61 f.; tr., 217. See no. **91**, and Kokovtzov, *Evr. — Khazar. perepiska*, 117, n. 10.

ca. 930   **93**

Afterwards there will arise a king who will cause them [the Jews] grief because of his expulsion, but it will not be extinction. It will be carried out mercifully.

Anon. apocalyptist (see no. **71**), ed. Ginzberg, *op. cit.*, 320. Cf. Krauss, *REJ*, LXXXVII, 14f. Unless we assume that Leo III and Basil I denied the right of recalcitrant Jews to emigrate, it is difficult to see wherein lay the «mercifulness» of Romanos I.

ca. 930   **94**

... The holy congregation of Otranto has lost three leaders, as a result of the execution of the accursed decree. Their names are: R. Isaiah, a prominent and learned man, a humble saint the like of whom we have not seen; R. Menahem, a pious and scrupulously observant scholar; Mar Elijah, their disciple, an upright man who was a merchant. R. Isaiah pierced his own throat with a knife... R. Menahem was thrust into prison, and Mar Elijah was strangled....

But — the Lord be praised! — not a letter of the Torah [or, «any Jewish writing»] was burned there. For the fire was first kindled in our town [Bari], whereupon we speedily notified them by secret messenger. Both here and there calamity prevailed for two days, but on the third we issued forth from the darkness into the light...

In our community there remains R. Abraham b. Jehoshaphat, formerly rabbi of the [now] scattered community of Oria, R. Samuel b. Judah, who was born and raised in our town, R. Abraham, R. Elijah b. Abraham, R. Moses *ha-kohen* b. Ephraim, R. Ebyatar b. Ezekiel, as well as the other scholars of the college. In Otranto there remain R. Hodaiah and his son Amittai, both learned men, R. Hīya *ha-kohen,* his [Hodaiah's] son-in-law, R. Mordecai, R. Leon, R. Shabbetai, ⟨and R. A⟩bra-b. Ezra.

All of them strive for the glory of our lord, and rejoice in his well-being... May his greatness increase and may his [political] power be firmly established....

Anon. correspondent at Bari to Hasdai Ibn Shaprūt, ed. Mann, *Texts,* I, 23-25; see also *ib.,* 12-14. Continued in no. **95**. On the settlement of the refugees from Oria in Bari and Otranto, see no. **116**. Cf. Cassuto, *Eshkol,* I, 837. On the problem of the identification of the Menahem mentioned here, see no. **89**. From the closing line (omitted from tr.) Poznanski, *REJ,* LXVIII, 1914, 270, n. 1, inferred that the addressee was still unmarried.

ca. 930   **95**

Moreover, we have to inform the leader of « the scattered flock » [Hasdai Ibn Shaprūt] concerning Mar Samuel, who has been as a faithful slave to his master... After he had escaped from «the defilement of that curse» [the danger of enforced conversion], he undertook nine months ago to make a copy of the book of Joseph b. Gurion [*Yosippon*] in a short time. On his way hither [Bari], when he got twelve miles away from NPIAH, he was held up by robbers who deprived him of the book as well as of the letters, and whatever else they found on him... Then out of esteem for you, Mar Abraham ⟨b.⟩ Sassōn, the doctor and head of the community, was stirred up. He and some other men of his rode off on horses [but failed to recover anything]...

Mann, *Texts,* I, 25 f.; continuing no. **94.** Samuel was evidently sent by Hasdai partly for the purpose of securing a copy of the Yosippon chronicle, a work which may have been composed in s. Italy a short time before; see Cassuto, *EJ,* IX, 420-25. (It is cited contemporaneously by Dunashb. Tamin of Kairwan; see S. Munk, *JA.* LVII, 1850, 18, n. 2. Cf. H. Malter. *Saadia Gaon.* Philadelphia, 1921. p. 51, n. 84.) See further R. Eisler. *The Messiah Jesus,* etc., tr. A. H. Krappe. New York, 1932. pp. 31, 77, 83 f., 93-108; ct. S. Zeitlin, *JQR,* XX, 1929, 32-40, XXI, 388, 416. See also F. Baer, *Siyon,* VI, 1934, 166 f.

ca. 945   **96**

When God bestowed upon you the marvellous yet real imperial nature as a special endowment, O beloved monarch, ... in you alone of all men did he so wonderfully unite those diverse qualities, emperorhood and learning, the glory of the purple robe and a talent for reasoning. Wherefore have you already converted numerous Hebrews from their ancestral error (πολλοὺς μὲν ἤδη τῶν Ἑβραίων τῆς πατροπαραδότου πλάνης ἐπέστρεψας), and refuted Athinganoi and Paulicians....

Demetrios, metropolitan of Cyzicus, introd. to an anti-Monophysite tract, in G. Ficker. *Erlasse des Patriarchen von Konstantinopel Alexios Studites.* Kiel, 1911. p. 22, n. Cf. Starr, *Harvard Theol. Rev.,* XXIX, 97, n. 19.

ca. 950   **97**

Mar Isaac b. Nathan volunteered to carry my letter to his Majesty [Joseph]. I paid him handsomely and provided him with gold and silver for his own and his attendants' expenses during the journey. Moreover, from my own funds I sent an expensive gift to the king of Constantinople [Constantine VII], with the request that he assist my messenger in whatever way necessary for his journey to his Majesty's land [Khazaria]. My messenger came to Constantinople where he presented himself to the king and gave him my letter and gift. The king showed him due honor, and he tarried there for some six months with the envoys of our lord, the king of Cordova ['Abd ar-Rahmān III]. But one day he told them to return to us, at the same time sending back my messenger with a letter, which read thus: The distance between us and them is ⟨15 days' sail⟩. The nations lying between us are at war, aud the sea is tempestuous. It cannot be crossed except during a limited season.»

Hasdai Ibn Shaprūt to Joseph, khagan of the Khazars, ed. Kahana, *Sifrut*, I, 38; tr. Adler, *Jewish Travellers*, 27 f. Cf. the allusion in Schechter's document, *JQR*, III, 210, line 87, tr. 219, and Mann, *Texts*, I, 9, n. 13; *HUC An.*, X, 301. On the chronology, *id.*, *Texts*, I, 12; Dölger, *Regesten*, I, pt. 1, 82 f., nos. 657, 659. The exports from the Khazars are said in the same source, *ib.*, to have been mentioned by the Byzantine embassy in Cordova. On the imperial reception of foreign envoys see Runciman, *Byz. Civ.*, 157 f.

ca. 950   **98**

We have already treated this subject [lunar phases] and illustrated it with diagrams in the book which we composed and sent to Abū Joseph Hasdai b. Isaac, in reply to questions which reached us via the city of Constantinople (or « Constantine »). It consists of three parts: part one on the spheres, part two on the indispensabillty of this science for purposes of calculation, and part three on the path of the stars.

Dunash b. Tamim, one of three Hebrew versions of the lost Arabic commentary on *Sefer Yesirah* completed in 955-56; ms. Oratoire 160, f. 72r, cited by Munk, «Notice sur Abou'l-Walid Merwan ibn-Djanah et sur quelques autres grammairiens hébreux du Xe et du XIe siècle.» *JA*, LVII, 16, n. 1. Cf. Mann, *Texts*, I, 7, n. 9a.

ca. 950 ?   **99**

.... request the two matters contained in this letter ... I cast
my supplication be⟨fore⟩ your ⟨royal⟩ Highness... on behalf of
the remnant of the ⟨Jewish⟩ nation abiding among you... who
have survived the captivity and persecution... The Lord has
commanded them not to cease from the observance of their laws,
nor... from the customs to which they adhere....

... Now if you will fulfill my earnest request by spreading
your wings over them.... ⟨Appoint⟩ one of your subjects... regularly
over them.... so that their enemies will be deterred from harm-
ing them....

Hasdai to the Empress Helena (?), ed. Mann, *Texts,* I, 21 f.;
cf. pp. 10, 22 f. See also Assaf, *Tarbiz,* III, 1932, 340. The discussion
of this fragment has been re-opened by Krauss, «Zu Dr. Mann's
neuen historischen Texten.» *HUC An.,* X, 1935. 265-74; his sugges-
tions for restoring the lost portions of lines 13, 16 f. (p. 269, nn. 9,
12 f.) should be considered, but his theory as to the events involved is
utterly demolished by Mann, «Rejoinder», *l.c.,* 297-307.

ca. 950 - 60   **100**

I took great pains to learn the science of medicine and that
of the stars and planets, and I made copies for myself of the works
of ancient Jewish scholars. However, I found no Jewish scholar
in all those regions [Byzantium] who understood them, although
some of these Jewish scholars would say that the astronomic books
written by Jews were not good, because of their failure to understand them, and they would add that the only good ones were
those of Gentile authorship, which differed widely from the Jewish
works.

For this reason I took it upon myself to search out the science
of the Greeks, the Moslems, the Babylonians, and the Indians,
and I gave myself no rest until I had copied the works of the
ancient Greek and the «Macedonian» [Byzantine] scholars, as
well as those of the Babylonians and Indians, in the original language with their commentaries. And after studying them, I found

them in complete agreement with the astronomic science of the Jewish works. Moreover, I perceived that the whole science of stars and planets is based on the *Baraita of Samuel the homilist (hadoresh)*, and that the works of the Gentile scholars agree with it, although Samuel did write his book in a very obscure fashion.

After having copied those works I toured various lands (*arasot;* or, « the Empire ») for the purpose of finding Gentile astronomers under whom I might study, and I did find one or two. Later I found a Gentile scholar from Babylonia, BGDS by name, who was a very learned astronomer, and also knew the art of determining correctly the past and the future from a study of the planets and stars...

After seeing that Gentile's ability tested many times,... I offered him a great deal of money and many gifts if he would teach me astronomy, and so he taught me....

Shabbetai Donnolo. *Hakmoni,* ed. Castelli, 4 f. On the *Baraita* see no. **101**. An attempt has been made to identify the Gentile scholar with a certain Kairwan physician by S. Fried, introd. to his ed. of Isaac Israeli's *Sefer ha-yesodot,* Leipzig, 1884. I, 56 f. But there is no evidence that Donnolo ever studied outside the Empire; cf. Steinschneider, «Die Mathematik bei den Juden.» *Bibliotheca Mathematica,* XCV, 1894, 44 f. On Constantinus Africanus, M. Meyerhof, *En. Is.,* Supplement, I, 48 f.

On *Moqedon* in medieval Hebrew usage see Krauss, *Studien,* 104, n. 4. A variant reading for BGDS is BGDT; Neubauer, *REJ,* XXII, 1891, 214.

ca. 950-60   **101**

... This firmament is built as an arched room, resembling a tent pitched over the earth, as it is written: «That spreadeth them [the heavens] out as a tent to dwell in,» [Is. 40:22]... like the dome of a bath-house...

In the works of the Jewish scholars it is noted that the extremities of the firmament in the north are not attached to the earth....

Should you inquire as to how the two luminaries, the stars,

and the 12 planets revolve, then learn that when the Lord created those, he also created the « dragon » (*Teli*) to serve as a beam for them, in the manner of the « weavers' beam » [1 S. 17:7] ... So it is written in Job [26:13]: «By his spirit the heavens are garnished; his hand hath pierced the swift serpent.» By «the swift serpent» is meant the « dragon »... Likewise the Gentile scholars, Babylonians, Indians, and Moslems, hold that the « dragon » has a head and a tail...

Donnolo, *Sefer ha-Mazzalot,* or commentary on the *Baraita of R. Samuel.* The only extant portions are those preserved in the citations of Joseph b. Simeon Qara (12th c.), in his commentary on Job. These were published separately with notes by S. D. Luzzatto, *Kerem Hemed,* VII, 1843, 61-67; cf. S. Sachs, *Monats.,* I, 1852, 278, n. 3. The commentary itself was published later in an edition in which the text of the citations from Donnolo is quite inferior to Luzzatto's; *Monats.,* VI, 1857, 271, 273; VII, 26of., 348-50.

The text of the Baraita is conveniently reprinted in J. D. Eisenstein. *Osar Midrashim.* New York, 1915. pp. 542-47. It comprises both astronomy and astrology and in its present form is later than the year 776. See Zunz, *Ges. Schr.,* III, 242-5; M. Steinschneider. *Gesammelte Schriften.* Berlin, 1925. I, 570-74.

It appears that this work was supplied with illustrations, which are alluded to by Hadassī, *Eshkol ha-Kofer,* s. 63, pp. 30b-31a. For other citations see *Sefer Raziel.* Amsterdam, 1701. pp. 18f. (ed. Kapust, 21a); cf. S. D. Luzzatto. *Iggarot,* ed. I. Luzzatto. Cracow, 1891. VI, 917, no. 364. The Tosafists on *Pesahim* 94a, mention the threefold division of the earth given here *(Monats.,* VII, 260): seas, wilderness, and habitable land. This occurs also in «*Midrash Konen*», *Osar Mid.,* 255, but, it is difficult to say whether Rashi's comment on Is. 40:12 drew the idea from this or some other anonymous source, or from Donnolo.

Note also the following items. With his twice 183 windows of the firmament *(l. c.,* 26of.) cf. the number 365 in *j. Rosh ha-Shanah,* II, 4, 12d. In connection with Job 9:9 he gives the foreign equivalents for the three planetary names: 1. *kimah=rās at-tāur,* and Πλειάδα, the etymology of the latter being traced to πλείων, which is precisely analogous to the notion held by Arabic writers (J. Ruska, *En. Is.,* IV, 740); as alternative for the latter he gives πούλαδα; 2. *kesil=kapernea,* Orion *falx.* 3. *'ash=banāt na'sh (l. c.,* VII, 349 f.). For his citation of a

lost *qerobah* by Kalir, see *l. c.*, 350. For his remark on the loss of astronomic knowledge among Jews, *l. c.*, VI, 273.
The term *Teli* in the sense of the line connecting the lunar nodes was thoroughly clarified by Harkavy, « *Teli-Atalyā* » (Hebrew).
Ben-'Ami, ed. J. L. Kantor. Petrograd, 1887. (Referring to the Syriac
cognate; C. Brockelmann. *Lexicon Syriacum*. Halle, 1928. p. 25.). Cf.
S. Geffen, « *Teli*». *Sefer Zikkaron le-yobel ha-shib'im shel A. Z. Rabbi-
nowitz*. Tel Aviv, 1924. pp. 126-28. It corresponds to the Arabic *Jau-
zahar*, on which see H. Suter, *En. Is.*, I, 1030. Like the latter it is
partly synonymous with *tannin*, yet must not be confused with the
constellation of the dragon. Cf. A. Epstein, *REJ*, XXIX, 1894, 63-66.
On the opposite qualities of its «head» and «tail», see *Ḥakmoni*, ed.
Castelli, p. 24.

[*ca.* 950 - 1000   **102**

When R. Amittai died, he left a son named 'Abdīel. The
latter had a son named Baruk, who, unlike his ancestors, was not
versed in the Torah. He had at home the *Book of the Merkabah*
which R. Shefatiah had used all his life. One Sabbath eve...
at sundown it happened that there was none to light the candle
before the *Book of the Merkabah*, and a certain woman came (the
accursed one was menstrually unclean...), and lit the candle before
the book. Thereupon the wrath of the Lord was kindled against
the family, and many of them died of the plague, leaving only a
few survivors.

There was a certain Jew there who understood the situation...
He took the book and put it into a leaden vessel in order to sink
it in the ocean. The waters had receded about a mile, but when
he threw the vessel in, they returned to their usual place. Forthwith the divine decree was revoked, and the plague ceased. But
the memory of Baruk perished..., for he left none to devote himself to the Torah. He had no son, but only one daughter.

Aḥīma'as, ed Neubauer, 125; ed. Kahana., 132; tr. Salzman, 87f.
For *Merkabah* see no. **49**. Cf. the sinking of the demon, no. **60**.]

ca. 952   **103**

R. Hasadiah b. R. Hananel had a son named R. Paltīel. He

begot a son named R. Hananel [II], and a daughter named Kassia [II]..... She bore a son named R. Paltiel [II], who was an
expert in the observation of the stars.

About this time the Arab soldiers under the general, (κάϊτ) al-
Mu'izz overran Italy. They devastated the whole of Calabria, and
penetrated as far as Oria.... They laid siege to the city and anni-
hilated all of its troops. As the siege continued the inhabitants of
the city found it impossible to resist any longer, and it was stor-
med.... Many were slain and the survivors were taken captive.

The general (κάϊτ) asked for the family of R. Shefatiah. He
summoned them and they were brought before him. But God
caused them to find mercy before him, and bestowed his kindness
upon his servant R. Paltiel, causing him to find favor in the eyes
of the prince....

Ahīma'as, *ib.* Referring to the invasion during the reign of the
first Fātimid caliph of Egypt, Abū Tamim Ma'ad. See Amari, *op. cit.,*
II, 288-90; Gay, *op. cit.,* 214; H. Lammens, *En. Is.,* II, 274 (limited to
Calabria?). On κάϊτ cf. Amari, *op. cit.,* III, 260-6, and Latin *Caytus.*
The orthography of the surname is somewhat troublesome; for emen-
dations see B. Halper, *Hatequfah,* XVIII, 1923, 177; Mann *Tarbiz,* X,
1934, 232; ct.Kaufmann, *ZDMG,* LI, 427, n. 2. On the identity of
Paltiel as an Egyptian personality, Marx, *JQR,* I, 1910, 78-85; Mann,
Jews in Egypt, I, 16, 49.

ca. 952   **104**

... Paltiel was carried away captive from the city of Oria in
the land of *Lonbardia,* together with those righteous men, who
were transported across the sea in ships as captives ...

Judah b. Samuel (13th c.). *Sefer ha-Ḥassidim.* ed. J. Wistinetzki.
Berlin, 1893 (2nd ed., J. Freimann. Frankfort, 1924). s. 545, p. 152; tr.
Marx, *l. c.,* 80. Due to the fact that this tale occurs here directly following a version of no. **87,** Marx took this as well as no. **103** to refer
to the sack of the town in 925. Reference to the family-tree **(Exc. A)**
will show the impossibility of this dating.

Cf. the reference to contemporary Byzantine prisoners in n. Africa
(al-Mahdīya), in the life of Nilos, jr., *PG,* CXX, 117-20; cf. Runciman, *Byz. Civ.,* 156.

ca. 960 **105**

The following incident occurred in the town of Bisignano [Calabria]. A certain young ruffian met a Hebrew returning from business and, enticed by his merchandise, stabbed him to death with a dagger. Then he seized his ass with its load and took to flight. Thereupon a relative of the murderer was arrested by the authorities, and was turned over to the Jews to be crucified in expiation of the murder of the Hebrew. When the wise Nilos learned that this individual had been condemned by his own co-religionists, he wrote to the unjust judges as follows:

« It is necessary for you who know the law to rule in accordance with it, for it commands judges to execute one Christian for seven Hebrews. Therefore, either let six other Hebrews be given over for execution for the man about to be crucified, or, if indeed it seems best to you to disregard those laws which were so wisely laid down, let he whom I am sending with this letter, a scion of one of the first families of Rossano, be handed over to the Jews to be crucified. And let the poor fellow go free...»

Then he called the holy monk George and, saying nothing to him regarding what he had written, gave him the letter with which he then sent him to Bisignano. When the judges had received and read the letter, they said to the old man, « O caloyer, the Father has written to us to hand you over to the Jews to be crucified. Is that satisfactory to you?»

He replied, «I am ready to fulfill whatever my master has written...» When they saw the devotion of the old man and the noble soul of his sender, they freed the poor fellow, and dismissed the old man with all honor.

Bartholomaios (? 11th c.). Life of St. Nilos, jr., ed. J. Cleus. *Acta Sanct.*, Sept., VII. Paris-Rome, 1867. v, 35f., pp. 282f. = *PG*, CXX, 72. Tr. by D. A. Rocchi. *Vita di S. Nilo Abate*. Rome, 1892 (inaccessible).

See N. Tamassia. « Stranieri ed ebrei nell'Italia meridionale dall'età Romana alla sueva.» *Atti* of the R. Istituto Veneto di Scienze, Lettere ed Arti, LXIII, pt. 2, 1904, 837. Cf. the loose remarks of O. Dito. *Gli ebrei di Calabria*. Rocca S. Cassiano, 1914-16. pp. 8f.

The Frankish law mentioned by Tamassia is cited by Aronius, *Regesten*, 26 f., no. 73.

ca. 960   **106**

When he [Nilos] came into the town [Rossano], there came to him a certain Jew, Domnoulos by name, who had enjoyed his acquaintance since his youth, being highly cultured (σφόδρα φιλομαθῆ) and a skilled physician. He entered upon the following conversation with the saint, «I have heard of your asceticism and your extreme abstinence, and knowing what your physical condition is, I have marvelled that you do not fall into an epileptic fit. However, with your permission, I will give you a remedy for your condition to use through the rest of your life, thus freeing you of illness.»

The great man replied, «One of you Hebrews has told us: 'Better is it to trust in the Lord than to trust in man.' [Ps. 117:8] The physician in whom we trust is our God and Lord Jesus Christ. Thus we have no need of your remedies, and this will deprive you of the opportunity to delude simple-minded Christians by boasting that you provide remedies for Nilos.» The physician listened to this, but made no reply to the saint.

Then the other Jew who had come with him, said to him, «Speak to us concerning God, for we desire to hear your words.»

The Father said to him, «Your request, O Jew, is comparable to commanding a baby to grasp the top of a tree and bend it to the ground. Nevertheless, if you wish to hear somewhat on the subject, take your prophets and Law, and come with me into the desert whither I retire. And after you have spent in reading as many days as Moses did on the mount, then ask and I shall answer you....»

Both answered at the same time, «That we cannot do lest we be excommunicated and stoned by our co-religionists.....»

Id., vii, 50., pp. 290 f. = *PG*, CXX, 92f. Donnolo shows some familiarity with the vicinity of this town in his antidotarium, no. **110**.

ca. 960   **107**

There was present also the Jew Domnoulos, whom I have already mentioned as physician, and he witnessed everything that went on. On his way out he expressed his surprise at what had taken place to those present, «Today I have witnessed a remarkable feat such as we hear of from olden times, for I have seen the prophet Daniel tame the lions. For who has ever dared to lay hand on this lion [Eupraxios]? Yet this latter-day Daniel [Nilos] has cut off his mane and put a cowl over him.»

Id., vii, 56, p. 293 = *PG,* CXX, 100. See G. Schlumberger. *L'épopée byzantine à la fin du dixième siècle.* Paris, 1896. I, 478f.

963 - 8 ?   **108**

The guild of dealers in raw silk must not sell any raw silk to Hebrews or to merchants who intend to dispose of it outside of the city [Cp.]. Violators will be flogged and shorn. (Οἱ μεταξοπράται μὴ ἀπεμπολείτωσαν τὴν μέταξαν Ἑβραίοις ἢ ἐμπόροις πρὸς τὸ διαπιπράσκειν αὐτὴν ἔξω τῆς πόλεως:...)

Τό ἐπαρχικόν βιβλίον, ed. J. Nicole. Geneva, 1893. [*Mémoires* of the Institut national génévois, XVIII] vi, 16, p. 33 = Zepos, *Jus graecor.,* II, 379; tr. A.E. Boak, «The book of the prefect.» *Journal of business and economic history,* I, 1929, 608. Cf. A Stöckle. *Spätrömische und byzantinische Zünfte.* Leipzig, 1911, p. 120; on the dating, *ib.*, 142-48. The analogous Frankish phrase (early 10th c.) is cited in Aronius, *Regesten,* p. 52, no. 122; cf. nos. 129, 132f. On silk-exportation, Heyd, *op. cit.,* I, 54f., 72.

963 - 8 ?   **109**

First, he [the Jewish litigant] must gird himself with bramble, and then, grasping the [Torah-] scroll in his hands shall say thus: «In the name of the blessed Lord, the God of our fathers, Who made the heaven and the earth and led us on dry land across the Red Sea, I do not testify falsely. If I be found a perjurer, may the Lord God afflict me with the leprosy of Gehazi and Naaman [Ἄμμα] and with the punishment of Eli; may the earth swallow me alive, even as Dathan and Abiram.»

164

Zepos, *Jus graecor.*, I, 375; *PG,* CXXXIII, 117. Cf. Janin, *Echos d' O.,* XV, 131. For its 12th c. context see no. **171.** The corresponding western formula is quoted by Aronius, *op. cit.,* p. 28, no. 77; on its spurious assignment to the Carolingian period, S. F. Katz, *EJ,* IX, 533. Cf J. Régné. *Étude sur la condition des juifs de Narbonne.* Narbonne, 1912. pp. 149f.; S. W. Baron. *A Social and Religious History of the Jews.* New York, 1937. III, 118f.

On this type of curse in general see H. Martin, *American Journal of Philology,* XXXVII, 1916, 434-51. Cf. the very similar Byzantine texts: no. **121** (s. II, 18), the praetorian prefect's oath of Justinian's time cited by Beneshevich, *Evr. Mysl,* 307, n. 5, and the monastic one in Michael Attaleiates' Διάταξις, ed. K. N. Sathas. Βιβλιοθήκη Μεσαιωνική. Venice, 1872. I, 13 (11th c.). For the Arabic formula, E. Fagnan, *REJ,* 1910, 228f.; cf. I. Goldziher, *l. c.,* XLV, 1902, 1-7.

ca. 970   **110**

This is the book of drugs, potions, powders, etc... composed by Shabbetai the physician, known as Donnolo, son of Abraham, (who was taken captive from the city of Oria,) for Jewish physicians, in order to instruct them regarding the preparation of drugs as known to Moslem and Byzantine physicians, and on the basis of his personal experience and study of medicine for 40 years.....

..... Therefore did the wise Hippocrates prescribe for all potions the mixing therewith of honey, i. e., *Attikon hédion,* which is the same as that prepared in Otranto, in Oria, and in the land of Calabria, in the locality called *Martis* (?), near Rossano.....

«*Sefer ha-yaqqar,*» ed M. Steinschneider. *Donnolo, Fragment des ältesten medizinischen Werkes in hebräischer Sprache.* Berlin, 1867; tr., *id.,* « Donnolo, Pharmakologische Fragmente aus dem X. Jahrhundert, nebst Beiträgen zur Literatur der Salernitaner, hauptsächlich nach handschriftlichen hebräischen Quellen.» (Virchow's) *Archiv für pathologische Anatomie und Physiologie und für klinische Medicin,* XLII, 1872, 124-33 (entire study, *l. c.,* XXXVIII, 65-91, XXXIX, 296-336, XL, 80-124, XLII, 51-174; reprinted with the Hebrew text, Berlin, 1872). (On a newly discovered second ms. of this work see H. Friedenwald. «The use of the Hebrew language in medical literature.» *Bulletin of the Institute of the History of Medicine,* II, no. 2, 1934, pp. 8of.)

In the clause following «Jewish physicians», read with the editor *Yishma'el* for *Yisrael.* The Arabic, Greek, and Latin glosses, numbering 120, have been collected by I. Löw. *Die Flora der Juden.* Vienna, 1934. IV, 176f. The reference to Hippocrates is false, but see Dioscorides, II, 101.

For the cultural atmosphere see C. and D. Singer. «The origin of the medical school of Salerno.» *Essays on the history of medicine presented to K. Sudhoff.* London, 1924. pp. 121-36; «The School of Salerno», *History,* X, 1925, 242-56. Not, however, entirely reliable with respect to our author himself.

972?   **111**

... A naval commander named Ibn Riyahīn [? text, DMAHIN] left Cordova, having been sent by the Moslem king of Spain, 'Abd ar-Rahmān an-Nasr. This commander had set out to capture the ships of the Christians and the coast-towns. They sailed as far as the Palestinian coast and then swung around to the Greek sea and the islands therein. Here they found a ship carrying four great scholars, who were on their way from the city of Bari to another called SPSTIN. These scholars were travelling for the purpose of collecting funds for the [Babylonian] academy (? *le-haknasat kallah).*Ibn Riyahīn capturedt his ship and took these scholars as his prisoners. One of them was R. Hushiel.., R. Moses, with whom were taken his wife and his young son Hanok, ... R. Shemariah b. Elhanan. As for the fourth, I do not know his name...

Abraham b. David (12th c.). «*Sefer ha-Qabbalah*», ed. Neubauer, *Mediaeval Jewish Chron.,* I, 67 f. Halper, *Post-Bib. Heb. Lit.: Texts,* 93-96, 239-41; *Tr.,* 123-26. See Mann, *Texts,* I, 86, and M. Schmitz, *En. Is.,* II, 223. The extensive literature on this passage is reviewed in M. Auerbach. *Die Erzählung von die vier Gefangenen.* [*Jahresbericht* of the Berlin Rabbiner-Seminar for 1925-7] Berlin, 1928.

On the identification of the 1st and 3rd individuals see V. Aptowitzer, «R. Chushiel und R. Chananel.» *Jahresbericht* of the Vienna Israelitisch-theologische Lehranstalt, XXXVII-IX, 1929-32, 3-50; cf. Mann's rejoinder, *Tarbiz,* V. 286-301.

The legend told by Samuel of Babenberg in which Shefatiah and Amittai were brought in this fashion to Italy (under Titus!) may be influenced by this; no. **49 n.**

ca. 975   **112**

...I have found another writing which a Jew wrote in his language in Constantinople, concerning the kings of Constantinople. He mentions the wars that were fought between the kings of Constantinople and King Aaron [of the Khazars], as well as those of the sons of those kings and King Joseph, son of Aaron...

Judah b. Barzillai (Barcelona, *ca.* 1100), «*Sefer ha-ʿIttim*», ms. cited by Assaf, *Jeschurun*, XI, 1924, 116; cf. Kokovtzov, *op. cit.*, 127. Dubnow, *Weltgesch.*, IV, 481f., identified the work with the letter published by Schechter (no. **13**), but the latter in no way answers to the description of the work mentioned here; Mann, *Texts,* I, 8, n. 1.

For Hebrew fragments dealing with the Byzantine emperors see Krauss, *Studien,* 140-44.

982   **113**

David did not compose these verses [Ps. 145:12] for the instruction of subsequent generations.... only insofar as they would be great men, but even for those generations which are as base, as despicable, and as devoid of wisdom as the present one in the year 4942 of the creation of the world...

Neubauer, «Un chapitre inédit de Sabbetai Donnolo». *REJ,* XXII, 215.

982   **114**
Shabbetai Donnolo's *Ḥakmoni*

The best edition is Castelli, *Il commento di Sabbetai Donnolo,* 1-86. (Reprinted in the Warsaw, 1884 ed. of *Sefer Yesirah* with commentaries pp. 121-48.). The rhymed portion of the introd. is republished in Schirmann, *Mibhar,* 15. Another ms. of the introd. was published by Neubauer, *REJ,* XXII, 215-18. For discussions of the content see Castelli's analysis, *op. cit.,* 39-69; on c. 1, see A. Jellinek. *Der Mensch als Gottes Ebenbild von dem Arzte und Astronomen R. Schabtai Donnolo.* Leipzig, 1854. pp. xii-xiv; cf. B. Beer, *Monats.* IV, 1855, 238-40. On the *Sefer Yesirah:* text in Eisenstein, *Osar Mid.,* 239-43, and a variant one with tr., P. Mordell, *JQR,* III, 1913, 536-44; tr. K. Stenring. *The book of Formation.* London, 1923; cf. Scholem, *EJ,* IX, 104-10; on the classification of the consonants, Bacher *ZDMG,* XLIX, 1895, 20-23. On the microcosm idea, including reference to the Jewish material, see G. P. Conger. *Theories of macrocosms and microcosms in the history of philosophy.* New York, 1922. On its correlation with astrology, *ibid.,*27. On the mystical significance of the alphabet, Horodetzky, *EJ,* II, 446-51; cf. Leclerq, *Dictionnaire d'Archéologie chrétienne et de Liturgie.* VI, 1589f.

The following glosses occur: p. 22, παράλυσις=*falij;* p. 28, ἴσκα-esca, in connection with the experiment of concentrating the sun's rays by means of a glass vessel full of water; p. 29, μιλιάρ(ιον), p. 77, *kalendas,* τάρταρον-*tartarum.* Occasional neologisms: p. 39, *gallul,* «round»; 81, ʿ*oqel,* central part of the body of the *Teli* (no. **101 n.**).

Citations by later medieval writers: 1. Rashi on *Besah* 33a, and ʿ*Erubin* 56a. 2. Judah b. Barzillai; Epstein, *Monats.,* XXXVII, 459, n. 3. 3. Abraham b. David; *id., l. c.,* 268. 4. Tobiah b. Eliezer. *Leqah Tob,* ed. S. Buber. Vilna, 1880. Gen. p. 6; cf. introd., 42f. 5. Eleazar Roqeah; Epstein, «Pseudo-Saadjaʿs und Eleasar Rokeach's Commentare zum Jezira-Buche.» *l. c.,* 117-20. 6. ps.-Saadia; Steinschneider, *Magazin,* XIX, 1892, 79-85. A Franco-German writer probably citing at second-hand; Epstein, *l. c.,* 75, n. 1. 7. Anon. commentary on Job (*ca.* 1200), ed. A. Sulzbach. Frankfort, 1911. p. 49: a comment on 38: 19f., not contained in our text, which is referred to as *Tahkemoni (sic)* which is lost.» 8. Solomon b. Judah (14th c.); Epstein, *l. c.,* 77f.

ca. 985   **115**

...He [Nikon] promised them [the delegation from Sparta] that the epidemic would cease if they would expel from their town those of the Jewish race who were residing among them, so that it should no longer be contaminated by their disgusting customs and by the pollution of their religion... Upon his arrival, after the removal of the Jews from the town, the pest disappeared....

But that fool [John Aratos] declared that the expulsion of the Jews from the town was neither just nor praiseworthy... Using some job as a pretext, the bold dastard brought into the town one of those Jews whom he was wont to employ in the finishing of woven fabrics (δὶ οὗ εἴωθε στιλβοῦσθαι τὰ ὑφάσματα). Thereupon he [Nikon] seized a club lying there and administered many blows to the Jew, whom he drove out of the town... For so abominable was the Jewish race to the saint that he advised all neither to hear nor to utter their name...

Life of Nikon the *Metanoeite,* ed S. F. Lampros, Νέος Ἑλληνο-μνήμων, III, 1906, 163, 165f., cf. 224,=M. E. Galanopoulos. Βίος.... Νίκωνος τοῦ « Μετανοεῖτε » Athens, 1933. pp. 97, 101f., 210. Cf. Caro, *Sozial- u. Wirtschaft.,* I, 255, 491f., who, however, cites the Latin tr. of J. Sirmond in E. Martène and U. Durand. *Veterum scriptorum et monumentorum... amplissima collectio.* Paris, 1729. VII, 859-62. This is based on another ms., Barberini 583 (now in the Vatican), where our extract occurs, fols. 636a-39a, without any noteworthy variant other than the surname of Nikon's opponent: Ἰωάννης δὲ ἐκεῖνος ᾧ Ἄρατος τὸ ἐπώνυμον. The work is believed to have been composed in the 11th c.; Nikos A. Bees, *Revue Byzantine,* II, 1916, 23 (Greek).

There is no real basis for dating this event in the year 982, as did C. Baronius. *Annales ecclesiastici.* Rome, 1602. X, 844f.; cf. *PG, CXIII,* 969-82.

For a western parallel see G. Deutsch, *JE,* VIII, 198.

ea. 985   **116**

R. Hananel b. Paltīel asked permission of the king of Africa to cross the sea to Italy, for at the time of the capture of Oria the fugitives fled to Bari and Otranto, taking along some of their household goods and whatever funds they could rescue, both their own and others'. R. Hananel went to Constantinople,... and petitioned the king [Basil II] to graciously furnish him with [an official document bearing] the royal seal, with which he might travel throughout the cities of his realm and recover his family possessions wherever he might find them. He received the seal and sailed to the city of Bari, where he found an old Pentateuch of of his [family's], some feminine effects, and some clothing.

The learned rabbis of Bari [contesting his right to these articles] cited in opposition: If a man saved some articles from an invading army, or from a flood, or from a fire, they are his as though by presentation [cf. *Baba Qamma,* X, 2].... «But,» he countered, «...our rabbis ruled that 'the law of the government takes precedence' [*ib.,* 113a], and here is the document with the seal which the king gave me.»

By way of compromise with him they gave him the clothing and the Pentateuch, and he waived the rest. He went on to Benevento, and the entire community welcomed him. After a year's sojourn he established his residence there, and married Esther b. R. Shabbetai, of the family of R. Amittai....

He [God] favored him in his old age with worthy sons: R. Samuel,... R. Shabbetai, Pappoleon, and Hasadiah. Hasadiah sailed off to Africa with R. Hananel to stay with R. Paltīel [II] the son of his [the latter's] sister Kassia. R. Samuel went to the town of Capua... Some time later Shabbetai and Pappoleon sailed away to deliver a gift to R.Paltīel from the duke of Amalfi...

Ahīma'as, ed. Neubauer, 127; ed. Kahana, 134f.; tr. Salzman, 91f. The saying respecting the two communities is quoted by Jacob b. Meir («Rabbenu Tam»; ca. 1150), *Sefer ha-yashar,* ed. S. Rosenthal. Berlin, 1898. s. 46, p. 90; cf. Zunz, *Ges. Schr.,* I, 105.

For the activities of the Arabs in this region during 974-81, see Gay, *L'Italie mérid.,* 325.

962   **117**

.... And the Venetians, moreover, shall not transport in their ships others who have business in Constantinople, such as Amalfitans, Jews, and Lombards, from the city of Bari and elsewhere, in order to reap advantage from their [the Venetians'] privilege, but shall carry only their own merchandise... (et ipsi autem Venetici pro occasione defensionis eorum alioquin quod negotium habent de Constantinopolim in suis navigiis levare, scilicet, Amalfitanos, Iudeos, Longombardos, de civitate Bari et aliorum, sed solum illorum negotium adduxerint.)

Basil II and Constantine VIII, chrysobull to Doge Pietro [II] Orseolo; Zepos, *Jus graecor.,* I, 261; *PG,* CXVII, 616f. Cf. the variant version in C. Romanin *Storia documentata di Venezia.* Venice, 1853 (repr. 1712). I, 382. See also Heyd, *op. cit.,* I, 114f.; Caro, *op. cit.,* I, 193, Dölger, *Regesten,* I, pt. 1, 100, no. 781. The earlier Venetian law reads: «nec etiam aliquis homo negotiare, vel Iudeum in navi sua levare debeat;» Romanin, *op. cit.,* I, 371.

In those days there was an archbishop at Thessalonica, ... a friend of these Fathers [John and Euthymios] .... Now there was in Thessalonica a certain Jew who was learned in the Law and whom the archbishop desired to convert to Christianity, wherefore he often conversed with him. Once when Father Euthymios was with him, he asked him to dispute with the Jew. Unwilling though he was, he entered into an argument concerning the Law. When the Jew had been drawn into a tight corner and was stuck, he burst out into loud abuse against the uncorrupted Christian faith in the presence of the blessed Father Euthymios. When the latter heard this, he, moved by resentment and flaming anger, said to him, «May your mouth be stricken dumb, you impure Jew!»

Immediately he became dumb and his mouth was distorted. The other Jews who were standing about, threw themselves at the feet of Father Euthymios and besought him to pardon the man. He replied to them, «Let him obtain the indulgence of him whom he has reviled, and let him enter his faith; then will he obtain indulgence from me.» Thereupon the bishop requested him to forgive him and to pray for him. When he had prayed, he made the sign of the cross over him. Immediately his mouth was straightened and he began to speak. He threw himself at the feet of the saint, and after he had been made a Christian, he conducted himself as a man of signal faith.

There was a certain other Jew, who was learned in the Law, very erudite, and famed for his cunning in disputation. This man, impelled by his Jewish arrogance, desired to hold a conversation with him. This was hardly pleasing to the saint, but being under orders from John, he was forced to meet him. After the Jew had opened the disputation and had put some questions, Euthymios began to unravel and explain, being because of his great learning the better man. Thereupon that cunning fellow, sensing defeat, resorted to revilement. The saint resented this and said to him,

«See here, if you raised a question touching some word of Scripture, we would explain it to you. Or if asked us something, we would respond. However, inasmuch as you have instead spoken revilingly against the Lord, may your cursing mouth be stricken dumb.» Having heard this, he immediately became dumb, and on the morrow gave up his soul.

St. George the Hagiorite (contemporary), lives of St. John and St. Euthymios; Latin tr. from the Georgian, P. Peeters, «Histoires monastiques géorgiennes». *Analecta Bollandiana,* XXXVI-VII, 1917-19, 38f.

See the reference to the local Jews in an anon. writing, *Acta Sanct.,* Oct., IV, s. 164, p. 164. According to its author the period is the latter seventh century; cf. Bury, *Later R. E.,* II, 337f. Yet the events narrated seem to have occurred early in the reign of Heraclius. See O. Tafrali. *Thessalonique au quatorzième siècle.* Paris, 1912. pp. 3f.

ca. 1000 ? **119**

... To the most highly esteemed congregations of the holy nation, the scattered remnant of Jeshurun....

We send you our greetings and wish to apprise you of the case of X b. Y, of the community of Russia, who was a visitor among us, the community of Saloniki... Here he found a relative of his, R. Z., who had returned from Jerusalem ... Now this relative had a letter from our honored master A, who extolled the beauty of the land so highly to him that his [the Russian's] spirit impelled him also to go and bow down at the site of the Sanctuary. He requested of us these few lines to serve as an introduction to your worthiness, so that you might lend him a helping hand, and guide him along the best road from city to city and from ⟨isle⟩ to isle, through trustworthy persons. For he knows neither Hebrew nor Greek nor Arabic, but only his native Russian [lit., «Canaanitish»]....

The power of charity and the great value of kindness, with its intrinsic reward, is known to you. For it is written first in the Torah, secondly in the Prophets, thirdly in the Hagiographa, fourthly in the Mishnah, and fifthly in the Talmud; it is symbolized by the letter *gimmel* and *dalet* [*Sabbath* 104a]....

Accept the greetings of B, a poor youth who requests your honorable attention to his plight and poverty. Do with me as I deserve for Heaven's sake, for my situation is not like that of others who can work and ply a craft... I lack food.

Marmorstein, «Nouveaux renseignements sur Tobiya ben Eliézer.» *REJ*, LXXIII, 1921, 92-97; in part, Mann, *Jews in Egypt*, II, 192, cf. J 165f. The former took it to be a draft of the letter given to the traveller, but as the latter says, it is rather a copy, or, more precisely, a form kept in the communal file at Thessalonica, which could be used repeatedly *mutatis mutandis*. The last paragraph is from the margin and there is no way of determining the authorship. For a similar document from the west see Mann, *ib.*, I, 165.

Marmorstein's theory that the letter was written by Tobiah b. Eliezer (no. **163**) as rabbi of the community is based on very flimsy evidence. He finds the word *tob* at the beginning of the long rhetorical salutation (omitted from the tr.), and then selects from three other lines the letters of «b. R. Eliezer», thus very ingeniously obtaining a unique signature-acrostic. It must be emphasized that even though the presence of the man in question in this city at the end of the c., is accepted by all (no. **153n.**), there is no proof that he resided there regularly. The dating of our document is suggested by Mann on the basis of the handwriting.

ca. 1000 ?   **120**

The following question was placed before the court of Bari: «Regarding the statement made by R. Giddal in the name of Rab ... This illustrates acquisition by mere declaration, [*Ketubot* 102a]', is this confined to the [respective] parents of the bride and bridegroom, and does it then exclude similar acquisitions between husband and wife [the parents of either bride or bridegroom], or between a grandfather and another at the time of the marriage-ceremony?»

They responded to the questioner as follows: «In our opinion this is not confined to the parents of the bride and bridegroom, but applies equally to all persons involved in the situation. For the parents are mentioned by the rabbis [not to the exclusion of others, but] because they are the parties customarily involved. Hence, all persons engaged in arranging the match are to be considered as the parents. Now let us explain why... We derive this principle from the law of the surety [citing *Baba Batra* 173b]...

«This responsum to the inquiry directed to us, is given in accordance with the teaching which God has vouchsafed us, and is thus written down, signed and given to the questioner.

«Leon b. R. Shabbetai. Joel b. R. Moses. Elijah b. Shemaiah. Hananel b. R. Joshua. Moses b. R. Abraham. Benjamen b. R. Yequtīel. Shemaiah b. R. Shabbetai.»

We, the undersigned, have verified the signatures of all signatories to this responsum, and have assented to it, for they have rendered the decision correctly. We have delivered it into his [the questioner's] hand in the presence of Abraham b. R. Elijah. Abraham b. R. Yohanan. Shabbetai b. R. Zechariah. Pappoleon b. R. Shabbetai. Hushīel b. R. Yohanan. Caleb b. R. Samuel.

Eleazar b. Nathan (latter 12th c.). *Sefer Raben,* ed. S. Albeck. Warsaw, 1904. s. 38, p. 30. The portion containing the signatures is preserved only by Abraham b. David of Posquières, who cites it in the name of Samuel b. Natronai, a disciple of Eleazar; « *Hagahot Maimoniot, Ishut,*» XIII, 14. The chronology is, of course, uncertain; cf. Cassuto, *EJ*, VII, 1076. Another local scholar who is perhaps to be assigned to the early 11th c. is Moses Kalfo, who is cited as deceased in 1100 by Nathan b. Yehīel of Rome. *«Sefer ha-'Aruk»*, ed. A. Kohut. *Aruch completum.* Vienna-Berlin, 1926. VII, 138a, 218b; VIII, 292a.

Cassuto identifies the 3rd signature as that of a liturgical poet, for whose compositions (40 in number) see Davidson, *Osar,* IV, 362; cf. Schirmann, *Eshkol,* II, 588f., who erroneously makes him the master of Samuel b. Natronai; *id., Mibhar,* 41-47.

ca. 1000-27   **121**

A stricter Exposition concerning the Reception of a Hebrew entering into the Christian Faith.

I. First, it is necessary for him to confess, and to renounce every Hebrew law, custom, and ceremony. Secondly, to show that he wishes to become a Christian with his whole heart and out of pure faith, and openly to withdraw from the entire Jewish religion and all its laws into the Church. Lastly, to anathematize the ceremonies and customs invented against the will of God, and thus to make a eovenant with Christ and with his religion. The priest first reads it and he, or in the case of of a minor, his godfather, repeats in order,

II. As follows:

1. I, so-and-so of the Hebrews, who enter this day into the Christian faith, do not do so because of force, nor of compulsion, nor of a special levy (ἐπήρεια), nor of fear, nor of poverty, nor of a criminal charge against me, nor for the sake of worldly honor, nor for any gain, nor for money, nor for things promised by someone, nor because of any kind of need or human glory whatsoever, nor for the purpose of avenging myself on the Christians, as a zealot for the Law, nor because of having been wronged by them, but because I love Christ and his faith with my whole soul and heart. I abjure the entire Jewish faith, the Feast of Unleavened Bread, the Passover, the sacrifice of the lamb, the Feast of Weeks, the Jubilee, the Feast of Trumpets, the Atonement, the Tabernacles, and all the other feasts of the Hebrews, the sacrifices, prayers, sprinklings, purifications, hallowings, fasts, Sabbaths, New Moons, and their foods and drinks. I utterly abjure every Jewish law, custom and ceremony.

2. In addition, I anathematize the following Jewish sects and their founders: The Sadducees.... The Pharisees.... The Nazarenes.... The Hossaioi.... The Herodians.... The Hemerobaptists.... The Scribes....

3. After them I anathematize those who celebrate the festival of Mordecai, during the first week of the Christian fasts [Lent], and those who nail Haman to a piece of wood, and joining it to the sign of the cross, burn them together while hurling various curses and the anathema against the Christians.

4. I also anathematize those who at the beginning of the

indiction [Sept. 1], during the Feast of Trumpets, wrap the candles in silks dyed in various colors. Then they recite certain hymns which, they imagine, serve to ward off the chill and every other illness.

5. I also anathematize those who in the month of July observe the fast called by them « Sorrow» (Λυπηρά), or the fall of Jerusalem, when they sprinkle ashes on their heads and observe a fast through the entire night and day, while with myriads of lamentations they voice their woes.

6. I also anathematize all those who hope for the coming of the Messiah, or rather, of Antichrist. They expect him to prepare a great table for them, on which he is to serve them the *Ziz*, the *Machemôth*, and Leviathan. (The Ziz is a winged creature, the Machemôth a quadruped, and the Leviathan a sea-creature. They are so huge and fleshy as to suffice for the food of untold myriads.)

7. I anathematize every Hebrew custom and ceremony not handed down by Moses, and all their witchcraft, incantations, sorcery, soothsaying, amulets, and phylacteries.

8. I also anathematize every ῥέμβι or ῥάμβι who shall or who does teach anything other than the Mosaic law, and all their ἀρχιφερέκιται or ἀρχιρεμβῖται or ἀρχιραμβῖται or teachers, whose impious teachings they term traditional.

9. In addition to the ancient ἀρχιραμβῖται, I anathematize the later teachers of the Jews, viz., Lazaros, who invited the wicked feast called μονοποδαρία, Elijah, not inferior to him in impiety, Benjamin, Zebedaios, Abraham, Sabbatios, etc.

10. In addition to all these I doubly anathematize... [6. repeated].

11-17. And I believe in the Father, the Son,... [Catechism].

18. Thus I enter into the Christian faith with whole soul and heart, and with sincere intention. However, if I say these things in hypocrisy and deceit, and do not love Christ who cometh with whole-souled faith and heart, but because of compulsion.... [1. repeated] If I pretend now to be a Christian, and later desire to

deny him and to return to the Jewish religion, or if I be found
secretly sharing a meal or a celebration or a fast or a conversation with them, or going to their synagogues and house of worship, or observing or pretending such things, rather than openly
working against them and rejecting their deeds and their erring
faith, then may there come upon me all the curses which Moses
wrote in Deuteronomy, the quivering of Cain, and the leprosy of
Gehazi, in addition to the penalties of the civil laws, being guilty
without extenuating circumstances. May I be double anathema,
and may my soul be troubled by Satan and the demons.

[Appendix:] The Festivals of the Jews

1. The Hebrews celebrate the festival of unleavened bread
as follows. For eight days they eat nothing leavened, but only
unleavened bread (λιπανάβατον). They throw [into a dish] raisins,
walnuts, and three little crumbs of unleavened bread and mix
them together. In another vessel they have parsley, bitter herbs,
and whatever meat is available, mutton, beef, or buffalo, salted or
fresh, and they eat it with the bitter herbs and the rest. But they
do not slaughter a lamb, ⟨fearing⟩ it is said, the Christians. The
point of the observance is not the meat, but the unleavened
bread, the purpose being not to desecrate the day by eating leaven. They do this on the fourteenth day of the month [Nisan],
when the sun is in the west, holding the so-called «spear-handle»
[? κονταρόξυλον]. On the morrow of the festival, being the ninth
day, they prepare leaven with chick-peas and eat it again at the
same hour.

2. The Tabernacles is as follows:

a. On the third and fourth of the month of September they
celebrate the Trumpets. It is said that when Abraham was about
to sacrifice Isaac, he shouted. On this model the trumpets were
prescribed. Some trace it to the trumpets of Gideon, and others
again to the trumpets of Joshua, son of Nun, who, when he
overthrew Jericho, said, ⟨«Shout!»⟩ [Josh. 6:16].

b. And after eight days comes the «Great Day» or fast called μονοποδαρέα. Some of them place their feet together and remain standing from morning to evening, from star to star, saying they are atoning. From that evening to the beginning of the next one not one of them eats, neither does his servant (παίδιον) or beast. In the evening, however, they slaughter a rooster each. The others who, as may happen, do not have any, must do with fish.

c. Seven days later comes the Tabernacles. In the courtyards of their synagogues (μασγίδια), which they term prayer-houses (εὐχαί), they construct huts (? καρ-ἀγλύβαι) where everyone eats according to his means, the rich inviting the poor.

3. At the end of the seventh day each one contributes as much as he wishes, they assemble, and having set the table invite the poor to eat with them.

4. At the New Moon, for two days only, the married and unmarried women rest.

[Scholia]

1. The Ziz is a very huge bird which flies everywhere.

2. The Mechemoth is a very huge beast which grazes over the entire earth.

3. The Leviathan is the largest fish in the sea. The Hebrews say that at the resurrection God is expected to give each one three portions from these three creatures, the bird, the beast, and the fish, and that these will suffice them for food forever...

4. The ῥαβὶς is the ruler (δεσπότης). The αρχιερεμβός is the more learned and greater teacher.

5. The interpreter of texts, i.e., of the difficult words of the Law and the post-biblical literature (δευτέρωσις), is called ἀρχιφερεκίτης, φερέκ being a passage. For they say that they received two Laws from God, one written, the other unwritten. Hence those who interpret the difficulties of the written Law and the commentaries of the unwritten, are called ἀρχιφερεκῖται.

6. The Montanists are those who have been separated from the Hebrew religion and community, and for some reason or other have been expelled from the synagogue. If they return,

12

they receive them as being like-minded, and include them among themselves as in the beginning.

Beneshevich, *Evr. Mysl,* 308-18; from a ms. dated 1027. Previous editions of the abjuration: *PG,* I, 1455-62 (tr. Parkes, *op. cit.,* 397-400); Cumont, «Une formule grecque de rénonciation au Judaïsme». *Wiener Studien,* XXXIV, 1902, 466-69 (tr. with notes, Krauss, «Eine byzantinische Abschwörungsformel.» *Festkrift i Anledning D. Simonsens.* Copenhagen, 1923. pp. 134-57); cf. Juster, I, 116-19. On the dating, Beneshevich, *l. c.,* 200-02, 218-23. See also J. Davreux. «Le Codex Bruxellensis Græcus III 4836 *(De Hæresibus).*» *Byzantion,* X, 1935, 101.

For texts of and references to parallel Byzantine materials see G. Ficker. «Eine Sammlung von Abschwörungsformeln». *Zeit. f. Kircheng.,* XXVII, 1906, 446-52. These are severally assigned to *ca.* 800, but without great assurance. Cf. Starr, *Harvard Theol. Rev.,* XXIX, 98-100. For extra-Byzantine texts see Juster, I, 115, n. 2; P. Lonardo. «Un abiura di ebrei a Lucera nel 1454.» *Studi Storici,* XVI, 1908, 581-91.

For the tradition regarding false converts in the time of Constantine, see no. **84n.** A citation from Romanos alluding to forced converts in the 6th c. is given by P. Maas, *BZ,* XV, 1906, 32; for the problem of his date see Bardenhewer, *op. cit.,* V, 159-61. On Borion see Juster, I, 472; ct. Beneshevich, *l.c.,* 200. The period 565-638 is treated in the present writer's study, *Jour. of the Pal. Or. Soc.,,* XV, 280-93; see also R. Devreesse. «La fin inédite d'une lettre de Saint Maxime: un baptême forcé de juifs et de samaritains à Carthage en 632». *Revue des Sciences religieuses,* XVII, 1937, 25-35. On the 13th c. instance, Mann, *REJ,* LXXXII, 1926, 372 f.

The extent of the incorporation of the phraseology of the earlier formula in ss. I, II, 1, 7, 10-12, 15 f., 18, is indicated by Beneshevich by sublineation.

Detailed annotations:

I. With the first two sentences cf. no. **18.** On the godfather, J. Pargoire, *Dict. d'arch. chr.,* I, 1873.

II., 1. The first part recurs *verbatim* in the other Byzantine formulæ, so that Dölger's remarks on the abuse of the defenceless Jews by officials, which he infers from the term ἐπήρεια, are unwarranted; *Viertel.,* XXVI, 11. Cf. nos. **14, 83, n.**; Beneshevich, *l. c.,* 309, n.3. The archaic list of 8 holidays is fuller than those given by certain Byzantine exegetes, where the Jubilee is omitted, and which have only the Passover for the first 3 of the present one; see *id.,* 198 and n. 1.

II., 2. See Juster, I, 117, n.

II., 3. Juster, II, 207, n. 2. Krauss, *l.c.*, 145. n. 5. The omission of the law (*C. I.* 1.9.11) prohibiting this celebration from the extant defective text of the *Basilika* is no proof that it was not originally contained therein. At any rate, *ca.* 600 a Greek version of the law was included in the «Collectio tripartita», ed. W. Vœll and H. Justell. *Bibliotheca Iuris Canonici.* Paris, 1661. II, 1294. For the survival of the prescribed custom in Persia, see Ginzberg, *Geonica*, II, 1, 419. Cf. Aronius, *Regesten*, 149, no. 330. Beneshevich, *l. c.*, 223, calculates this to be the Purim of 1014, but see below on Appendix 2a.

II., 4. See H. Lewy. «Kleine Beiträge zur Volkskunde und Religionswissenschaft». *Archiv für Religionswissenschaft*, XXV, 1927, 197 f.

II., 5. The reference to the use of ashes may have been inspired merely by the Bible, but the the custom is known later in Palestine (*Ta'anit*, II, 1), and as late as the 19th c. in Yemen; S. Bialoblocki, *EJ*, I, 103.

II., 6. On Antichrist cf. no. **25.** For the joys of the Messianic era, *Lev. R.*, s. 22.

II., 8. On the *resh pirka*, Mann, *Jews in Egypt*, II, 269 f.; *Texts*, I, 197 f. Among local titles, nothing higher than rabbi occurs in the earlier period; Juster I, 450-53.

II., 9. See Lewy, *l. c.*, 198-200. Beneshevich's identifications, *l. c.*, 220-23, are as follows: Eleazar Kalir (7th c., no. **89n.**); the author of the midrash *Seder Eliyahu* (the title alludes to the prophet!), on which see no. **22n.**; Benjamin b. Zerah, who, though supposed to have lived in the Empire, is assigned to the latter 11th c. (Horodetzky, *EJ*, IV, 130); Zebadiah (9th c., no. **80n.**); Amram Gaon (9th c., M. Zobel, *EJ*, II, 712-15); Shabbetai Donnolo (Pt. I, c. VI).

II., 18. Cf. no. **18.** See also the very similar phraseology of the monastic text, to which reference is made in no. **109n.** The «trembling of Cain» is derived from the Sept., Gen. 4:12. The death-penalty for apostasy does not seem to be implied here; see no. **84n.** Cf. tr. by C. Michel, *Dict. d'arch. chr.*, I, 1931.

Appendix. Cf. Beneshevich's tr., *l.c.*, 217 f.

1. The lexicon gives the masculine form λειπανάβατος (*EL*, VIII, 573). Cf. however, the commentary of Jacob b. Reuben, a Byzantine Karaite of the 12th c., on Prov. 12:27, where he remarks on «the knave who is too lazy to cook his food or to bake his bread, but bakes only *phasiton* (?), which becomes *lipanabaton*»; *Sefer ha-'Osher*, ed. A. Firkowicz. Eupatoria, 1836. Prov., p. 2a, bot. On the alleged

prohibition of eating lamb at Passover, see Procopius. *Anecdota,* XXVIII, 17, ed. and tr. Dewing, Cambridge (U.S.A.), 1935. pp. 332 f.

2. The heading is obviously incorrect.

2a. Beneshevich, *l.c.*, 223, calculates that the dates indicated apply to the years 932, 981, 989, and 1019, none of which, however, coincides with the dating of Purim above (II, 3). The traditional connection with the sacrifice of Isaac specifies the ram's horn, and not the angel's voice; *Roshha-Shanah* 16a.

2b. «The Great Day» recalls the rabbinic *yoma rabba, ib.* 21a. The alternative sense of παιδίον is «child», which, if intended here, would point to a tendency in Karaism where we find the followers of Benjamin of Nahawand making children subject to all the laws as soon as they learned to speak. See al-Qirqisānī, tr. L. Nemoy, *HUC An.,* VII, 1930, 387.

2c. With μασψιδία cf. *moscheta*=«synagogue», in a 15th c. Italian source; Ferorelli, *op. cit.*, 100 f. On the Baghdad practice see B. M. Lewin. *Oṣar ha-Geonim.* Jerusalem, 1934. VI, pt. 2, 33 f. On καλύβη= *sukkah,* cf. the Byzantine-Jewish version of Jonah, ed. D. C. Hesseling, *BZ,* X, 1901, 217, line 100.

4. Cf. j. *Pesaḥim,* IV, 1, 30d.

Scholia. These relate to the 6th c. formula, ed. Beneshevich, *l. c.,* 305-07. 2. On the change of β to μ see the editor, *l. c., 222.* 3. Cf. the extraneous remarks which have crept into II, 3.

4. With ῥαβὶς (pronounced *ravis*), cf. the plural *rividi* cited from a ms. Mahzor Romaniah; Brann, *Monats.,* LXII, 1918, 276. (The modern ῥαββῖνος is a relatively late loan-word).

5. The etymology is incorrect, since the writer is unaware of the sense of the Aramaic *pirqa,* «an academic session».

6. Cf. the Montanists' alleged agreement with the Jewish date of the Passover; ps.-Chrysostom, *PG,* LIX, 747 (tr. de Labriolle, *Sources du Montanisme,* 225). This was not true, however, in the 4th c.; see Sozomen, *Ecclesiastical history,* VII, 18, *PG,* LXVII, 1469, 1472.

ca. 1000-38   **122**

We have put the question before the Greek students from Constantinople who are here with us. They replied that from the Greek language it is clear that anything which is lost, or any matter which is useless and worthless, is termed in the Greek language ANPDI (?).

Hai to an anon. correspondent, ed. A. Harkavy. *Zikkaron la-risho-nim ve-gam la-aharonim.* [Verein *Mekize Nirdamim,* IX] Berlin, 1887. I, no. 225, pp. 105 f. The Talmudic loan-word in question is either *'andipi* (*Sabbath,* VIII, 4) or *'anporia* (*Baba Mesia,* II, 2), but the sense given here seems to refer to ἀνωφελής, as Harkavy suggested (p. 362); ct. Perles, *BZ,* II, 1893, 570; Krauss, *Studien,* 112, n. 2. See also the eulogy by Samuel ha-Nagid, (*Ben-Tehillim,* XI, 56), ed. D. S. Sasoon. *Diwan Shemuel ha-Nagid.* London, 1934. p. 12.

Certain students from «Edom» are mentioned *ca.* 1025 as studying in SRMUB, having reached it via Aleppo. Two of them are named Judah and Karmī, and it has been suggested that they came from the Empire. See the letter of Elijah b. Abraham to Jacob b. Joseph, ed. Schechter, *Festschrift... Berliners.* Frankfort, 1903, p. 110, lines 9-14; cf. Mann, *Jews in Egypt.* I, 37, n. 1, II, 341; Poznanski, *REJ,* XLVII, 1903, 139.

ca. 1000 - 38 **123**

Certainly one ought not deliberately do so [write a bill of divorcement] in a foreign language, lest he be unable to frame the document in that language with sufficient precision, and lest the case require investigation and a fault be found in it. It is otherwise however, if a court of high standing be convened in Greece, in Rome, or in Persia.

Hai, *op. cit.,* no. 255, p. 130; cf. *ibid.,* no. 14, p. 6. Cf. also the criticism of the abandonment of Hebrew for Greek among other languages by Saadia in the introd. to his *Agron,* ed. Steinschneider, *Jüdische Zeitschrift,* X, 1872, 257, line 1.

ca. 1000 - 38 **124**

You have asked regarding the statement of a *kohen*... to you to the effect that the seven days of Passover are of great signi-ficance... I have already admonished many communities not to inquire in such matters, for « It is the glory of God to conceal a thing» [Pr. 25:2].... Moreover. we have no time for such matters.... We have already written regarding these things in the letters which we sent to the inhabitants of Calabria and those of Apulia, that they have no right to inquire and we, none to reply.....

Attributed to Hai; *Shaaré Teshubah,* ed. E. B. Chasan. Livorno, 1859. no. 99, p. 38a. A late Kabbalistic pseudepigraph which is defended as authentic only by D. Kahana, *Ha-kedem,* III, 1912, 123 f.; *contra* Zunz, *Die Ritus des synagogalen Gottesdienstes geschichtlich entwickelt.* (Reprint) Berlin, 1919. p. 193. The rejection is supported from ms. evidence by E. E. Hildesheimer, in *Festschrift für J. Rosenheim.* Frankfort, 1931. p. 275, n. 8. Cf. Graetz, *Gesch.,* VI, 352.

There is a ms. responsum (spuriously?) attributed to Hai and addressed to Nathan, Shealtiel, and Kalonymos, which Zunz, by an emendation, would read as addressed to Otranto; *Die gottesdienstlichen Vorträge der Juden.* 2nd ed., Frankfort, 1892. p. 376, n. *e.*]

ca. 1000 - 1100   **125**

.... When Abū ʿAlī arrived there,... you had given him one letter addressed to us, and another to R. Elijah b. R. Shabbetai, the chief rabbi. It concerned the case of.... who had been imprisoned. You also sent a parchment scroll of Esther to me and our brother·... Those letters which you sent me by Abū ʿAlī, because I did not write them in an ordinary letter, but I had three sheets of prayers (*selihot*) ....., which I had composed, and I sent these to you in return for the scroll of Esther which you had sent as a memento between you and us. On half the sheet I wrote out replies in lieu of a letter. Then Abū ʿAlī said to me, « Give me the replies which you have written to your brother, and I will send them with a Christian MULFITIANIN together with my letters. »

So I gave them to him to send to you. Faith, I took great pains with those replies, for I said, « I will write them out clearly so that he will be informed of everything.» However, when you had sent some more letters to the sons of R. Obadiah the ⟨silversmith⟩, discussing the affair of the non-conformist Karaites— may they be accursed!—, and I received no answer for the prayers and replies as to whether or not they reached you, I was very much perturbed. But, as you know, my dear brother, the Karaites again fought against us last year. They desecrated the divine festivals, and celebrated the New Year in the eighth month, for

they had received letters from Palestine stating that the barley-
ripening had not yet been seen in Nisan and the Passover had
been celebrated in Iyyar....

A violent enmity developed between us, and many disputes
took place. They slandered the Rabbinites, and the congregation
was fined almost a thousand dinars IPRNIIR. In the midst of
all these disputes and great enmity, there arrived the letters
which you had sent to the sons of R. Obadiah. On one of the
intermediate days of the ⟨Sukko⟩t, a meeting was called and the
whole congregation gathered in the great synagogue. The letters
were read, and when the community had heard their contents
and realized that they had transgressed the precepts, they were
stirred, and blessed your name.... And now your good name has
spread.... throughout the whole world. Even from Russia...
some merchants arrived here, and when they had heard the contents of the letter,... they praised you highly. And when people
see me, they say, «This is the brother of R. Elljah, who wrote
down the whole story...»

[Postscript] I wish you to know, my dear brother,... what
befell this dear friend of ours, Isaac, who went to the trouble of
bringing these letters, which you sent by him, and who delivered
them to R. Joseph and our master David, the sons of R. Obadiah
the silversmith. They gave him not a penny, and paid attention
to him, even neglecting to invite him to a meal, or to send him a
present of the least value. Neither they nor any other member of
our community showed any interest in his welfare. However,
since he is related to my father-in-law, Samuel the elder, and
because of this tie stayed at his home, he confided in me and expressed his chagrin. He adjured me to tell you the true facts. As
for me, my dear brother, every day that I saw him, I was ashamed to face him, but I was unable to do anything for him because of my lack of means....

Mann, *Texts*, I, 48-51, cf. pp. 45-57, II, 1458. Cf. Krauss, *HUC
An.*, I, 49 and Mann, *l.c.*, 297-307. On lines 29, 64, see Assaf, *Tarbiz*,

III, 341, n. 1. The unintelligible word at the end of line 37 might be emended to read ὑπερπέρα, although that term did not replace *nomisma* until the end of the 12th c.; Andréadès, *Byzantion,* I, 75. Another suggestion, offered by Perles, is to read ὑπάργυρ(οι), «of silver»; *Orientalistische Literaturzeitung,* XXXVI, 1933, 538. But that overlooks the fact that *dinar* regularly denotes a gold coin.

As for provenance, Mann chooses Thessalonica because of the appearance there of Jews from Russia (cf. no. **118**). And, as it happens, the season in which these events took place is that of the fair of St. Demetrios (Oct. 20-26), when Russian merchants would be expected to visit that town. (See H. F. Tozer, *JHS,* II, 1882, 243-45; Miller, *English Historical Review,* XXXII, 167.) Nevertheless, Cp. is by far more probable, for here was the chief center of the Byzantine Karaites (Mann, *op. cit.,* II, 281-91), and the greater probability from the commercial side is self-evident. See Vasiliev, «Economic relations between Byzantium and Old Russia». *Jour. of econ. and bus. his.,* IV, 1931-2, 314-34.

On the Karaite position with respect to the calendar, see al-Qirqisānī, tr. Nemoy, *l.c.,* 387; cf. no. **154.** For the responsum received by Tobiah b. Moses from Jerusalem, see Hadassī, *op. cit.,* s. 187, p. 76a. Cf. a curious modern viewpoint cited by Poznanski, *ZfhB,* XIII, 1909, 113.

On the amount of the fine cf. the case of an individual who in 1256 was required to pay 1000 *nomismata,* at a time, however, when this coin had depreciated by about $^1/_4$; Ostrogorsky, *BZ,* XXXII, 306, 312, n.

1006-19   **126**

.... Previous to this time [1019] he [Caliph al-Hākim] had promulgated restrictions against the Christians and the Jews, with regard to riding [horses] and the baths, etc. This policy drove them to despair, and many of them left for Byzantium. He demolished their houses of worship and commanded them to live outwardly as Moslems. And so they did for a number of years.

Jamāl ad-Dīn Abū'l Hasan ʿAlī b. Dāfir al-Azdī (al-Halabī; 13th c.) *Kitāb ad-duwal al-munqatiʿa,* pt. 4, ed. in part, F. Wüstenfeld. *Geschichte der Fatimiden-Chalifen nach arabischen Quellen. (Abhandlungen* of the Göttingen Königliche Gesellschaft der Wissenschaften, XXVI-II) Göttingen, 1881. p. 210. See I. Chanoch, *EJ,* II, 309-11.

An earlier source makes it fairly certain that at least the Syrian Christians took refuge *ca.* 1011 in towns such as Laodicæa and Antioch, but mentions no similar act on the part of the Jews. See Yaḥyā ibn Saʿīd. *Histoire,* ed. and tr. I. Kratchkovsky and Vasiliev. *PO,* XXIII, 506, 511, 519. One scholar has stated that an expulsion of both groups took place in 1013, without citing his authority; S. de Sacy. *Exposé de la Religion des Druzes.* Paris, 1838, I, CCCLXVIII. A 15th c. source speaks of a decree of expulsion which was rescinded; Wüstenfeld, *Makrizi's Geschichte der Copten.* Göttingen, 1845. p. 65. In this connection a Jewish source mentions, aside from some non-Christian localities, only Rome (*Romah*); ed. Davidson, *JQR,* IV, 1913, 55.

1007 **127**

Then Basil [II] sent a second message to Armenia, to John Shahinshah, to the honorable catholicos Sarkis, and.... succeeded in getting them to send him Samuel, a very learned and profound scholar. The emperor put him up against the Greek scholars in an assembly. The latter employed all their writings against Samuel.... All of his arguments pleased the emperor. But the Greek savants said to Basil, «Sire, summon hither the great scholar of the Hebrews, who lives on the island of Cyprus, and who has, since his childhood, acquired such a vast erudition in the science of the calendar, and in all the branches of human knowledge.»

He sent to Cyprus and this scholar, whose name was Moses, was brought. This eloquent and wise man, standing in the assembly before the emperor, delivered a discourse on the principles of the calendar, exposed the error of the Greeks and covered them with confusion, while he heaped praises on the Armenian scholar for his demonstration.

Matthew of Edessa (12th c.). *Chronique,* tr. from the Armenian, E. Dulaurier *[Bibliothèque historique arménienne].* Paris, 1838. XXIV, p. 39; cf. 390 f. Dölger, *Regesten,* I, pt. 1, 103, no. 798. With respect to the Christians of Egypt, Palestine, and Syria, see Yaḥyā ibn Saʿīd, *l.c.,* 481-83.

1020-30   **128**

.... Some time later there came a report that a vessel of one of the Arabs, Jabārah ibn Mukhtār, had set out, and that it held ten Jews from the city of Attaleia. It had put in at Ramadah [n. Africa] on its westward course. But we refused to believe these things until their [the captives'] letter reached us [at Alexandria], as well as R. Netanel *ha-Kohen*, the elder.... Therein they informed us that there were ten of them, and that much money had been taken from them....

Mann, *Jews in Egypt*, II, 87, cf. I, 90. He took *'eres 'Antaliyah* = «land of Anatolia», overlooking Cowley's correct identification (no. **132n.**); for the use of *'eres* as an Arabism for the equivocal *balad* see, e. g., *ib.*, II, 91, last line. See also no. **167** and the notice regarding the local Jewish quarter *ca.* 1330 in Ibn Batūtah. *Voyages*, ed. and tr. C. Defrémery and B. R. Sanguinetti. Paris, 1914 (Reprint). II, 259. In general, see Heyd, *op. cit.*, Index, s. v. «Satalia»; Starr, «The place-name *Italiya-Antaliyah*,» *Rivista*, XVII, 1937.

A similar and apparently contemporary but more fragmentary document is given by Mann, *op. cit.*, II, 344 f. Only the addressee's title, *ha-rab ha-mubhaq*, survives, and the only proper name is that of the city (not land) whence came the five young captives involved. This is read by the editor ASSRBILU, which is not intelligible. However, from a photostat in my possession it is fairly clear that the place-name must be read otherwise, apparently, ASTSBILU; the possible connection with Pylæ was suggested by Prof. Vasiliev privately. Among the editor's other errors one should note the omission of line 18; for the corrected text see **App. B.** See also Mann, *Texts*, I, 139, lines 17 f.

1020-30   **129**

To the glorious and honorable R. Ephraim b. Shemariah [Fustāt] .... from the community of Alexandria....

Our purpose in writing to you.... is to inform you of the matter of the captive woman who was brought from the land of Edom, and whom we ransomed for 24 gold-pieces plus the government-tax. You sent us 12 dinārs and we paid the remainder, including the government-tax levied on her. In addition, the sailors brought us two more: one a handsome and educated youth, and the other a boy of about ten. When we saw them being beaten and terrorized by their captors, we took pity on them, and ransomed them from their captors. But before we could rest from this affair, another vessel arrived from the land of Edom with many captives.... Among them was a physician and his wife....

Mann, *Jews in Egypt*, II, 88 f., cf. I, 91. On line 8, Halper, *Hatc-qufah*, XVIII, 195.

1022 **130**

Friday, Nisan 4 [March 9], 4782 of the creation of the world, according to the customary era in use at the city of Mastaura, near the River Maeander.

Namer b. Elqanah came and declared to Eudokia b. Caleb: Be my wife in accordance with the law of Moses and Israel, and I will serve, honor, maintain and support you, in the manner in which Jewish husbands faithfully serve and honor their wives. As the matrimonial price for your virginity, I give you the sum of 200 *zūzīm*, which are equivalent to 8 $^1/_3$ dinars [*nomismata*], as required by the Torah, and which may be collected from my property. I assume responsibility for your sustenance, your clothing, your general needs, as well as for the normal conjugal relations. The aforementioned Eudokia brings from the home of her father Caleb to that of her husband Namer:

A cauldron (κακκάβιν), at 1 gold-piece.

A copper kettle (? *qumqum* λεβήτιν), at 1 gold-piece.

A wash-basin (λεκάνιν), a medium-sized small kettle, a copper spoon, at 1 gold-piece.

A veil with a silver clasp, at 2 gold-pieces.

A cloak and ANPLIN, at 1 gold-piece.

Two female garments, at 1 gold-piece.

A red cotton (βαβακερόν) double-coat, and a white coat, at 1 gold-piece.

A female scarf, hand-embroidered (χειρόπλουμον), at two gold-pieces. Two others, at two gold-pieces.

A female garment [bath-robe?] and bag (σάκουλ) for the bath, a small table-cloth (μεσσάλιν), at 1 gold-piece.

Two palm-fans (βαιεῖς) and a handsome woolen girdle, at a gold-piece.

A wig (ἐντρίχιν), and three handkerchiefs, at one-half gold-piece.

As the ceremonial marriage-gift the bridegroom presented to the bride Eudokia:

A gilded bracelet of ten and one-half shekels, and another of silver, at 2 gold-pieces.

Two armlets (ἀγκωνοβράχιλα) of 18 (eighteen) shekels, and another of silver, at 2 gold-pieces.

A woolen girdle, at one-half gold-piece.

A pair of gold ear-rings with triple pendants (*tribolata*), and a gold ring, of three shekels.

In addition, the mother of the bride presented to her daughter Eudokia a double red garment with hood (κουκουλλάρικον) at one and one-half gold-pieces.

The general total including her possessions, her marriage-gifts [from her husband], the matrimonial price for her as a virgin, and the additional (*tosefet*) marriage-settlement, is thirty-five and one-third gold-pieces.

In addition the bride's mother presents to her daughter the lower story of the house for which the egress shall be on the east, on the river-bank. Half of the well shall belong to her brother Caleb, who shall have the right to use the well. «Mercy and truth are met together; righteousness and peace have kissed each other.» [Ps. 85:11].

The bridegroom Namer assumes responsibility for the marriage-settlement, which will be binding both on him and on his heirs after him, and which is secured by the choicest of his possessions under the heavens, whether indoors or out, landed or movable, even to the coat on his back. It is not to be regarded as an *asmakhta* nor as a documentary form, but as valid to the full extent of every enactment of the rabbis.

We have received from the aforementioned bridegroom Namer the symbolical delivery by means of an article valid for the purpose [*Baba Mesi'a* 47a], confirming all statements and points enumerated on the reverse side of this instrument. Valid and established. UNHINDERED (ἀκωλύτως). Judah b. Nabon... Moses b. Leon... The scribe Shelahiah b. Joseph... Moses b. R. Shabbetai...

Mann, *Jews in Egypt,* II, 94-6, I, 92 f. For supplements to Mann's philological notes and the mosaic from Daphni illustrating some of the objects, see T. Reinach. «Un contrat de mariage du temps de Basile le Bulgaroctone». *Mélanges Schlumberger.* Paris, 1924. I, 118-32. (The mosaic is conveniently published also in *Dict. d'Arch. Chr.,* I, 2170).

The general form is closely related to the roughly contemporary *ketubot* published with full apparatus by Assaf, *Sefer ha-Shetarot le-Rab Hai bar Sherira Gaon.* (Supplement to *Tarbiz,* 1/3) Jerusalem, 1930. pp. 13-15, 54 f., 63 f. See Maimonides. *Mishneh Torah,* « *Yibbum*», IV, 33; tr. J. Z. Lauterbach, *JE*, VII, 472. See also D. J. Bornstein, *EJ,* IX, 1174-86.

Detailed annotations:

Line 4. Strictly speaking, the town is on the Chrysaoras, a n. branch of the Mæander.

Line 5. Read *le'intū,* lit., «be mine in wifehood», an idiom of great antiquity; cf. *Qiddushin,* IV, 8, and Assaf, *op. cit.,* p. 13, line 6, p. 54, line 4, p. 63, line 17. Our scribe consistently writes final *yodh.*

Line 8. Cf. *id.,* 54, line 6 and n. Mann takes the word *'ahid* in the sense of «seizable»; *Texts,* I, 431, n. 13.

Line 10. Read as in line 5.

Line 15. The Greek word is evidently explanatory, perhaps specifying the material, as Mann says. But Reinach renders «marmite à pieds».

Line 17. For *semikah* Mann gives «rug», citing Jud. 4:18. But «cloak» is the post-Biblical sense, and the context, apart from metal ware, deals almost exclusively with wearing apparel. The next item, ANPLIN, is connected by Mann with the loan-word *'apalion,* from *pallium,* giving the sense of «sheet used for a cloak and also bedcover».

Line 18. For βαβακερόν cf. *babakin* in a Hebrew work; Perles, *BZ,* II, 579.

Line 29. Mann read *'abiha*, but the photostat shows clearly *'immah*, confirming the correction of Halper, *JQR*, XIV, 1923, 97.

Line 32. The total includes the sum of 6¹/₂ *nomismata* as the value of the items for which no individual estimation is given.

Line 38. A menorah is drawn in the middle of the quotation.

Verso, line 10. This particular use of the Greek term is known only from Jewish documents. Mann cites the two other known cases both undated documents of Byzantine provenance. One is a new fragment forming the conclusion of a document, and the other is a Hebrew *ketubah* termed «Jerusalemite»!; A. Gulak. *Osar ha-shetarot ha-nehugim be-Yisrael.* Jerusalem, 1926. pp. 35 f. (Cf. Assaf, *op. cit.,* 54, n. 1). The latter gives the currency in use as «gold-pieces of Constantinople».

ca. 1025-50   **131**

a. ... the Byzantines, who tolerate a large population of Jews in their realm... They afford them protection, allow them openly to adhere to their religion, and to build their synagogues...

b. [As regards the Byzantines], the Jew in their lands may say, «I am a Jew.» He may adhere to his religion and recite his prayers. No one brings it up to him, restrains him, or puts any difficulties in his way...

c. ... even the Jews may enter the churches of the Byzantines...

d. ... in Byzantium... there are a large number of Jews, who endure humiliation and the hatred of those men as well as of all others....

Elīshā bar Shinayā. *«Al-būrhān alā sahīh al-'imān».* Vatican codex arabicus 180, fols. 157v, 158v, 202v, 213r (see **App. B**); tr. L. Horst. *Beweis der Wahrheit des Glaubens.* Colmar, 1886. pp. 42, 103, 117. Cited in part by Krauss, *Studien,* 67. The point of *c* is the laxity of the Byzantine clergy in ceremonial matters; *d* is part of a refutation of «cuius regio, eius religio».

1028   **132**

... To the community of... R. Ephraim b. Shemariah [Fustāt] ...from Yeshuah *ha-Kohen*... b. Joseph... and from the two congregations... of No-Amon [Alexandria]...

... The news reached us that some other captives had arrived. This we refused to believe until some of the men of Yabqī ibn Abū Razīn came with seven Jewish m⟨erchants⟩ from the city of Attaleia. Yabqī brought them to the home of our venerable leader R. Netanel *ha-Kohen*... b. R. Eleazar... The Arab said to us, « I want the ransom of these seven.» (Of these four were Rabbinites and three Karaites, and their ransom would amount to 233 1/3 dinars)...

The venerable R. Netanel... replied to him, «Seeing that you have not left these poor men [the local Jews] even enough to pay for their [the captives'] food, how can they possibly pay you the ransom?....»

... The seven captives are from the city of Attaleia, and include some of its elders and household-heads...

Written in the month of Kislev [December], in the year [1] 340 of the documentary [Seleucid] era...

A. Cowley, «Bodleian Genizah Fragments, IV». *JQR*, XIX, 1906, 251-54; for the identification of the place-name, *l.c.*, 250 and no. **128n.**; cf. Mann, *Jews in Egypt*, I, 88-90.

1028-35   **133**

... To R. Ephraim... b. R. Shemariah...

These lines are written to inform you of the following matter... during this year, and this week they returned to ⟨their land⟩.. We did what we could for them, and helped them to get to the territory of ⟨Byzantium⟩... But R. Shabbetai b. R. Netanel of the city of At⟨taleia⟩,... him, together with his fellow-captives, and that we should allow him to go... So we granted his request because he desires to... at the Holy Mount, the site of the resting-place of His glory... somewhat of a cantor and is alert... so that he might go to [the site of] the Temple...

From your affectionate friend, Yeshu'ah ha-Ko⟨hen⟩ b. Joseph⟩.

Mann, *Jews in Egypt*, II, 91, cf. I, 92. See nos. **128, 132.**

1028-35   **134**

... For many scholars have come hither [Egypt] from the
land of Edom and from Palestine. Let me be as one of them...

Letter to Ephraim b. Shemariah at Fusṭāt from a certain Isaac,
appealing for financial assistance; ed. Mann, *Jews in Egypt,* II, 110.
The reference to Byzantium is not questioned by Mann, *ib.,* I, 102
(cf. Krauss, *Hashiloah,* XLII, 1920, 240, n. 4). Yet it must not be
overlooked that precisely the same juxtaposition of the two countries
figures in a communication to Hai concerning the prevalence of
magical beliefs, and in his reply to this he substitutes Rome (the
city) for «Edom». Here again Mann, *op. cit.,* I, 47, n. 1, believes that
Byzantium is involved; ct. Assaf, *Hashiloah,* XXXV, 281, n. 2. Cf. also
the identical problem in another connection; Mann, *Tarbiz,* V, 296 f.,
and n. 182; Krauss, «Die hebräische Benennungen der modernen
Völker.» *Jew. Studies ... Kohut,* pp. 380-84.

1031   **135**

From the two congregations of Alexandria.... to our master
R. David... ⟨b. R. Isaac⟩...

... to inform you that the news reached us... ⟨the 1⟩and of
Edom. They took three of them to the land of ... then the captive
came... So we must request you... to send us thirty-three ⟨and
one-third dinars⟩... The other three will come from the land of...
Shebat [January], 4391 of the Creation....

Mann, *Jews in Egypt,* II, 91 f., cf. I, 92.

1031-40   **136**

... Some time later we heard that some Christians had brought
a boy to Prag for sale, and he said that he had been taken captive at Primush [now Przemysl, Poland; text, *Primut*]. He was
ransomed by a Greek [or, «Russian»] Jew. Another one who
had been freed and had returned from the land of *Canaan Yavan*
[Russia?] said, «I saw him in Constantinople.» And now will
the master give us his ruling whether the widow is permitted to
re-marry or not.

Responsum of R. Judah b. Meir *ha-Kohen* (Mayence; Horodetzky,
EJ, VIII, 1019), cited from his *Sefer ha-dinim* by Isaac b. Moses. *'Or*

Zarʿua, I, 196a, no. 694. The case deals with a widow whose husband is survived by a brother who, though unseen for years and inaccessible, is yet known to be alive and subject to the duty of levirate marriage.

For the historical interpretation the writer has followed Brutzkus, «The earliest notices of the Jews in Poland (10-11 cc.).» (Yiddish) *Historishe Shriften* of the Berlin Yidisher Visenshaftlicher Institut, *Historishe Sektzie*. Warsaw, 1929. I, 66 f.; cf. *id., Zeit. f. d. Gesch. d. Juden in Deutschland*, III, 102. He connects the notice in our source with the raid of Yaroslav and Mastislav of Kiev in Poland, the captives of which were settled on the shore of the Ros, as related in the Russian Primary Chronicle. See the tr. by S. H. Cross in *Harvard Studies and Notes in Philology and Literature*, XII, 1930, 225.

On Jewish merchants in contemporary Bohemia, Brann, *Germ. Jud.*, I, 30, 41, n. 42.

Brutzkus' interpretation of *Canaan Yavan* in the sense that either term by itself bore in the contemporary Hebrew of central Europe, though it fulfills the requirements of this particular situation best, is still not free from difficulty. Elsewhere in the *'Or Zarʿua*, the author uses *Canaan* consistently for his native Bohemia; see S. H. Tykocinski, *Monats.*, LV, 1910, 488-96, and Krauss, *Jew. Studies . . . Kohut*, 397-400. But it might be argued from this that he added the word *Yavan* to the text of the responsum in order to avoid ambiguity. This, however, is unlikely when one notes, on the one hand, that his designation for Russia is simply the Hebrew transcription of that word, and, on the other, that *Yavan* appears in his citations from R. Baruk in the sense of Magna Græcia; see J. Wellescz, *Jahrbuch der jüdisch-literarischen Gesellschaft*, IV, 1906, 101, 109; cf. Epstein, *Tarbiz*, I/4, 27-32, and Aptowitzer, Vienna *Jahresbericht*, XXXVII-IX, 36 f. For Greece=Russia in Gentile sources, see Heyd, *op. cit.*, I, 74, 77.

An earlier suggestion was Bulgaria; M. Güdemann. *Geschichte des Erziehungswesen und der Cultur der abendländischen Juden*. Vienna, 1882. I, 110. But during the period in question this country was a Byzantine province, and would probably not have received a special name. Cf. Krauss, *Studien*, 104, who takes it as designating both Greece and Russia. For *Yavan*=Hungary, *id.*, 103.

For the account of how some Jews purchased slaves in Bulgaria and then sold them in Venice in 885 to an envoy of Basil I, see the shorter life of Naum of Achrida, ed. Y. Ivanov. *B'lgarski Starini iz' Makedoniya*. Sofia, 1931. p. 306; Latin tr., F. Snopek. *Konstantinus-*

Cyrillus und Methodius die Slavenapostel. Kremsier, 1911. p. 429. Cf. the allusion in one version of the life of Clement of Achrida, *PG*, CXXVI, 1213, 1216, which is discussed by Snopek, *op. cit.*, 437-43. See further, S. Dvornik. *Les Slaves, Byzance et Rome au IXe siècle.* Paris, 1926. pp. 298 f.; S. Runciman. *A history of the first Bulgarian empire.* London, 1930. p. 124.

1033   **137**

.... I, the supersigned Leo, ... of the city of Taranto.... of my own free will and choice, sell to you Theophylaktos, also called Chimaria, a Hebrew by race, a plot of 2 vineyards, 50 square ὄϱδινοι, from my share of my paternal inheritance, which lies near the property of the Holy Angel below Raskla, at a price agreed on between us 5 gold inscribed and undefaced Roman nomismata. The boundaries, etc.....

F. Trinchera. *Syllabus græcarum membranarum.* Naples, 1865. pp. 29-31. On the specification of full valued currency as a necessary safeguard, see Ostrogorsky, *Viertel.*, XXII, 1929, 141. The second name of the purchaser undoubtedly represents Shemariah, the exact equivalent of his Greek name; Cassuto, *Giornale della Società Asiatica Italiana*, XXIX, 109, n. 3. Yet the transcription of *shin* by χ is unparalleled.

1039   **138**

.... We, the supersigned husband and wife [Leo and Flavia],... of our own free will and choice, sell to you, Theophylaktos the Hebrew, a vineyard plot from our inheritance below the property of the Holy Angel of Raskla, consisting of 50 square ὄϱδινοι, at a price agreed upon between us at 3 gold inscribed Roman nomismata. The boundaries, etc.,... and from the west, the property of the aforementioned Theophylaktos the Hebrew...

Written at our order by the hand of the priest Basil,... in January of the year 6547 [A. M.].

Trinchera, *op. cit.*, 36-38.

ca 1040?   **139**

... May God spread His tent of peace... over our beloved brethren, the holy community of Ma⟨st⟩aur⟨a⟩,... the holy community which dwells in the land of Greece, scattered in the land of the Edomites, de⟨livered⟩ into the hand of the enemy, and subjected to the yoke of ⟨the⟩ adversaries, bearing the yokes of the crushers. May God help and ⟨keep them⟩!...

We are obliged... for the sake of our brethren, captives from your midst, because of present hardships, and the multitude of troubles and disturbances,... who are with us, Elijah and Leo, sons of... He came to us... Elijah... and told us of your generosity and solicitude toward... this Leo to you, and will convey our greetings... And with the help of Heaven he set out... until this Leo reaches you...

Mann, *Jews in Egypt,* II, 92 f., cf. I, 92 f. Presumably from Alexandria, reflecting a time when the communal resources had been exhausted by a series of such activities.

[1044   **140**

At this time when there were many aliens, Armenians, Arabs, and Jews in the royal capital, a great tumult broke out against King Constantine [ĪX]. The foreigners gathered together at the gate of the palace and cried out, « Constantine has killed our two queens [the βασιλίσσαι, Empress Zoé and Princess Theodora, her sister]» (The purpose of their shouting was to loot the palace and the mansions of the nobles.) Then King Constantine gathered the nobles together and brought out Theodora and Zoé dressed in the royal robes. When the trio appeared there was quiet.

When the king inquired into the cause of the tumult, he was told that the aliens had stirred up disorder in order to loot the city. Thereupon the king decreed that there should not remain in it any one who had entered it during the last 30 years; whoever stayed should be blinded. About 100,000 persons left.

Bar Hebræus, 227; tr. Budge, 203 (among other inaccuracies, he misread *malkathē* as masculine). Cf. Ibn al-Athīr. *Kitāb al-kamīl fī't-tā'-rīkh,* ed. Tornberg, C. J. Leyden, 1863. X, 352. His account involves «Moslems, Christians, and other kinds». The actual occurrence was quite otherwise. As the emperor was about to take part in the procession in honor of the Forty Martyrs (March 9), the populace expressed their resentment at the favor shown his mistress at the expense of Zoé and Theodora. Only the timely intervention of the empress averted imminent bloodshed; Kedrenos, *PG*, CXXII, 288. Cf. Schlumberger, *L'épopée byz.*, III, 424-26; ct. Vogt, *CMH*, IV, 109, who combines the data of both the Greek and Semitic sources.

Note that the population of the city is estimated to have been half a million or more. See Andréadès, «La population de l'empire byzantin». *Bulletin de l'Institut Archéologique Bulgare*, IX, 1935, 118-21.]

ca. 1045   **141**

... He [the monk Gregorios] having had his senses blinded by them [he demons], began to dispute with him [Lazaros], saying, « It is no demonic guile, it is a manifestation of the Holy Spirit. Behold,» he continued, «the Holy Spirit has ordered me to go to the Theologos [Ephesus] to teach the metropolitan and all the clergy... Unless you permit me to go soon, all the local Jews will come hither [Mt. Galésion]. For God has revealed to me through the Holy Spirit, that in this ravine water will gush forth like a river in order to baptize all the Jews coming to me.»....

... Then a certain Jew came by, and seeing him [Lazaros] out in the open, wearing a leathern shirt and seated on a pillar, asked, and thereupon learned that he had worn it all of the dozen years during which he had been there, and had never changed into another. He was greatly amazed, and said, «This man, it seems to me, has surpassed the righteous men of old. For in the ancient time we find only Elijah wearing a leathern shirt. But even he had two of them, and changed from one into the other after having worn it not more than six months.»

At another time seven other Jews came up to the monastery. And when they caught sight of him, they did not need to learn more of his life than had the previous one, before they were astonished and sang hymns.

Gregorios (contemporary). Life of Lazaros. ed. H. Delehaye. *Acta Sanct.*, Nov., III (1910), cc. 49, 112, pp. 524, 542. On Theologos= Ephesus, and the monastery, see W. M. Ramsay. *The historical geo-*

graphy of Asia Minor. London, 1890. pp. 109 f. On the chronology, E. Kurtz, *BZ,* VII, 1898, 477-79.

There is one other reference of Byzantine date to the Jews of Ephesus. It seems that during the fourth decade of the sixth century they served the city as undertakers. See the epigraphic pastoral letter of Bishop Hypatios, fully discussed with photograph and tr. by J. N. Bakhuizen van den Brink. *De Oud-christelijke Monumenten van Ephesus.* Hague, 1923. pp. 129 f., 137 f.

1047   **142**

From all of the lands of the Greeks, too, and from other countries, the Christians and Jews come up to Jerusalem in great numbers in order to make their visitation of the Church and the Synagogue that is there.

Nasir-i-Khusrau. *(Sefer Nameh) Diary of a journey through Syria and Palestine, 1047 A. D.,* tr. from the Persian, G. Le Strange *[Palestine Pilgrims' Text Society].* London, 1888. p. 23.

1049   **143**

God, the great king, rejected the old Israel and chose the new one, which, since he preferred the latter to the former as the superior people and the desired portion, he called his own inheritance. Then he made the Jewish race subject to the Christian and appointed the believing, orthodox people to rule over the unbelieving, misguided one. Now in pursuance of this divine economy, His Imperial Majesty, in addition to the previous gifts which he has bestowed on the Nea Moné of the Virgin on the island of Chios, assigns to the monastery the Jews on this island, who are everywhere free and subordinate to no one (ἐλευθέρους παντάπασιν ὄντας καὶ μηδαμοῦ ὑποκειμένους). He decrees that they should be subject to it as enacted in this chrysobull, so that the Jews on Chios should pay the tax to the aforesaid Nea Moné, and that they should enjoy exemption [from all other taxes]; they shall pay the capitation-tax (*kephalétion*) to the monastery, so that it shall act as the mistress of those families from whom the members of the Nea Moné shall have the right of collecting the *kephalétion.*

We assign all the fifteen families to it, from whom the *kephalétion* shall annually be collected by the monks. These fifteen families of Jews shall be exempt from every special charge *(epéreia)* or corvée (ἀγγαρεία), whether authorized by Imperial decree or by the strategos, or by the judge, or by anyone else who has been entrusted with the business of the fisc. No one at all, whether a strategos, as has been said, or a judge, or a πρωτονοτάριος, or some other collector, or the bishop of the island, or the civil ruler, or the χαρτυλάριος or the μεράρχης, or the δρουγγάριος,.... or the πρωτοκεντάρχοι, or the deputies of the strategos or of the judge, shall take occasion to subject them to any *angareia* or *epéreia*, or, in general, to get anything out of them through an *epéreia* or with the pretext of a *Rôs* or other foreign invasion, or of the threatening Arabs; neither may they introduce any innovations, nor injure, nor extort anything from them. For we render them free from every hand, with exemption from civil and ecclesiastical authorities before all; we decree that they be subject only to the Nea Moné.... July, 6557 [A.M.]....

Constantine IX, ed. Zepos, *Jus graecor.*, I, 633 f.; G. Zolôtas. Ἱστορία τῆς Χίου. Athens, 1924. II, 282. (Earliest reference in 1866: F. de Coulanges, «Mémoire sur l'île de Chio», repr., *Questions historiques*. Paris, 1893. pp. 333 f.) See Andréadès, *Mélanges Diehl*, I, 22-25; Dölger, *Regesten*, I, pt. 2, 8, no. 892; *id.*, *Viertel.*, XXVI, 12-14, taking ἐλευθέρους in the technical sense: «unlisted on the tax-rolls».

On the theory that these Jews worked in the silk and purples industry, see Zolôtas, *op. cit.*, 284, n. 1. On the *angareia* and *epéreia*, Dölger, *Beiträge*, 61 f.; Ostrogorsky, *Viertel.*, XX, 1928, 60.

1051 **144**

Argyros, the *magistros* [of Italy] arrived,... bearing money, gifts, and honors, from the emperor [Constantine IX] Monomachos for the Normans. And in the month of April he entered Bari. Mel Malopezza and Liboni were put to death, and he burned the Jewish quarter.... (Venit Argiro Magistri... cum thesauro et dona et honores a Monomacho Imp. Et in mense Aprili intravit in Bari. Et occisus est Mel Malopezza et Liboni; et zalavit ipse Iudeam).

Anon. Chronicle of Bari (12th c.), ed. Muratori, *Rerum Italicarum Scriptores.* V, 151. See Gay, *L'Italie mérid.,* 485 f.; cf. F. Carabellese. *L'Apulià e il suo commune nell'alto medio evo.* Bari, 1905, p. 227, who considers the burning incidental.

For another possibly contemporary reference to Bari see the obscure Judeo-Arabic fragment cited by Mann, *JQR,* XI, 1921, 454 f. (The unintelligible SRLYVN looks like a misreading for *'eres Yavan,* and may thus be synonymous with *Rūm,* which occurs on the same line).

1054 **145**

I, Ahīma'as b. R. Paltīel [III] b. R. Samuel [II] b. R. Hananel [II] b. [a descendant of] R. Amittai, ... in the first month of the year 4814 [A.M.] ... investigated ... and discovered my genealogy, ... which I have written down in rhymed form. Taking as my beginning the exile from Jerusalem, ... I reached the time of the exile from Oria (the city of my own residence), and the arrival of my ancestors in Capua... I completed it in the month of Sivan....

Ahīma'as, ed. Neubauer, 131 f.; ed. Kahana, 140; tr. Salzman, 100 f. The material relating to his father and grandfather immediately precedes this. Cf. Cassuto, *EJ,* V, 36.

On the style of the work see Kaufmann, *Ges. Schr.,* III, 41-46; Brody, *ZfhB,* II, 1897, 160-64. (From a study of the rhyming syllables the latter finds that the chronicler make no distinction in the pronunciation of certain consonants and vowels, viz., the 3 *t* sounds, *kaf* with and without *dagesh, sin* and *shin, holam* and broad *qames, sere* and *segol.* Some of these may be due to the exigencies of the rhyme rather than to the prevalent phonetics). See also Kahana, *op cit.,* 115 f. On the *saj* or *mamzuj* in Arabic literature, F. Krenkow, *En. Is.,* IV, 44.

The chronicler's liturgical compositions are listed in Davidson, *Osar,* IV, 360, one of them being included in the chronicle. This is an elegy constructed as an alphabetic acrostic, and is now best read in Schirmann, *Mibhar,* 78 f.

ca. 1060-75 **146**

... From Jerusalem, ... the eve of Tabernacles, after my having left Byzantium - may the God of Israel desolate it! The Lord has been gracious unto me and has saved me from great tribula-

tion [lines 2-4] ... The Lord has rescued me from prison in Constantinople, and while I was in Byzantium, I vowed that if He
would save me, I would live in Jerusalem [7-9] ...
[Verso] To... Abū Yahyā Nahrai b. Nissīm ... b. Nahrai....
From Israel b. Nathan.... b. Nahrai ..., his cousin.... [Arabic
characters] From Isrā'īl b. Sahalūn.... To Fustāt.

Genizah letter, ed. with Hebrew tr. by Starr, «On Nahrai b.
Nissīm of Fustāt», *Zion,* I, 1936, 443; II, 92. A later letter refers to
the death of the writer's son in Byzantium, leaving a child surviving;
l. c., 446, lines 25 f.

The quaestor had jurisdiction over foreigners sojourning in the
capital; Zachariä, *Gesch. d. griech.-röm. Rechts,* 368. But he apparently
relegated this function to a lesser official termed for short ὁ βάρβαρος.
See Bury, *The imperial administrative system in the ninth century.*
London, 1911, p. 93.

With the curse on Cp. cf. no. **63**, and the Byzantine Karaite
exegetes who apply Biblical threats directed against the Edomites to
the capital of «Edom». Jacob b. Reuben on Ezek. 35:7, *Sefer ha-ʿOsher,*
9b; Aaron b. Elijah (14th c.). *Keter Torah,* ed. J. Savsakan. Eupatoria,
1866-67. IV, 38b (on Obad. 18, in the name of «our sages», i. e. the
standard interpretation).

1062   **147**
It is not just that requests which come from holy and pious
men,... whatever they may be, should be rejected. Especially
since they concern the grant of the Jews, or rather, not the grant
but the overlordship (ἐπικυρώσεως) which has been presented by
others because of their pious virtue..., to the existent monastery
near them [the Jews], as the writing sets forth...

The emperor who preceded us [Isaac I ?] honored them and
rewarded their laborby bestowing many gifts on their newly-built
monastery. In addition to the multitude of gifts, he awarded to
their monastery the Jews inhabiting that island, who number 15
families. Hence they requested of our Majesty also to confirm
chrysobull 576 of the grant of the Jews.

* These fifteen families shall remain in the dwellings owned
by the monastery and under its control, under penalty of triple

the *kephalétiôn* and the rent. The island is closed to any other Hebrews who may wish to settle on it. The children born to the residents shall also be subject to the monastery... May, 6570 [A.M.].

Constantine X. ed. Zepos, *Jus graecor.*, I, 640; Zolôtas, *op. cit.*, 297 f.; Dölger, *Regesten,* I, pt. 2, 14, no. 950. The last paragraph, lacking in the ms. published by Zolôtas (and repr. by Zepos), is based on the abstract from Adrianople codex 1156 (now lost) by B. K. Stephanides, *BZ*, XIV, 1905, 594. Its content agrees with the rubric περὶ τῆς ἐπαυξήσεως κτλ., which is borne by the published copy as well. Cf. Brutzkus, *EJ,* V, 486.

1065-80 **148**

.... To R. Judah,... the *Nagid* ... b. ... R. Saadiah [Fustāt]...

.... When our captors and mockers saw that the⟨y c⟩ould not, ... then the first fence was breached. They brought us into the market and we were sold for 49, 50, 70, 87, and 100 dinars, respectively, to Moslems and Ch⟨ristians⟩. We remained with our purchasers for 5 days, when the leaders of the community went weeping bitterly, and supplicated ⟨the officials of⟩ the city. God helped them and we were returned to the pirates against their will. They were so enraged that they threatened to kill us; they treated us very cruelly. They tied our hands behind our backs so tightly that they bled. They shackled our feet and beat us mercilessly. Then the leaders of the community came and took us, it being stipulated that the ransom be paid within a certain period.

And now, sirs,... take pity on us and save us from the sword. Those pirates cannot take us elsewhere to sell us, for they have collected a party ready for a raid in Byzantium (*Yavan*). This community [Alexandria?] is already weakened and cannot even maintain us... The pirates have sworn that on the day set they will either behead us in full view of the community, or will sell us to the Christians and Moslems.....

Mann, *Jews in Egypt,* II, 363-65; for the dating, I, 207 f. The assumption that these 5 captives came from the Empire is quite plausible, but there is, of course, no certainty.

1073 **149**

... They laid the task of piercing his [ex-emperor Romanos IV's] eyes, on a certain Jew who had no experience in such matters (τινα Ἰουδαῖον ἀμαθῆ.... τὴν διαχείρεισιν ἐπιτρέπουσι).... They brought the Jew to pierce his eyes with an iron.... He [Romanos] was not to suffer once and be quit of the agony, but three times did that scion of the deicide thrust the iron into his eyes...

Michael Attaleiates (contemporary). *Historia,* ed. W. Brunet. [*CSHB*, L] Bonn, 1853. p. 178. See Dölger, *Regesten,* I, pt. 2, 18. no. 991. On the institution in general, Schlumberger, *L'epopée byz.,* I, 66. The later materials on the use of Jews for such a purpose may be found as follows: 1. In the Empire and Bulgaria, end of 13th c., Georgios Pachymeres. Ἀνδρόνικος Παλαιολόγος, ed. Bekker. Bonn, 1835. [*CSHB*, XXV] pp. 229, 265. 2. Earlier in the same c. in the latter country, Mann, *REJ,* LXXXII, 372. 3. Under the Venetians, C. Roth. *History of the Jews in Venice.* Philadelphia, 1930. pp. 296, 311; I. Levy, *REJ,* XXVI, 1893, 202 f. 4. Serbia *ca.* 1350, Miller, *CMH,* IV, 548. 5. Under the Turks *ca.* 1500 in Morocco, and Palermo; Assaf, *Tarbiz,* V, 224-26.

See Bees, *Byz.-neugr. Jahr.,* II, 164, n. 4, who denies that it was a Byzantine custom. Ct. M. Lewin. «Eine Notiz zur Geschichte der Juden im byzantinischen Reiche». *Monats.,* XIX, 1870, 119; apparently the earliest writer to express a contrary opinion.

1077 **150**

He [the rebel John Bryennios] hurled fire on the houses stretching from St. Panteleémôn to the highest parts of the Stenon. The flame caught on and consumed all but a few of the houses... Especially of the Jewish ones, since they were all built of wood, none escaped the rush of the flames. (καὶ μᾶλλον τῶν Ἰουδάϊκων, διὰ τὸ ξύλοις καρτηρτίσθαι πάσας, οὐδεμία διέφυγε τὴν τοῦ πυρὸς ἐρωήν).

Attaleiates, *op. cit.,* 252. Cf. Heyd, *op. cit.,* I, 250.

1079 **151**

... and the *kephalétiôn* of the fifteen families of Jews with their exemption from taxation... June, 6687 [A.M.]...

Nikephoros III, in a renewal of the previous grants made to the

Nea Moné; ed. Zepos, *op. cit.*, 643; Zolôtas, II, 303. Dölger, *Regesten*, I, pt. 2, 21, no. 1030; date 1078 corrected by V. Laurent, *Echos d'O.*, XXVI, 1927, 349.

1082 **152**

He [Alexios I] also gave the Venetians all the shops running from the old Hebraic anchorage (παλαιὰ Ἑβραϊκὴ σκάλα) to that called *Bigla*.

Anna Comnena. Ἀλέξιας, ed. A. Reifferscheid. Leipzig, 1884. vi, 5, vol. I, 195; tr. E. A. S. Dawes. *The Alexiad.* London, 1928. p. 147. Dölger, *Regesten*, I, pt. 2, 27; no. 1081.

This pier figures under other names, such as *Hebraika*, and *Iudeca*, in various later connections. The chief difficulty in fixing its location is the question whether or not it is identical with the *Porta Hebraika*, also called *Porta de Perama;* see the map in *Dict. d'arch. chr.*, II, 1389. See the discussion in H. F. Brown, *JHS*, XL, 1920, 71-77; ct. A. van Millingen. *Byzantine Constantinople.* London, 1899. pp. 216 f., 221, n. 8. Heyd, *op. cit.*, I, 250.

The fact that this was once actually a «Jewish pier» is emphasized by Beés, *EL*, VIII, 389, 392, who also offers the hypothesis that it contained the residences of the Jewish community during the early part of our period; see also no. **2 n.**

For the theory which takes the name in the sense of the stairway to the Jewish cemetery, see Krauss, *Studien*, 81; Brown, *l. c.*, 78. It conflicts with the fact that this cemetery was located, like the Jewish quarter, on the *opposite* shore of the Golden Horn; no. **190.**

1096 **153**

a. .... Now although «the threshing-floor» is not yet filled, know you, our brethren, blessed of the Lord, that in this year the promise of our God has been fulfilled: an innumerable multitude of Franks (*'Ashkenazim*) has come, with their wives and all their money, and the Lord has gathered them into «the threshing-floor». When the Gentiles and the Jews asked of them, «Why have you abandoned your homes and your land?», their leaders reply, «'The mountains of darkness' have drawn near to us, and now they are revealed to us in a great light. We saw a nation with innumerable tents, and we did not recognize their language.

One man stepped forth from their midst, and said to us, 'Go on your way.' Thus have we come to you. Thus have we been pursued [*nirdafim;* or, «persecuted»] and have arrived».

b. We said, «Surely, God has fulfilled his promise: 'To them that are in darkness, show yourselves'. These are the other [ten] tribes. And when all the Franks shall have gone to Palestine, and 'the threshing-floor' shall have been filled, then will God say, 'Arise and thresh, O daughter of Zion', etc.».

c. All the congregations have been stirred, and have repented before God with fasting and almsgiving, ... those from Khazaria. As they said, 17 communites went out to the wilderness of the Gentiles, but we do not know whether they have met with the tribes or not... from the land of France whence they had despatched a messenger bearing letters to Constantinople. But we do not as yet know exactly what they contained, hence, we cannot communicate it to you.

d. Now at Constantinople [or rather], at Abydos near Constantinople, some small congregations have arisen, in accordance with the words of Daniel, ... «The children of the violent», etc. They said, «Elijah has revealed himself unto us». But instead of receiving them, both we and the community of Constantinople utterly excommunicated them.

e. Permit us now to relate what transpired in Saloniki, in the holy community. There came foreigners, Jewish and Christian, and officials *(shiltonim),* who reported that Elijah... had revealed himself openly, and not in a dream, to certain men of standing. They witnessed many signs and miracles there which the Jews and Christians relate. He revealed himself to R. Eliezer b. R. Judah b. R. Eliezer the Great, and as the foreigners say, he gave him a staff. It was the Christians, however, who in good faith gave the clearest version of the miracles which took place in Saloniki. The Jews are idly neglecting their work. R. Tobiah also sent a scholar *[talmid]* with an open letter to Constantinople to apprise them of the good news. A Jewish fellow-townsman of ours was there, who is somewhat learned. He saw the letter sent by R. Tobiah, and it said, «Signs and miracles have taken place among us. Yea, Elijah has manifested himself to us». Moreover, thus testified the Jew, Michael the German: he saw in R. Tobiah's letter that a totally blind man, Michael b. R. Aaron *he-ḥaber*, who was in Saloniki, regained his eyesight. R. Nissīm also knows that man. By an oversight, this Michael neglected to make a copy of the letter. Had he brought us one, we would have forwarded it to you to convince you.

f. Moreover, we have definite information that R. Ebyatar *ha-Kohen*, the head of the academy, sent a letter from Tripolis [Syria] to the community of Constantinople. Four men were there who saw the letter in the care of Lugiz the Christian. But they likewise did not take the trouble to bring us a copy, being ignoramuses.

g. At the present time, we are looking forward to receiving letters from R. Tobiah, and from the holy congregations. For we are amazed at the great miracle that has occurred in Saloniki, where the Christians have always hated the Jews most intensely, as R. Nissīm knows. For had the sign and great miracle not taken place, and had the king not heard of it, not one of the Jews would have escaped. At the present time they dwell in great security; free of the poll-tax *(gulgolet)* and the other levies *(ʿonashim)*, they sit garbed in prayer-shawls and do no work. We do not know what they are expecting, and we are in constant dread lest it become known to the Gentiles and they kill us. But at the present time the governor *(shilton)* himself and the archbishop *(hegmon ha-gadol)* say, «O Jews, why remain in Saloniki? Sell your homes and property (the emperor protects *[ʿozer]* them and no man may harm them). You have not yet set out despite the fact that we have definitely learned that your Messiah has appeared».

h. Praise be to God that we have no fear, and that we too have repented with fasting and alms-giving. Many fast daily and others on Monday and Thursday. They receive stripes, and confess their sins. Before we got this report that in Saloniki both Jews and Christians were seeing visions, we knew nothing of the events in Saloniki. We refused to believe their words, and used to rebuke them until a Jewish *kohen* saw in his dream, before the matter was announced, that all the Byzantine congregations were to gather in Saloniki, and would leave from there. We rebuked him, and said that they were the enemies of Israel, until Tobiah came from Thebes, bringing a letter saying that signs and miracles had transpired in Saloniki, and that other congregations were gathering there. Soon Tobiah will come thither [to you] and will relate to you what he has heard and seen; thus the dream which the Jewish *kohen* saw will come true.

i. Now, our brethren, if God has vouchsafed you some happy report or good news, — for we are aware of the things which our master, the head of the academy, has heard and knows — then do us the kindness of writing us what you know and have heard. Have no fear, for even the king has heard of it, and we are not afraid. And if a letter should come from you, our entire community would be encouraged in their repentance. May God reward you well; may you be deemed worthy of experiencing His graciousness, and of visiting His Temple. I, Menahem, should like to go to Palestine [or, «Syria»] to see the Frankish soldiers passing in great number — I know not whither they will spread. May God defend you and us, Amen!

This is copied from the original in the possession of the illustrious R. Nissīm. . . .

[Margin] This is the letter which R. Menahem b. R. Elijah sent. [Interlinear] Written on 8 Ab [July]. Solomon.

Mann, «The Messianic movements during the first Crusades». (Hebrew) *Hatequfah,* XXIII, 1924, 253-59; tr. Kaufmann, «Ein Brief aus dem byzantinischen Reiche über eine messianische Bewegung den Judenheit und der zehn Stämme aus dem Jahre 1096». *BZ,* VII, 1898, 85-90. (Based on the original ed. of Neubauer, *JQR,* IX, 1896, 26-9). Cf. the 12th c. (?) situation in Sicily and elsewhere, apparently including Morea, Mann, *Texts,* I, 34-44; Krauss, *HUC An.,* X, 275-96.

Annotations: Lines 1-3: Quotation from Micah 4: 11 f. omitted from tr.

a. Line 4: See *ib.* The traditional interpretation of this passage, e. g., by Rashī, pictures the Gentile armies assembling for combat in Jerusalem, on the eve of the advent of the Messiah, without realizing the import of their movements. Line 5: For *Ashkenazim* in this sense, see Poznanski, *ZfhB,* XV, 1911, 76; also no. **154.** Krauss' hypothesis that it denotes Khazars is extremely rash; *Tarbiz,* III, 1932, 423-30. See Mann's refutation, *l. c.,* IV, 391-94, and Krauss, *Jewish Studies . . . Kohut,* 387 f. Line 6: Evidently indicating one of the groups which comprised the People's Crusade. See H. von Sybel. *Geschichte des ersten Kreuzzugs.* 2nd ed. Leipzig, 1881. pp. 81 f. Although no specific mention of such a band passing through Thessalonica occurs, that town did lie on the overland route of some of the later knights' corps. See Fulcher of Chartres. *Historia Hierosolymitana,* ed. H. Hagenmeyer. Heidelberg, 1913. I, viii, 7, p. 174, and n. 25. Lines 10-14: The terms of the reply are unquestionably Jewish, and consequently Kaufmann, followed by Dubnow, *Weltgesch.,* IV, 418, n. 1, jumped to the conclusion that the *Ashkenazim* are German Jews. Mann, however, dissents, and more plausibly attributes the Jewish connotations of their reply to the coloring supplied by the excited local Jews. Concurring in this one may add that it is inconceivable that a band of Jews should have come through Central Europe at this time, and have lived to tell the tale. Krauss, *Tarbiz,* III, 429, n. 30, restores the word *'eslekem* at the beginning of line 14. Kaufmann's emendation, *nifradim,* is unnecessary; *l. c.,* 86, n. 2.

b. Line 15: In the traditional interpretation these words are made to refer to that portion of the lost ten tribes which had settled near the «mountains of darkness» (line 10). See S. M. Lazar, *Hashiloah,* IX, 1902, 51 f.

c. Line 20: Lacuna after *ben;* for emendations, Krauss, *l. c.;* Mann, *REJ,* LXXXIX, 1930, 254, n. Note the Arabism *al-Khazaria;* cf. lines 24-6. It undoubtedly denotes the Crimea (Mann, *Tarbiz,* IV, 392 f.), termed *Gazaria* in Genoese documents; Heyd, *op. cit.,* II, 171, 195, 296. Line 21: Ezek. 20:35. Line 24: French Jewry had experienced a Messianic movement earlier in the c.; Friedlaender, *JQR,* II, 1912, 492, 506 f.; Mann, *Hatequfah,* XXIV, 356-68.

d. Line 25: The only other reference to a Jew in Abydos is, if correctly interpreted, the epitaph of Joseph b. Aaron of ABUDN,

found n. of Jerusalem; S. Klein, *Qobes* of the Jewish Palestine Explo-
ration Society, I, 1925, 94. Line 27: Dan. 11:14. Lines 28-9: The first
two words are Arabic. The repetition of the biblical quotation is to
be deleted.

e. Line 40: This Tobiah (cf. lines 43, 46) is evidently an important local figure, known to the addressee. All have agreed in identi-
fying him with T. b. Eliezer (no. **164**), on the theory that he came
with other members of his community to Thessalonica, the general
gathering-place (line 84). Line 47: On the title, Mann, *Jews in Egypt*,
I, 272-77. Line 49: on Nissīm, the addressee, who succeeded his
father Nahrai (no. **140**) to the leadership of Fustāt, see Mann, *op. cit.*,
I, 206f.

f. Line 62. With *gulgolet* cf. *kephalétiòn* no. **143n**. Line 63: Dölger, *Viertel.*, XXVI, 14, n. 3, (following Kaufmann) takes *'onashim*
in its basic sense, and hence, corresponding to the ζημίαι and κακώσεις.
But note its use in the sense of the annual *kharāj*, Cowley, *JQR*,
XIX, 108, line 6. Line 69: Mann would relieve the awkwardness by
reading *lakem* twice.

i. *Verso,* Line 2, *me'esel* (Arabism)=*min 'and*; cf. *infra*, line 10.
Line 5: On the ambiguity of *Sha'm* in Jewish documents, see Mann,
Texts, I, 264, n. 1. The possibility that it might mean Syria here is
suggested by our writer's use of the usual Hebrew designation for
Palestine in line 17.

1096-97 **154**

Some Karaite scholars narrate in their writings that it happened once that the [waning] moon appeared in the morning in
the east while the Rabbinites were reciting the New Year's Day
hymns. This took place in Constantinople in the reign of King
Alexios, at the time when the Franks *(Ashkenazim)* came to
Constantinople.

Then with regard to another time we are informed by trustworthy witnesses that the appearance of the new moon was noted
[in Palestine]. Thereupon the Karaites proclaimed the new month
[Nīsan], whereas the Rabbinites had calculated it for the next
day. This took place at the time of the arrival of R. Shemaria
Alexander at Constantinople. The author giving this incident
relates, moreover, that some of the Rabbinites took this into

consideration and performed the burning of the leaven on the same evening as the Karaites.

Aaron b. Elijah (14th c.). *Gan 'Eden,* ed. J. Savsakan. Eupatoria, 1866. i, 8, p. 8d. Cf. Mann, *Texts,* II, 43. In determining the exact year of the first incident, it should be borne in mind that whereas the band led by Peter the Hermit arrived on August 1, 1096, the knights did not come until the end of that year; Chalandon, *CMH,* IV, 336f. On *Ashkenazim,* see no. **153 n.**, and Mann, *Hatequfah,* XXIII, 260, line 12. Cf. the ambiguity of Γερμανοί, noted by G. L. F. Tafel. *Komnenen nnd Normannen.* 2nd ed., Stuttgart, 1870. p. 118, n. 194. The second item is ambiguous, and one cannot determine whether it refers to any time prior to the 13th c. For a similar situation in Palestine see Sahl b. Maslīah, in S. Pinsker. *Liqquté Qadmoniot.* Vienna, 1860. Appendix, p. 33.

1096-*ca.* 1100   **155**

... This saint [Eustratios] was taken captive together with other Christians and was sold to a certain Jew among many others. Instructing and exhorting the captives he warned them thus: «Brethren, if you have been baptized and believe in God, let us not violate our vow taken in holy baptism ... » Thus had Eustratios been taken captive by the godless Hagarenes [Polovtzi] and had been sold to a Jew. After several days had passed, they began to die from hunger and faint from thirst, some after three days, others after seven, the stronger ones after ten days, and so all died of hunger and thirst. They had been 50 in all: 30 monastic laborers, and 20 from Kiev; but after 14 days had passed, only this one monk remained alive, being a habitual faster since his youth. The Jew seeing this now turned his attention to the captives, and prepared his Passover for them. With the day of the Lord's resurrection approaching he committed an outrage upon St. Eustratios, after the manner described in the Gospel, as well as upon our Lord Jesus Christ... For on that day the Jews nailed him to a cross, whereupon he thanked God for it and lived 15 days more. The Jew said to him: «Come now, you fool, eat food according to the Law, yea, in order that you

14

may live. For Moses, after having received the Law from God, gave it to us, and in those books it is said: 'Cursed are all who are hanged on a tree'» [cf. Dt. 21 : 23].

But the monk replied: «God has deemed me worthy of a signal blessing — to suffer martyrdom on this day. He says to me as to the robber: 'This day shall you be with Me in Paradise'. [Lk. 23 : 43].... But you and the Jews who are with you will weep and wail this day, for there has come an answer from God unto you, for the sake of my blood and that of all Christians....».

Hearing how the crucified man was reviling him, the Jew seized a spear and pierced him through. In this wise did he give up his soul to his Lord... Then on account of this affair an announcement *(vyest)* was sent out by the emperor about this time concerning the Jews, viz., that they should all be expelled, their possessions confiscated and elders executed. For such was the situation: A certain wealthy and very enterprising Jew had turned Christian, and because of this the emperor received him in audience, and a few days later appointed him eparch [of Cherson]. Having obtained this office he continued to despise Christ and his faith, and granted the Jews throughout the Greek Empire permission to purchase Christians for their service. But this impious eparch was discovered and was executed, in accordance with the words of St. Eustratios, together with all the other Jews living in Cherson. And the Jew's property was confiscated, as well as that of the saint's murderer... When the accursed Jews witnessed the awful miracle [disappearance of E. 's corpse], they were converted and became Christians.

Simon, bishop of Vladimir-Suzdal (13th c.), on the monks of the Pechera monastery at Kiev, in *Kievo-Pecherskii Paterik,* ed. D. Abramovich. Kiev, 1930. pp. 106-08. The chronology is assured by the account of the capture of the monks of this monastery by the Polovtzi on July 20, 1096 in the *Russian Primary Chronicle,* tr. Cross, *l. c.,* 274. See I. Malishevsky. *Evrei v' yuzhnoi Rusi i Kievye v' X-XII vyekakh'.* Kiev, 1878. pp. 96-100. (Repr. from *Trudy* of the Kievskaya Dukhovnaye Akademiia, 1878, no. 3.) See also Vasiliev, *Jour. of ec.*

and bus. his., IV, 327. On the basis of the last words of Eustratios the Gustynski chronicle (17th c.) states that he prophesied the massacres in the West; *Polmoye Sobranie Russkikh Letopisei.* Petrograd, 1843. II, p. 282.

1097 **156**

... Therein [Cp.] are assembled Greeks, Bulgars,.... also Jews and proselytes, Cretans, and Arabs, and members of all the nations. (...in ea Graeci, Bulgari,... Iudaei quoque et proselyti, Cretes et Arabes, omniumque nationum gentes conveniunt.)

Bartolf de Nangis (12th c.). « Gesta Francorum Iherusalem expugnantium.» *Recueil des historiens des croisades: Historiens occidentaux*, III. Paris, 1866. v, p. 494. The passage is modelled on Acts 2:11, and constitutes an extension of a passage in Fulcher, *op. cit.*, ed. Hagenmeyer, ix, p. 116, and n. 1. Bartolf is in turn copied by the « Anonymi Rhenani Historia et Gesta Ducis Gotfridi.» *Recueil*, V, vii, p. 448.

1097 **157**

They [Bohemond and his men] departed from Castoria and encamped at Pelagonia.... Here they justly burned all travellers, Jews, heretics, and Saracens, whom everybody calls enemies of God.

Baudri (Baldricus) of Bourgueil (12th c.), « Historia Jerosolimitana,» i, 17; *Recueil*, IV, 23. The source on which this is based mentions only the heretics (Paulicians) as the victims. See L. Bréhier, ed. and tr., *Histoire anonyme de la première Croisade*. Paris, 1924. pp. xiv, 22.

ca. 1100-75 **158**

... This custom prevails in Germany, in Rome, and elsewhere in the diaspora, but not in the land of Greece. There the cantor recites the benediction [introducing the *Hallel*], and all others remain silent. This I do not approve of....

Joseph b. Plat, cited in *Sefer ha-Pardes le-Rashi,* ed. H. L. Ehrenreich. Budapest, 1924. p. 208. The scholar quoted lived in Lunel in the 12th c.; Horodetzky, *EJ*, IX, 37. Epstein has suggested that he was acquainted with the customs of the places mentioned at first hand, although, of course, there are other possibilities; *Monats.*, XLIV,

1900, 291. (He also mentions a *paytan* named Benjamin b. Samuel, who is said to have been Joseph's grandfather, and whom he supposed to have lived in the Empire; *l.c.*, 295f. A w. European provenience is, however, the accepted one; J. Heller, *EJ*, IX, 371.)

Excursus B:

On the Byzantine-Jewish Liturgy

For the three editions ef the *Mahzor Romaniah,* see Davidson *Osar,* I, lvi. Analysis of contents, Zunz, *Ritus,* 79-83. For noteworthy citations of additional material in mss., see Zunz, *ZfhB,* XIX, 1916, 56; Brann, *Monats.,* LXII, 1918, 276f. L. Belléli, *JQR,* XVII, 1905, 163-67, 585; Neubauer and Cowley. *Catalogue of the Hebrew mss. in the Bodleian Library.* Oxford, 1906. II, no. 2895, pp. 408f. (This deals with a lengthy *yoser* for Passover by Abraham Ezrah b. Mattitiah, on whom see Schirmann, *EJ,* VI, 794, and *Mibhar,* 78f.)

On the *Haggadah,* A. Spanier, *EJ,* VII, 788, 792f. For the peculiar recitation of the prayer '*al ha-nissim,* Rosanes, *Dibré yemé yisrael be-Tugarmah.* Tel Aviv, 1930. I, 207. For miscellaneous details, Ginzberg, *ZfhB,* IX, 1905, 106f.; *id., Geonica,* I, 124, n. 1, 127, n. 2, 203, II, 110, 112, 260, n. 3. L. Finkelstein, *JQR,* XVI, 1925, 137f. (the '*amidah).*

The announcement of the New Moon in Greek is given by Brann, *l.c.;* cf. Zunz, *l.c.* A *qinah* for the Ninth of Ab is said to be found in a 13th c. ms.; Papadopoulos-Kerameus, «Ein vulgärgriechisches Klagelied griechischer Juden.» *Hakedem,* I, 35-39. See also, Schwab, *Rapport sur une Mission de Philologie en Grèce: Épigraphie et Chirographie.* Paris, 1913. pp. 119-43; Krauss, *Studien.* 124, n. 2.

On the reading of Jonah in Greek, see Meir b. Israel Katzenellenbogen. (16th c.) *Sheelot u-teshubot.* Cracow, 1882. no. 78, p. 112. The text in Greek transcription is given by D.C. Hesseling. « Le livre de Jonas.» *BZ,* X, 1901, 208-17. For facsimile of the first page of the Oxford ms, see *EJ,* IX, 554. The text in Hebrew characters of 1:1-3 and 3:1-3 was published by L. Modona. *Catalogo dei codici ebraici della Università di Bologna (Cataloghi dei codici orientali di alcune biblioteche d'Italia,* IV). Florence, 1889. no. 12, pp. 333-38. For theories as to the provenance of these two mss., see Belléli, *REJ,* XXII, 251; *id., JE,* VII, 311; Romanos, *REJ,* XXIII, 64. Cf. Krauss, *Studien,* 122f.

ca. 1100   **159**

Leo the Stammerer (Μοῦγγος), formerly a Jew, called from
his ancestors to serve as teacher unto the Gentiles.

H. Gelzer. *Der Patriarchat von Achrida. (Abhandlungen* of the
Königliche Sächsischen Gesellschaft der Wissenschaften: philoso-
phisch-historisch Classe, XX, no. 5) Leipzig, 1902. p. 7, no. 18. Ivanov,
B'lgarski Starini, 567. From an ancient list of the patriarchs of Bulgaria; the incumbency of this convert falls somewhere between 1092-
1134. Cf. S. Mézan, *EJ,* IV, 1191, who takes the epithet as a proper
name, «Mung»!

This is the earliest reference to a Jew in Bulgaria cited up to
the present, and no faith is to be placed in statements concerning
the transfer of Byzantine Jews thither in the 9th and 10th cc.: M.
Franco, *JE,* III, 425 f.; and most recently, Mézan, *l.c.,* who, however,
admits elsewhere that such statements cannot be supported. See his
Les juifs espagnols en Bulgarie. Sofia, 1925. I, 9. Nor is it correct for
Franco and Mézan to mention the well-known Christian writer,
Simeon Seth, as a Jew; see Krumbacher, *Gesch. der byz. Litt.,* 896.

** *ca.* 1100 - 18   **160**

The doctrine of the Trinity can be supported from passages
in the Old Testament. Not only does God speak in the plural on
occasion, and His Person seen to be threefold but His Word
and Spirit are mentioned. Secondly, Christ eminently fulfilled
the prophecies regarding the Messiah. He is the «son of man»,
the son of the Virgin, and he was born in Bethlehem. He is sin-
less, a wonder-worker, and God. Christendom is the realization of
the Messianic age in that it is eternal, all-embracing, and bears
a new name. Christ has experienced both the sufferings and the
resurrection prophesied for the Messiah. The time indicated in
Daniel for the end of the Jewish cult is past, as the destruction
of the Temple shows. In place of the former sacrifices, there is
now the eucharist, for the Law of servitude, the law of freedom,
for circumcision, baptism, for the Sabbath, the Lord's Day. Hence,
the Jew cannot cite the Old Testament to justify his attitude
toward Christianity.

Euthymios Zigabénos. Πανοπλία Δογματική, c. VIII: «Against the Hebrews»; *PG,* CXXX, 257-305. See J. Wickert, «Die Panoplia dogmatica des Euthymios Zigabenos». *Or. chr.,* VIII, 1907, 337-39.

ca. 1100? **161**

... In this case the reason is to avoid discouraging him [the money-lender]. Such is the explanation given by R. Moses Dābā of Greece, may the memory of a righteous man be blessed!

Isaac b. Abba Marī (Marseilles, *ca.* 1180). *Sefer ha-ʿIttur,* ed. M. Katz. Vilna, 1874-75. II, 37a, line 2. With reference to *Shebuʿot* 41b.

1100-1200? **162**

... To my dear brothers Abū Saʿīd and Solomon, from your sister Malīhah,... and my little daughter Zoé respectfully greets you...

I have been separated from you for several years and desire greatly to see you again... But I cannot [journey to you], for the time is inauspicious. For I had prepared to go with these people, when I looked into the Torah-scroll and struck an unfavorable prognostication; hence, I could not go with them. Now, by Heaven, you have seen that when men from the communities of Byzantium *(Romaniah)* are taken captive, their relatives go to ransom them. So why should not one of you risk his life to come for me and take me back? I cannot allow myself to accompany another... But if I come thither and that disaster befall me, it were better that I died.... merchandise and come hither to Byzantium... and let one of you take some merchandise...

Man, *Jews in Egypt,* II, 306 f.; cf. I, 241 f. On bibliomancy see Grünwald and Kohler, *JE,* III, 202-205; E. von Dobschütz, *Encyclopedia of Religion and Ethics,* II, 611. This specific practice is known in contemporary Egypt, according to the statement of Maimonides cited by Mann, *op. cit.,* II, 307, n. 1. Among Byzantine Christians the practice is said to have been rare; Krumbacher, *Gesch. der byz. Litt.,* 631.

1102- *ca.* 1105 **163**

.... To the holy congregations, ... who live in the land of Edom, in the royal city of Bosrah, called Constantinople....

I wish to inform you that I am a former official of the king of Egypt, ... al-Afdal... Time and time again did slanderers and enemies lie about me to him, but he paid no attention to them, until there came a season of visitation, and they caused me to become subject to a heavy fine....

Following these events, the king promoted a Christian, Yuhanna [?], the brother of *NVUpatriarki,* who last year accompanied the king's envoy from Egypt to Constantinople. It pleased this Christian to try to expel all the Jews from the government offices. Now there was a pious and saintly Jewish physician inthe court of this greatking,... and his name was Meborak... Whenthis *Nagid* died [1098]... the hand of the Christians waslaid heavily upon them...

Neubauer, «Egyptian fragments, C.» *JQR,* IX, 29-36; tr. Kaufmann, «Letter sent to Constantinople by Alafdhal's ex-minister of finances». *l.c.,* X, 430-44 (introd.); *id.,* «Beiträge zur Geschichte Ägyptens aus jüdischen Quellen». *ZDMG,* LI, 1897, 444-47 (body). See also Mann, *Jews in Egypt,* I, 211 f., for corrections and historical discussion. Cf. Dinaburg, *Yisrael ba-golah,* II, 100 f., 218 (bizarre interpretation of the address). Communications between Alexios I and the contemporary ruler of Egypt are recorded for the years 1098, 1102, 1104, and 1105; Dölger, *Regesten,* I, pt. 2, 47 f., nos. 1209, 1216, 1220, 1222, However, Abū'l Qasim Shāhānshāh, surnamed *al-Malik al-Afdal,* served as vizir until 1121; Graefe, *En. Is.,* II, 91. On «Bosrah», Krauss, *Studien,* 109.

1107- *ca.* 1120 **164**

a. ... The fourth method of exegesis ... is that of the scholars of Greece, who ignore rational and grammatical considerations, and rely on the homiletical method *(derash),* as in *Leqah Tob* and *Or 'Enayim.* Now in view of the fact that homiletical interpretations abound in the works of the ancients, why should modern scholars go to the trouble of re-writing them?....

Abraham Ibn Ezra (*ca.* 1150), introd. to commentary on the Pentateuch, ed. and tr. D. Rosin. *Die Reime und Gedichte des Abraham Ibn Ezra.* Breslau, 1885. I, 35 f. See Bacher, «Die Bibelexegese vom Anfang des 10ten bis zum 16ten Jahrhundert», in Winter and Wünsche, *Die jüdische Litteratur,* II, 271, *b.* ... The author of *Leqah Tob* begins every weekly section with the word *tob* or *tobah*. He is the great scholar R. Tobiah of Byzantium *(Yavan)* of the city of Castoria, who lived about three [ms. «six»] hundred years ago....

Judah b. Moses Mosconi (1362). *« Eben ha-'Ezer»* (super-commentary on Ibn Ezra), cited by Buber, introd. to *Leqah Tob* on Gen.-Ex., p. 20. (On the ms., H. Hirschfeld, *JQR,* XIV, 1902, 168 f., no. 149.)

Editions of the commentary are as follows: Gen.-Ex., ed. S. Buber. Vilna, 1880; reviewed by Steinschneider, *HB,* XXI, 1882, 29-32; N. Brüll, *Jahrbücher für jüdische Geschichte und Litteratur,* V, 1883, 132-38. Lev.-Dt., ed. A. M. Padua. Vilna, 1884. Cant., ed. A. W. Greenup. London, 1909; reviewed by Poznanski, *ZfhB,* XIII, 1909, 75-80, XIV, 131, n. 1. See also S. Salfeld, *Magazin,* V, 1878, 141-44; *ZfhB,* III, 1899, 3. Ruth, ed. S. Bamberger. Mayence, 1887. Lam., ed. J. Nacht. Frankfort, 1895; ed. Greenup. London, 1908. Eccl., ed. G. Feinberg, Berlin, 1904. Esther, ed. Buber, *Sifré d'Agadta 'al Megillat Esther.* Vilna, 1886. pp. 85-112.

References to scholars with whom he studied: his father, Buber, introd. to Gen., 15 f., and Cant., ed. Greenup, pp. 10, 12, 14, etc.; Samson, Buber, *op. cit.,* 22 f.; R. Moses, as the source of an oral citation from Saadia, Lam., 61 (identified with a scholar at Rome by Nacht, 30, n. 123). Full list of literary sources, Buber, *op. cit.,* 36-45.

He gives the year 1107-08 as the date of the composition of his commentary on Gen.; *ibid.,* 23-66. See also the references to the massacre at Mayence in 1096; Ex., 123, Cant., 15. Cf. Marx, *TQR,* XX, 1907, 241, 258.

On his treatment of occasional points of grammar and law, see Buber, *op. cit.,* 29.; Feinberg, 13-15. Note, e. g., his remarks on the custom (corresponding to the modern Sephardic procedure) of sounding the Shofar during the silent prayer of the New Year service, which he considered justifiable as an ancient tradition, although not obligatory; Lev.-Num., 131. See also an unnoticed reference to «the mourners of Zion», who on Purim shed their habitual black garments, and celebrated the holiday by washing and dressing in white; Esther, 111. Since such groups existed in Palestine, Yemen, and in Germany, it is plausible to suppose that Tobiah had seen them somewhere in the Empire; cf. Mann, *EJ,* I, 217-19.

Strictures on the Karaites: with reference to the interpretation of Lev. 18:18 (p. 102), and Dt. 21:15 (p. 70), on which see Poznanski,

REJ, XLV, 1902, 186, n., and ct. Schechter, *JQR,* IV, 1914, 456; against the *poter* of the Karaites who misinterpreted *mamzer,* Dt. 23:2 (p. 77), as a synonym for one with a sexual defect, as in the preceding verse (cf., however, the fact that certain Karaite commentators, including 3 from the Empire, referred the word *mamzer* to the Khazars; Harkavy, *Monats.,* XXXI, 1882, 170-72); without explicit mention, the remarks on *yibbum,* the Sabbath light, «the morrow of the Sabbath,» and, in general, against the innovators influenced by Islam (Gen., 192, Ex., 106, 115, Lev.-Num., 38 f.). See further, Buber, *op. cit.,* 34 f. and Marmorstein, in *Festschrift A. Schwartz,* Berlin, 1917, p. 469. See also the tr. of some selections by Bacher, *l. c.,* 273-75.

On the Greek glosses see Buber's introd., 27, and Perles, *BZ,* II, 574 f. But note the misrendering of *ochlosin* as «heroes» (Gen.-Ex., 150 end), and his evasion of the word δίκαιον in citing a rabbinic passage containing it (*ib.,* 73).

A lengthy list of the later writers who used these works is given in Buber's introd., 45-57. Cf. also H. P. Chajes. *Perush maseket Mashqin le-R. Shelomoh b. ha-yatom.* Berlin, 1909. (Verein Mek. Nird., ser. 3, I) p. XXVI. On their use by Solomon b. Parhon in Salerno (*ca.* 1200), Bacher, *Zeitschrift für die alttestamentliche Wissenschaft,* X, 1890, 138.

Excursus C:
An anonymous composition attributed to
Tobiah b. Eliezer.

A fragment of a commentary on Kalir's *qerobah* for the Ninth of Ab, *Zakor'ekah 'onu,* was published by Ginzberg, *Ginzé Schechter,* I, 246-97. (This *piyut* is still to be found in the *Mahzor Romaniah,* and the Byzantine provenance of the commentary thereon is assured by the six Greek glosses which it contains.) Ginzberg's theory of the authorship (accepted by Davidson, *Osar,* II, 210-12) is based on the following points: 1. Certain similarities between its content and Tobiah's introd. to Lam. (which he does not trouble to specify). Both follow the Talmud in citing Jer. 36 as a basis for the dating of Lam., and both cite the same passage from *Lam. R.* (Yet each manifests different errors of omission and misquotation!) 2. Certain minor stylistic evidence, such as the use of the expression *dabar'aher.* 3. The system of transliteration of glosses, which is, however, essentially common to all the Byzantine-Jewish writers who employ them. 4. The same ms.

contains the *Leqah Tob* on Ruth. Cf. Mann, *Am. Jour. of Sem. Lang. and Lit.*, XLVI, 269. *A priori* one would be justified in assuming that Tobiah b. Eliezer wrote no more than the relatively extensive commentaries on the Pentateuch and the Scrolls.

ca. 1110   **165**

The priests, to whom it was formerly necessary to offer a portion of one's life, now contribute a share of the taxes. O crucified Savior, Christians, thine own worshippers, O only son of God, are ruled by descendants of the Hebrews and are chastised by them!... These depraved modern Jews, such friends of Judas as they would have found, they stir them up against the teachers, prosecuting the defenders of God and defending his prosecutors, assessing upon them (?) tens of thousands of silver-pieces... Verily these latter-day Bellerophontes have been imported against their own clerks. They have brought them here in order to outcry their trusted men in antistrophe..... (Χριστιανῶν κρατοῦντας Ἑβραίων γόνους, — τοὺς σοὺς κολάστας..... τοὺς παμπονήρους νῦγ Ἰουδαίους νέους — ὅσους ἂν εὑρήσωσιν Ἰούδα φίλους, — κινοῦντας αὐτοὺς κατὰ τῶν διδασκάλων, — κατηγόρους μὲν τῶν Θεοῦ συνηγόρων, — ἱστῶντας αὐτοῖς ἀργύρια μυρία...... κἂν αὐτόχρημα Βελλερόφονται νέοι — τῶν καθ᾽ ἑαυτῶν εἰσκομισταὶ γραμμάτων. — οὓς γὰρ παρεισάγουσιν ὡς πιστευτέους — αὐτῶν κατακράζουσιν ἐξ ἀντιστρόφου....)

S. I. Doanidou. «The resignation of Nikolaos Mouzalôn from the archbishopric of Cyprus. An unpublished apologetic poem». Ἑλληνικά, VII, 1934, pp. 130 f., lines 656-60, 679-84, 691-95. Cf. Dölger, «Zu dem Abdankungsgedicht des Nikolaos Muzalôn. II. Politisches und Kulturgeschichtliches.» *BZ*, XXXV, 1935, 12.

ca. 1125   **166**

The author of *'Or 'Enayim* begins every weekly section with the word *'ôr* or *'ôrah*. He is the worthy scholar, R. Meir of Byzantium, who likewise lived in the city of Castoria, where for many years he was a student of R. Tobiah's. This information is derived from our local tradition which has been handed down from generation to generation.

Mosconi, *op. cit.*, continuing no. **164.**

ca. 1140 **167**

I, the humble and insignificant subject of your powerful and sacred Majesty [Manuel I], take the liberty of supplicating you, my sacred lord. Your subject is a former Jew in your loyal town of Attaleia,... who, realizing his sins, received in repentance the sacred baptism. Then, with the good fortune of your divine power, I baptized my three other brothers. Thereupon our thrice-blessed... emperor, your Majesty's... father [John II], was supplicated by us to award us the synagogue ('Ιουδαϊκόν) and residence (οἴκημα) of our [deceased] parents, and the few articles therein, which had been seized by the Jews. Our supplication was heard by... his sacred Majesty, and there were sent to us the rescript (λύσις) requested for the *praktôr*, ruling that the house must be turned over to us...

Zepos, *Jus graecor.*, I, 373 f.; *PG*, CXXXIII, 716 f. Cf. Dölger, *Regesten*, I, pt. 2, 62, no. 1327. On the emperor's court of appeal, Zachariä, *Gesch. d. gr.-röm. Rechts*, 355-61; on the *praktôr*, Dölger, *Beiträge*, 71-74.

On the contemporary importance of this town see Chalandon, *Les Comnènes*, II, 310-15, 626.

ca. 1140 **168**

... Some waters have curative properties for those who drink them, but others have an injurious effect. An example of the latter is the spring APTS... in the Orient. Its appearance is that of pure, clear waters which all may drink safely... It is located in the distant East, as we were told by Jacob Gargirin who had been there. Later he visited Constantinople... with his companions and told us what he had seen there. He told us that the name of the place was Khalqī Nasūr..., and that the king who rules there is named Sultan Sanyar...

Judah Hadassī, *Eshkol ha-Kofer*, s. 61, p. 30a. The passage occurs between two extracts from the work of Eldad ha-Danī (on whom see B. Suler, *EJ*, VI, 394-98). In addition the author (s. 60) gives a tale concerning a voyager from Cp., whose ship was driven to the land of the pygmies, where he fought a fierce battle with the birds of that region; cf. S. T. H. Hurwitz, *JQR,* VI, 1915, 355-57.

On the Seljuq ruler Sanjar (1086-1156), see Zetterstéen, *En. Is.,* IV, 151 f. The name of the spring is taken to be Νάφθα by Frankl, *Monats.,* XXIII, 1884, 516, but it is probably Oriental.

1141-50   169

... To our esteemed master, R. Samuel the Nagīd [b. Hananiah of Fustāt],... from Elijah b. R. Caleb b. R. L⟨eo⟩...

I, the undersigned, am obliged to inform my lord that I have come as he ordered me and am now in Benhē. When I arrived at Alexandria and observed their behavior, I ascribed it to the distance which separates them from your presence, and thought that perhaps those nearer to our master would show his influence. But behold them unwashed of their filth, so that men of learning are as animals to them, while the Torah and the statutes are of no account in their eyes...

If then I have found favor in the eyes of our master, do not put me off any longer, but for the sake of the glory of Heaven, enable me to present myself before you... May I receive your reply by my messenger, informing me how to transport some books which I have? Also, will I be able to enter in my present costume? For men have given me cause to fear on account of my language and costume...

Mann, *Jews in Egypt,* II, 288 f., cf. I, 230 f. Although there is no certainty that the writer did not come from a place in Latin Europe, the names in his signature are more frequent in the Empire. (The name Leo is assured by the signature in the last line of the *verso.*) He had spent the spring and summer in Alexandria, whence he had evidently first written to the Nagīd, who attempted to secure aid for him in the form of rabbinical work in a provincial community.

1141-50   170

... Account of the sum collected in the *Rif* for the ransom of the captives...

To our glorious master, Samuel the great Nagīd...

... There was expended on the captives from Byzantium *(Rūm)* the sum of forty-five *dirhems* or one and one-eighth *dīnars*...

Mann, *Jews in Egypt,* II, 289-91, cf. I, 232. The collection totaled 226 1/8 *dīnars,* which were contributed by 10 provincial communities. Cf. the famous autograph letter of Maimonides regarding a similar collection in 1173; ed. S. H. Margulies, *Monats.,* XLIV, 1900, 10 f.

1143-7   **171**

... Under your reign, this house was transformed by your humble servants into a church, the Hagia Anastasis, and we settled some monks in it... We broached the matter of our articles to the *praktôr* in order that he should turn them over to us. The Jews denied [having them]. Thereupon the *praktôr* ordered us to settle our suit by the charge of falsehood (συκοφάντικον) and by the termination-oath (τέλειον). I, being a Christian, was to formulate the *teleion,* which they were to accept, not in the form they desired but as I should set before them in writing, thus:

At first he should gird himself with bramble, sit astride a leathern bag, go down to the sea, spit three times on his circumcision, and say: «By Barassé Baraa Adonai Elôi Who led Israel across the Red Sea with dry feet, and gave them water to drink from a rock, and fed them manna and quails (although they became ungrateful and refrained from pork), by the Law which Adonai gave, and the spitting on the circumcision of the flesh, and the bramble with which my loins are girded, I do not invoke the name of the Lord Sabaoth for a falsehood. If I do, cursed be my children, may I grope along the wall like a blind man, and fall down a sightless one; may the earth open its mouth and swallow me like Dathan and Abiram.»

They shamelessly accepted this oath, and then after I had sworn to the *sykophantikon,* they refused to pronounce the *teleion.* And by bribing the *praktôr* they evaded the oath. It is for this reason that I supplicate and appeal to your... Majesty, to furnish me with a... rescript, ordering the present *praktôr* to make these Jews, even if unwilling, take this oath, or without further dispute to turn over to us the articles so much desired by us...

Imperial Rescript

Show this rescript... to the... duke of the Kybyrrhaiot theme, so that he may summon the Jews sued by you. And if after you have sworn, as you have stated, to the *sykophantikon,* they refuse the *teleion* mentioned by you in your supplication, then persuade them to accept the *teleion* cited below, or to surrender those things which you mention to you. In the month of November, 11th Indiction...

Zepos, *Jus graecor.,* I, 374 f.; *PG,* CXXXIII, 717. Dölger, *Regesten,* I, pt. 2, p. 67, no. 1369. The opening words of the oath are a partial transliteration of the Hebrew of Gen. 1:1, as was recognized by S. Cassel (in Ersch and Gruber's *Allgemeine Encyclopädie der Wissenschaften und Künste.* Leipzig, 1850. 2nd section. XXVII, 53, n. 3). The formula preserved in s. Italy reads as follows:

Loosen his belt, scratch him with thorns, and throw him into the sea neck-deep; and with his hand let him grasp the sea and say, «By God Who created Adam and Eve, and gave the Law to Moses and mighty tokens, leading Israel through the wilderness, and spreading a table in the desert, and feeding the people with the bread of heaven, I speak the truth, thus and thus, and do not lie».

«Ecloga mutata», xxxvii, 14; ed. Zepos, *op. cit.,* VI, 298; tr. Freshfield. *A manual of later Roman law.* Cambridge, 1928. p. 151; Janin, *Echos d'O.,* XV, 130.

1143-80   **172**

... It had been the custom for the Jews [of Cp.] to be judged only by the strategos of the Stenon. Our mighty and holy emperor [Manuel] decreed that they be should judged before every court in accordance with the laws.

Balsamon on Nomocanon, I, 3; ed. Rhallés and Potlés, *Syntagma,* I, 41; Zepos, *op. cit.,* I, 426 f. Dölger, *Regesten,* I, pt. 2, p. 88, no. 1536. Cf. Krauss, *EJ,* IV, 1241. Broydé saw in this the influence of the emperor's Jewish physician (no. **182**; *JE,* XI, 451). Andréadès, *Econ. His.,* III, 15, n. 5, likewise views the change as motivated by a favorable attitude toward the Jews.

For this emperor's general reforms, see Dölger, *op. cit.,* 78 f., no. 1465. This use of the title *stratégos* for a relatively minor office is noteworthy in contrast to its earlier higher denotation; E. Stein, *Mitteilungen zur osmanischen Geschichte*, II, 21.

1147 **173**

... King Roger [II] sent his fleet against Byzantium, and took Corfu, Cephallonia, Thebes, Corinth, and the rest of the coast as far as Malvasia... He led all the Jews of that land captive to Sicily. (Rex Rogerius stolium suum in Romaniam misit et Corpho et Cephaloniam et Estivam et Corinthum omnemque aliam usque ad Malvasiam cepit... et cunctos Iudeos illius terrae captivos ad Siciliam duxit.)

Annales Cavenses (13th c.), ed. G. H. Pertz (*MGH,* Script., III). Hannover, 1839. p. 132. See Chalandon, *Les Comnène,* II, 319; E. Weigand, *BZ,* XXXIV, 466. Cf. Otto of Freising (12th c.). «Gesta Frederici Imperatoris», ed. R. Wilmans (*MGH,* Script., XX). Hannover, 1868. I, 33, p. 370: «opifices... qui sericos pannos texere solent.» Nevertheless, silk-weaving was not a Jewish monopoly, as Caro would have it; *Sozial- und Wirt.,* I, 251, 490. See E. Weigand, «Die Helladisch-byzantinische Seidenweberei,» Εἰς μνήμην Σπ. Λάμπρου. Athens, 1935. pp. 503-14.

(The foregoing sources do not deal with the transfer of «Seidenzucht», as Krauss, *Studien,* 73, following Graetz, *Gesch.,* V, 256, supposes. It is true, however, that the Peloponnesus was contemporaneously noted for sericulture; Beés, *En. Is.,* III, 567. And yet the Gaonic responsum touching this matter, cited by Krauss, *op. cit.,* 74, n. 1, formerly believed to have been addressed to a Byzantine correspondent turns out, according to a document recently published, to have been sent either to Spain or to n. Africa. See S. Assaf. *Misifrut ha-Geonim.* Jerusalem, 1933. p. 224, line 20, cf. p. 220.)

Excursus D:

Aaron Isaakios a Jew?

Among the captives taken from Corinth to Sicily was a certain Aaron Isaakios, who later had a noteworthy career as Latin interpreter and soothsayer to Manuel II, which was terminated by mutilation as punishment for his treachery. Because of his name he is gratuitously assumed to be a Jew by L. Oeconomos. *La vie religieuse*

dans l'empire byzantin au temps des Comnènes et des Anges. Paris, 1918.
pp. 79-82. This notion was also adopted by Rosanes, *EJ*, X, 276.
But see Laurent, *Echos d'O.*, 1934, 394.

ca. 1150 **174**

« Nineveh »... The Jewish scholars in the land of Greece
indentify this with Troy...

Abraham Ibn Ezra, on Jonah 1:2. The Greek name is misspelt
here, but is given correctly in the comment on Zeph. 2:13; Rosin,
Monats., XLII, 1898, 401. This commentary was completed in 1155 in
the Provence, subsequent to his sojourn in Italy; Bernfeld, *EJ*, VIII,
328.

On Homer among the Byzantines, see Runciman, *Byz. Civ.*, 223 f.

ca. 1150 **175**

... Let but a Greek locust come, and he will be exalted among
them... Has not this riotous fellow desecrated the sacred covenant? Avoid him for he curses good men in the manner of Shi-
me'ī, his namesake...

Place a Greek among them; his acts will be an abomination...
He will say to the erring ones, « I am replete with knowledge of
the Talmudic tractates.» Yet he is ignorant of the simple sections
of the Mishnah...

Abraham Ibn Ezra, «*Nedod hesir 'oni,*» stanzas 22-34, ed. and tr.
Rosin, *Reime u. Ged. des Abr. Ibn E.*, II, 90 f. Bernfeld, *l. c.*, and others
believe the object of the attack to be R. Moses *ha-Kohen* of Salerno,
and the issue to be the emphasis on Biblical scholarship, for which
Ibn Ezra stood, versus specialization in Talmud. See also Güdemann,
Gesch. d. Erziehungs., II, 47 f., and Appendix III; Cassuto, *EJ*, VIII, 528.

ca. 1150 **176**

He [Nikétas, archbishop of Chonai] abhorred the Jews likewise, and would never permit them to dwell in his diocese. For
he hearkened to Paul's cry: « Beware of the bad dogs, the evil-
doers» [Phill. 3:2], and accordingly he refused to receive them
when they offered to serve the Church by contributing of those
arts in which they delight. Wherefore they were ejected from

their residences, and like hungry, leather-gnawing dogs they prowled about the towns, as tanners and dyers of old clothes. From old they have been steeped in dark-hued iniquity, and they are incapable of ridding themselves of that stain by divine purification. Thus he banished them thence so that these offenders of God might not with impunity contaminate the cloak of the Savior Jesus and the festive garment of Christ, which we don after the spiritual bath, with the dye of blasphemy, and that they might not tint His pure limbs with the black dye of evil. In this wise did he hate with utter hatred those who hate the Lord.

(ἐκεῖνος καὶ τοὺς Ἰουδαίους οὕτω τι ἐβδελύξατο, ὡς μηδὲ τὴν αὐτοῦ παροικεῖν ἐφεῖναί ποτε. Ἠκροᾶτο γὰρ Παύλου βοῶντος .... καὶ παρὰ τοῦτο οὐ προσίετο ἐπαγγελλομένους ὑπηρετεῖσθαι τῇ ἐκκλησίᾳ καὶ εἰσφέρειν τὰ ἐκ τῶν τεχνῶν ὅσας ἠγάπησαν. Ἐξ οὗ δῆτα τῶν οἰκοπέδων αὐτῶν ἐκβέβληνται καὶ οἷα λιμηρὰ καὶ σκυτοτράγα κυνάρια εἰσκυκλοῦσι τὰς πόλεις σκυτοδέψαι καὶ τριβωνίων δευσποιοί,...)

Michael Choniates. «Eulogy over Nikétas of Chonai,» ed. Lampros, Μιχαὴλ Ἀκομινάτου τὰ σωζόμενα. Athens, 1879-80. I, 53; editor's note, II, 439 f. On the chronology, G. Stadtmüller. *Michael Choniates, Metropolit von Athen (ca. 1138-ca. 1222).* Rome, 1934 (*Orientalia-christiana*, 91). p. 118. The Paulicians (Εὐχαῖται) shared in this persecution.

Cf. Benjamin on the Jewish tanners of Cp., no. **182,** and Solomon Ibn Virga (*ca.* 1500). *Shebet Yehudah,* ed. and tr. M. Wiener. Berlin, 1924 (Reprint). c. 28, pp. 47 f., tr., 94. The dependence of Ibn Virga upon Benjamin is overlooked by Krauss, *Studien,* 80 f. Cf. Caro, *Sozial- u. Wirt.,* I, 254. For the 15th c., Dölger, *Viertel.,* XXVI, 10. (On Athens' tradition of being *Judenrein,* see F. Gregorovius. *Geschichte der Stadt Athen im Mittelalter.* Stuttgart, 1889. I, 201 f.)

1150-1200   **177**

Meyuhas b. Elijah, Biblical commentator.

For the ms. of the commentary on the Pentateuch see G. Margoliouth. *Catalogue of the Hebrew and Samaritan mss. in the British Museum.* London, 1899. I, no. 201, pp. 152-54; cf. Poznanski, *REJ,* XLI, 1900, 303. Gen. was published by Greenup and C. H. Titterton. London, 1909; (rev. by Poznanski, *REJ,* LX, 1910, 154-60). Ex. by Greenup, *Hasofeh,* XIII, 1929, 1-81, 121-82. The commentaries on Chron. and Job are contained in Warsaw synagogue ms. 77, fols. 69v-

15

82v, 82v-106r; *id.*, «Eine wertvolle hebräische Handschrift.» *ZfhB*, XVI, 1913, 178-84, XVII, 18 f. (Another copy of the latter, dated 1436, is extant in a Bodleian ms., Neubauer, *Catalogue*, I, 777 f., no. 2243, s. 7.) The author's *Sefer ha-Middot* is known only from his own references to it; Gen., pp. 1, 10, 21, 23, 62, 64, 85, 114, and Job, Poznanski *l.c.*; Neubauer, *op. cit., ib.*

The indications of a Byzantine provenance are few, but sufficient. See the comment on Ex. 39:8 (*l. c.*, 180), with reference to the «breast-plate»: «Similar to it is the garment worn by the Greek priests, who, however, do not fasten it at the belt.» The reference here is perhaps to the φℯλόνιον, illustrated in *EL,* I, 937. See also the following glosses: ἀνδρεῖα, Gen., *l.c.,* 31; *skapernea* and DRMUDANA (Tramon-tana?), cited by Poznanski, *l. c.,* XVII, 18 f. The former term appears likewise in Hadassī, s. 63, 31a. The commentator in drawing on Rashi never reproduces his French glosses. In one instance, on Ex. 30:34 (*l. c.,* 157), he substitutes a Greek word, *balsamon*, which is, however, a common rabbinic loan-word. (Cf. the very much similar comment in a Byzantine Karaite work; Aaron b. Joseph (1294). *Sefer ha-Mibhar.* Eupatoria, 1835. II, 62a.)

In addition to Rashi he cites Nathan b. Yehīel, an obscure Isaac b. Samuel, an Aramaic version as *ha-melīs,* and Abraham Ibn Ezra. It is clear, however, that he did not use Ibn Ezra's commentaries, and this is thus far the chief clue to dating Meyuhas. Had he written in the latter 13th c., he would undoubtedly have cited the works of later scholars, notably David Kimhi and Nahmanides, whom Aaron b. Joseph used.

On the terminology of his grammatical notes, see Poznanski, *REJ*, LX, 157 f.

ca. 1150-1200   **178**

R. Abraham Zutra of Thebes, commentator on rabbinic texts.

His commentaries on *Sifra,* on the tractate *Sabbath,* and on the order of *Tohorot* are cited in the ms. responsa of Isaiah da Trani (13th c.), after the former's death. S. Schechter, «Notes on Hebrew mss. in the University Library of Cambridge.» *JQR,* IV, 1891, 94; Gross, «Jesaja b. Mali da Trani.» *ZfhB,* XIII, 1909, 120. Certain of his opinions are directed explicitly against the views of Hillel b. Eliaqim (no. **179**).

References to his first-named work are found also in Elijah

Mizrahī's super-commentary to Rashi (on Lev.). *Sefer Mizrahi*. Warsaw, 1864, e.g., II, 44b, 47b, 51a (with surname Ze'īra); cf. 42b, where
he mentions R. *Isaac* Zutra, which is thought to be a possible error
for Abraham. See Simhoni, *Eshkol*, I, 383 f.

ca. 1150-1200   **179**

... Due to the fact that the [late] R. Hillel... wrote in his
commentary to *Sifra* that the use of well or spring-water [in the
ritual bath] is a rabbinic enactment, all the congregations of
Romaniah have adopted the custom of laxity in the post-menstrual
purification-bath. Thus there is not even one community in all of
Romaniah which does more than bathe in the stagnant water of
the bath-houses. Most of them, moreover, are married to unpuri-
fied wives *(niddot)* ...

Isaiah b. Mali, cited by Schechter, *l.c.*, 99; cf. Gross, *l.c.*, 53, and
Magazin, X, 71. The technical laxity may have been due to Karaite
influence, as Schechter suggested; cf. Krauss, *Studien*, 97. In Egypt a
similar situation was explicitly characterized as imitation of these
heretics by Maimonides; ed. Friedlaender, *Monats.*, LIII, 1909, 469-85.
Cf. A. H. Freimann, ed., *Teshubot ha-Rambam*. Jerusalem, 1934, no. 97,
pp. 91-94.

Hillel is said to have come from, or resided in, Silivri; Gross, *l.c.*,
121. This is one of the forms of Selymbria-Selybria, and the spelling
agrees with that appearing in a later source (*ca.* 1500); ed. A. Danon,
JQR, XVII, 1926, 170, line 2.

The text of the introductory section was edited from the Vienna
ms. by A. Freimann. «The commentary of R. Hillel on the *Baraita* of
R. Ishmael.» *Sefer zikkaron le-Kebod S. A. Poznanski*. Warsaw, 1927.
pp. 170-80. That of chapters 100 f. by Jellinek. *Qontres ha-Rambam*.
Vienna, 1878 pp. 29-32. The Frankfort Stadtsbibliothek ms. is described by R. N. Rabbinowicz *Diduqé Soferim*. Munich, 1873. V: '*Erubin*,
introd., end. (It was done at Fustāt in 1212 by Yehīel b. Eliaqīm,
not the author's brother, but apparently the local *dayyan*; Mann, *Jews
in Egypt*, I, 239-41.) For the glosses, Perles, *BZ*, II, 576-80.

The fullest description of the commentary on *Sifré* is given in
D. S. Sassoon. *Ohel Dawid*. London, 1932, I, 106-09. See also M.
Friedmann in his edition of *Sifré*, Vienna, 1864. Introd., VI, *c*., pp. 52b,
n. 15, 58b, n. 5. Cf. Schechter, *JQR*, VII, 1895, 732. Herein he cites a

Hillel *masra'āh* (?), Rashbam, and, without naming him, ps.—Hai on *Tohorot*, on which see J. N. Epstein. *Der gaonische Kommentar zur Ordnung Tohoroth*. Berlin, 1915. pp. 104, 128 f., 154.

For other ms. notices, and for the wide use of these works by later scholars, see Seligman, *JE*, VI, 401; Horodetzky, *EJ*, VIII, 54; Gross, *REJ*, VII, 1883, 62; Steinschneider, *Jüdische Zeitschrift*, X, 1872, 316; Sassoon, *op. cit.*, 109, 111; Marmorstein, *REJ*, LXXVI, 124; Elijah Mizrahī *op. cit.*, II, 2a, 24a, 42b, 43b, 44a («of Romaniah»; cf. no. **180**).

ca. 1150-1200 **180**

... I have heard that R. Hillel of Romaniah invalidates it, whereas R. Shabbetai disagrees with him...

Isaac b. Abba Marī. *Sefer ha-'Ittur*, ed. Katz. I, VII, 54b, line 14. With reference to a bill of divorcement which bears a certain formula. The writer's source apparently cited a difference of opinion between two Byzantine scholars. Gross, *l.c.*, 121, however, thought that the Hillel in question is to be distinguished from the one of no. **179**. But he is cited in precisely the same fashion by Elijah Mizrahī; *ib.*, n.

1153 **181**

... And after the enumeration of those things, he says: « The Strobiliote Jews wherever found (παντᾳχοῦ εὑρισκόμενοι Στροβι-λιῶται Ἰουδαῖοι) and exemption of vessels of a capacity of 40,000...

Balsamon on the 2nd Nicaean Council, canon 12; *PG*, CXXXIII, 728, CXXXVII, 948; Zepos, *Ius graecor.*, I, 380. Dölger, *Regesten*, I, pt. 2, 69 f., no. 1390. The reference is in all probability to Strobilos on the Lycian coast; see W. Tomaschek. «Zur historischen Topographie von Kleinasien im Mittelalter.» *Sitzungsberichte*, philos.-hist. Cl., of the Vienna K. Akademie der Wiss., CXXIV, 1891, no. 8, 38 f. For other localities similarly named, Beés, *EL*, XI, 824; Krauss, *REJ*, LXXXVII, 24, n. 3.

ca. 1165 **182**

a. ... Thence [Otranto] one crosses the sea by a two-day voyage to the island of Corfu. Here there is one Jew. This is the end of the kingdom of Sicily.

b. Thence it is two days' voyage to the city of ⟨Leukas?⟩, which is the beginning of the dominions of Manuel, king of the Greeks. It is a place *(kefar)* containing about 100 Jews, at their head being R. Shelahiah and R. Herakles.

c. Thence it is two days to Acheloos [Aitolikon], a place in which reside about 30 Jews, at their head being R. Shabbetai...

d. Thence it takes a day to Patras... About 50 Jews live here, at their head being R. Isaac, R. Jacob, and R. Samuel.

e. Thence it is half a day by sea to Kifto [Naupaktos or Lepanto], where there are about 100 Jews who live on the seacoast. At their head are R. Gurī, R. Shalom, and R. Abraham.

f. Thence it is a day and a half's journey to Krisa, where about 200 Jews live apart. They sow and reap on their own land. At their head are R. Solomon, R. Hayīm, and R. Yediayah.

g. Thence it is two days' journey to the city of Corinth. Here are about 300 Jews, at their head being R. Leo, R. Jacob, and R. Hezekiah.

h. Thence it is two days' journey to the great city of Thebes, where there are about 2,000 Jews. They are the most skilled tailors of silk and purple garments in Greece. They have scholars learned in the Mishnah and the Talmud, including some prominent figures *(gedolê ha-dor)*. At their head are the chief rabbi, R. Qutī, and his brother R. Moses, as well as R. Hīya, R. Elijah Tirutot, and R. Yoqtan. There are none equal to them in all of Greece, except in Constantinople.

i. Thence it is a day's journey to Egripo [Chalkis], which is a large city on the sea-coast, whither come merchants from every direction. About two hundred Jews live there, at their head being R. Elijah Psaltiri, R. Emanuel, and R. Caleb.

j. Thence it is a day's journey to Jabustrissa, which is a city on the sea-coast. Here are about 100 Jews, at their head being R. Samuel and R. Netaniah.

k. Thence it is a day to Rabenika, where there are about 100 Jews, at their head being R. Joseph, R. Eleazar and R. Isaac.

l. Thence it is a day's journey to Sinon Potamou [Zeitun or Lamia] where there are about 50 Jews, at their head being R. Solomon and R. Jacob.

m. The city is situated at the foot of the mountains of Wallachia, where live the nation called Wallachians. They are as swift as hinds, and they sweep down from the mountains to despoil and ravage the land of Greece. No man can go up and wage war against them, nor can any king rule over them. They do not adhere to the Christian faith, but give themselves Jewish names. Some people say that they were Jews, and they call the Jews their brethren. When they happen to meet them, they rob them but refrain from killing them as they kill the Greeks. They belong to no religion.

n. Thence it is two days' journey to Gardiki, which is in ruins and contains but few inhabitants, both Greeks and Jews.

o. Thence it is two days' journey to Harmylo [or Halmyro] which is a large city on the sea-coast, frequented by Venetians, Pisans, and Genoese, and other merchants as well come there. It is an extensive place and contains about 400 Jews, at their head being the chief Rabbi Shiloh Lombardo, R. Joseph the *parnas,* and R. Solomon the *ro'sh.*

p. Thence it is a day's journey to Bissena, where there are about 100 Jews, at their head being the [chief] Rabbi Shabbetai, R. Solomon, and R. Jacob.

q. Thence it is two days by sea to the city of Saloniki . . . It is a very large city with about 500 Jews. Here live R. Samuel and his sons, who are scholars. He serves as the head of the Jews by royal authority. Besides him there are R. Shabbetai, his son-in-law, R. Elijah, and R. Michael. There are restrictions *(galut)* on the Jews, and they are engaged in the manufacture of silken garments *(mele'ket ha-mesih).*

r. Thence it is two days to Demetrizi, where there are about 50 Jews. Here live R. Isaiah, R. Makir, and R. Eliab.

s. Thence it is two days to Drama, where there are about 140 Jews, at their head being R. Michael and R. Joseph.

t. Thence it is one day to Christopoli, where about 50 Jews live . . .

u. . . . No Jews live among them inside the city [Cp.], for they have been transferred to the other side of the strait. On the other side they are bounded by the strait of . . . . . , so that they can go out to do business with the townspeople only by crossing the water. There are about 2,000 Rabbinite Jews, and about 500 Karaites, in one section *(sad),* and between the two is a fence *(meḥisah).* Among the Rabbinites there are some scholars. At their head is Rabbi *(ha-rab)* Abtalīōn, R. Obadiah, R. Aaron *Bekor-shoro,* R. Joseph *Sir-giro,* and R. Eliaqīm the *parnas.* Among them are workers in silk [garments], many merchants, und many rich men. No Jew is allowed to ride on a horse, except R. Solomon the Egyptian, the king's physician, through whom the Jews obtain alleviation of their alien status *(galut).* For their situation is very difficult: there is much hatred against them, which is engendered by the tanners, who throw out their slops in the streets at the doors of their homes, and thus defile the quarter *(migrash)* of the Jews. Thus the Greeks hate the Jews, good and bad alike, and subject them to severe restrictions; they beat them in the streets and force them to hard labor (?). Yet the Jews are rich and good men, charitable and religious; they cheerfully bear the burden of their situation *(galut).* The place in which the Jews live is called « Pera ».

v. Thence it is a journey of two days by sea to Rhodostos, where there is a Jewish community of about 400, at their head being R. Moses, R. Abiyah, and R. Jacob.

w. Thence it is two days to Kallipoli [Gallipoli], where there are about 200 Jews, at their head being R. Elijah Qabūr, R. Shabbetai Zutra, and R. Isaac Megas (which means «great» in Greek).

x. Thence it is two days to Kales, where there are about 50 Jews, at their head being R. Jacob and R. Judah.

y. Thence it is two days to the island of Mytilene, one of the islands of the sea, and that island [Lesbos] has Jewish communities « in ten places ».

z. Thence it is three days by sea to the island of Chios, where there are about 400 Jews, at their head being R. Elijah and R. Shabbetai . . . .

aa. Thence it is three days by sea to the island of Samos, where there are 300 Jews, at their head being R. Shemaiah, R. Obadiah, and R. Joel. Those islands have many Jewish communities.

bb. Thence it is three days by sea to Rhodes, where there are about 400 Jews, at their head being R. Abba, R. Hananel, and R. Elijah.

cc. Thence it is four days to Cyprus, where there are Rabbinite and Karaite Jews. There are some heretical Jews there . . . whom the Jews everywhere have excommunicated, for they profane the Sabbath eve, and observe instead Saturday night.

Benjamin of Tudela. *Sefer Masaʿot (Itinerary),* ed. and tr. M. N. Adler. London, 1907 (=*JQR,* XVI, 1904, 716-31). pp. 11-4, 16-8; tr. 10 f., 14 f. The present rendering departs from Adler's in a number of particulars.

The dating of this tour of the Empire may be determined within a few years from certain observations made in the sections dealing with Sicily and Armenia; Adler, *ib.,* 1, n. 2; Heisenberg, *BZ.* IX, 1900, 593 f.; C. R. Beazley. *The Dawn of Modern Geography.* London, 1901. II, 238. For detailed discussion, Tafel, *De Thess.,* 467-520; Uspenski, *Annaly,* III, 1923, 5-20 (Russian).

With regard to the communal organization, see Krauss, *Studien,* 87 f., 91. His notion of an ἔφορος functioning at this period is highly improbable; see no. **85n.** On *parnas* see Mann, *Jews in Egypt,* I, 259; Krauss, *op. cit.,* 89, n. 4. On *ro'sh,* Mann, *op. cit.,* 258.

As to the statistics, Krauss, *op. cit.,* 79 f., is quite inconsistent. Those given for the communities outside the Empire afford no certain basis for determining in general whether Benjamin counted families or adults or included the suburban communities with the nearby cities. The tendency, however, is to take his figures as denoting families;

e. g., Adler, *op. cit.,* 16, n. 2 ; Caro, *Soz. u. Wirt.,* I, 254-60; Baron, *Social and Rel. His.,* I, 315, III, 78. Ct. Andréadès, *Ec. His.,* III, 4.

For material on the economic life of the region in question see the following: Tomaschek, «Die Handelswege im 12. Jahrhundert nach den Erkundigungen des Arabers Idrisi». *Sitzungsb.* (Philos.-hist. Cl.) of the Vienna Akad.der Wissensch., CXIII, 1886, 285-373 ; Schaube, *Handelsgeschichte,* 222-260; *EL,* articles for each locality; W. Miller. *Essays on the Latin Orient.* Cambridge, 1921.

Detailed annotations:

a. True only in 1147-49, but evidently an error.

b. Place-name corrupt in all mss., and although *Larta* = Arta, (Schaube, *op. cit.,* 244), is the accepted reading, it is inland and distinctly off the course. More plausible is Leukas, as has been shown by Andréadès, «Sur Benjamin de Tudèle». *BZ,* XXX, 1930, 458 f. His point has not been weakened by M. A. Dendias, «Leukas or Arta ? A note on a place in the itinerary of Benjamin of Tudela». (Greek) Ἠπειρωτικὰ Χρονικά, VI, 1931, 23-8. Note that two of the mss. have a name beginning LB (V), which may be a survival of *Levkas,* as the name in question is pronounced. Yet *kefar,* «village», is a strange designation for either town.

h. For the petition of the Genoese shippers regarding the garments manufactured here, G. I. Bratianu. *Recherches sur le commerce génois dans la mer noire au XIIIe siècle.* Paris, 1929. p. 66. Cf. Michael Choniates, ed. Lampros, II, 83: οὖ τὰς ἀμπέχονας ὑμῖν ἱστορ^γοῦσι Θηβαῖοι καὶ Κορίνθιοι δάκτυλοι ...; For Harīzī's visit *ca.* 1218, see his *Macamac* («Taḥkemōnī»), ed. P. Lagarde. (repr.). Hannover, 1924. pp. 92, 184.

j. The names of the two local leaders are preceded in the text by three others, which are, however, identical with those in *k,* and are in the same order. Since 5 leaders for a community as small as this seems excessive, dittography should probably be assumed.

m. See M. Halevy, « On the history of the Roumanian Jews in the Middle Ages». (Hebrew) *Mizraḥ u-Maʿarab,* II 1929, 279.

o. Krauss, *Studien,* 88, assumes without warrant that the Italian merchants in question are Jews, who form a congregation presided over by the first-named; that this individual bears an Italian name does not strengthen his hypothesis.

q. Cf. the sense of the same phrase in Abraham b. David, *Sefer ha-Qabbalah,* ed. Neubauer, *Mediaeval Jew. Chron.,* p. 70, line 7.

u. Where one would expect a reference to the Bosphorus (a strait is required by the term *zeroʿa*), the mss. offer *Rūmi* (Mediterranean?),

Rusiah (Black Sea), and *Sophia,* none of which fits, unless one deletes *zeroͨa* as dittography and reads *yam Rusiah ;* cf. Krauss, *ib.,* n. 2. In the second sentence read *medīnah,* which the editor has unwisely rejected in favor of the meaningless *dīmah.* The surnames of Aaron and Joseph have apparently become interchanged. *Bekor - shoro* is found elsewhere only in connection with the name Joseph, in reminiscence of Dt. 33:17. The prohibition of horse-back riding is found also under certain Moslem rulers, no. **117**; E. Fagnan, *REJ,* XXVIII, 1894, 295, n.; in Cp. in 1758, A. Galanté. *Documents officiels turcs conçernant les juifs de Turquie.* Stambul, 1931. p. 60. With regard to occupations, Krauss, *EJ,* IV, 1242, and *Studien,* 75, asserts that the local Jews engaged in money-changing and lending, but this is unfounded; see no. **192n.** Bratianu, *op. cit.,* 64, calls attention to a Habacuc and an Ismael in the local Genoese quarter in 1174, and considers them to be Jews. The names, however, are just as unusual among medieval Jews as they are among Christians.

z. See Zolôtas, Ἱστορία, II, 323, who assumes the figure to stand for families, hence a 25-fold increase in the space of one c.! Ct. Andréadès, *BZ,* XXX, 461.

cc. On these heretics as followers of Meswī, Poznanski, *REJ,* XXXIV, 1897, 161-91; Harkavy, *Voskhod,* XVII, 1898, 16-9.

Our source gives the names of two Byzantine Jews, Elijah *ha-yevani* and Isaac *ha-yevani,* who were prominent in Siponto and Palmyra, respectively: pp. 10, 32. Note also that certain Jews from *Rūm* figure in a contemporary incident in Fustāt; R. Gottheil and W. H. Worrell. *Fragments from the Cairo Genizah in the Freer Collection.* New York, 1927. p. 54, line 6. Cf. also Mann, *Jews in Egypt,* II, 246, lines 9, 17; *id., JQR,* XI, 464, n.

Excursus E:

Communities Not Visited by Benjamin.

Europe: Macedonia (nos. **164, 166, 189**). Selymbria (no. **179**). Regarding Crete, the earliest mention is by Isaiah da Trani in the early 13th c.; Schechter *JQR,* IV, 99 Andréadès argues for its existence before 1204 in, «Were the Jews in Crete when the Venetians conquered the Archipelago?» (Greek) Πρακτικά of the Academy of Athens, IV, 1929, 32-37. In addition, attention should be called to the fact that the earliest version of the local *Taqqanot Candia* has been dated 1237-38; L. Finkelstein. *Jewish Self-Government in the Middle Ages.* New York, 1924. p. 84.

The absence of any reference to Adrianople before 1361 may be merely accidental; see Danon, *JE*, I, 214. On a local legend concerning a blood-accusation in the Byzantine period, see Rosanes, *EJ*, I, 912; first published by S. Loupo. «Les synagogues d'Andrianople.» *Bulletin* of the Alliance Israélite Universelle. 2nd s., no. 13, 1888, 112. But even if one grants its historical basis, it is perhaps to be attributed to Latin influence after 1204.

It has been stated that one of the synagogues in Janina possesses a Torah-crown inscribed with the date [4] 640 A. M., i. e., 1140 A. D.; Rosanes, *EJ*, II, 111. In the fall of 1934 I discussed the matter with the cantor of the Athens synagogue, a native of Janina, who assured me that no such object existed. The earliest evidence for the existence of this community is dated 1318-19; Bees, «Übersicht über die Geschichte des Judentums von Janina (Epirus)». *Byz.-neugr. Jahr.*, II, 162, 165 f.

Asia: Attaleia (no. **171**); Pylae? (no. **128n.**); Strobilos (no. **180**); Ephesus (no. **141**); Kotyaion (no. **149**); Phrygia (no. **176**). (Mastaura [no. **130**] had been devastated by the Turks.)

Excursus F:

Astafortis, Manuel II's «Jewish» Official.

The only document mentioning Astafortis is a letter sent in 1166 by Ugone Eteriano, a Pisan in Cp., to the consuls of Pisa, which was published by G. Müller. *Documenti sulle relazioni delle città toscane coll' oriente cristiano e coi turchi.* Florence, 1879. pp. 11-13. The statement by Müller that he was a Jew is repeated by Heyd, *op. cit.*, I, 200 f., and Chalandon, *Les Comnènes*, II, 124, 227. The letter reads, in essence, as follows:

« ... The emperor returned from the Hungarian campaign, and with him there came a certain new man, a savage tormentor, as tax-collector for the unlucky Latins, who are scattered throughout all of Greece ... Certain rascals of your people [Pisans] did, indeed, come to this circumcised fellow, a liar before God and man, and ... they testified that the burgher [Signoretto] had died intestate and had left more than 300,000 *hyperpera* ... This great scoundrel [Astafortis] came to me [Signoretto's executor] and by imperial order demanded that I turn over in entirety Signoretto's 300,000 gold-pieces ... But I replied in all truthfulness that I had never had any of this money ....

«While I was telling them [fellow-Pisans] what had taken place, Astafortis suddenly rushed in, surrounded by a band of his men, as though he wished to break down the gates of the hospice... He demanded of us the reason for our meeting. A brief reply was made: For that which you yourself have ordered. This that apostate with an oath declared a lie. [Unsuccessful search is made and a lieutenant is despatched by Astafortis to get whatever money was to be found in the Pisan churches. The writer quotes himself as speaking thus:] Astafortis, it behooves one to use foresight wisely, in order not to merit punishment by doing something which is punishable. This money has been devoted to God, and is quite outside both your province and ours.».....

ca. 1170?   **183**

On the island of Chios I saw in the possession of the learned R. Elijah, the grandson of the renowned and learned physician R. Benjamin, ... a commentary attributed to R. Caleb Korsinos of the city of Constantinople. He was the foremost authority on the subject of grammar, and not a thing expressed by Ibn Ezra in his book in the way of grammar, was overlooked by this R. Caleb. On the other hand, with respect to his secret meanings the latter knew nothing ....

In the city of Ṣaḥoq (?) I found a commentary attributed to a scholar named R. Isaiah of Trani, and its contents were nothing more than a plagiary of this R. Caleb.

Mosconi, *op. cit.,* ed. Berliner, *Osar Tob.* Berlin, 1878. p. 07; *id., Magazin,* III, 46. Cf. Steinschneider, *l. c.,* 96, n. 5 = *Ges. Schr..* I, 538.

The only clue to the dating is the section on a presumably contemporary super-commentator, Abishai of *Zagora* (= Bulgaria), immediately preceding. (Cf. the variant version published by Kaufmann, *Monats.,* XXXIII, 1884, 567, and M. Friedlaender, *Essays on the writings of Abraham Ibn Ezra.* London, 1877. IV, 214 f.) The manner in which Isaiah of Trani is mentioned here makes the otherwise possible identification with the well-known scholar (no. **179n.**) questionable. As a parallel to this early spread of Ibn Ezra's influence eastward, it may be noted that Hadassī seems to have used that writer's *Moaznayim;* Bacher, *Monats.,* XL, 1896, 69.

ca. 1175 **184**

.... During the incumbency of the saintly patriarchs [of Thessalonica] who preceded my worthless self, the Hebrews were permitted to spread out. I know not whether this happened by oversight or with their knowledge or because of an imperial rescript (Θεία τινὰ κέλευσιν), for that cannot be determined. Some of them occupied ruined Christian dwellings which they rebuilt, while others lived in houses occupied by Christians. Some of these houses had been decorated with religious pictures, before which hymns had been chanted, yet until the other day no one said a word of it. However, in the course of a certain recent dispute the matter was mentioned, and since I was naturally aroused by the situation, I took action. I have been given a list by certain persons, which covers not only the city but other people as well. Inasmuch as it seems to me that I cannot adjust this entire matter properly unless I receive instructions from your great Holiness and obtain aid from you, I venture to ask what am I to do in order to handle the affair in reverent obedience and to terminate the issue correctly.

Eustathios, Epistle 32, addressed to the patriarch of Cp., ed. Tafel, *PG,* CXXXVI, 1299. The writer was patriarch of Thessalonica from 1175 to *ca.* 1185. Cf. O. Tafrali. *Thessalonique au quatorzième siècle.* Paris, 1912. p. 40. I. S. Emmanuel. *Histoire des Israélites de Salonique.* Thonon, 1936. I, pp. 38-40.

1177 **185**

Kindly instruct us what to reply to the questioner regarding the *Shi'ur Qomah.* Is it true, as someone has said, that it is of Karaite authorship?... or that it is one of the secrets of the rabbis ?...

Responsum: I cannot see that it is a product of the rabbis ... It is merely a composition of one of the preachers of *Rūm* ....

Maimonides to the scholars of Tyre in a Judaeo-Arabic text, ed. and tr. A. Geiger and S. L. Heilberg. *Nit'é Na'amanim.* Breslau, 1847. I, 17. Cf. A. H. Freimann. *Teshubot ha-Rambam.* Jerusalem, 1934. no. 373, p. 343; see also p XLIII. The work in question is now dated in the 3-4th c.: Scholem, *EJ,* IX, 639.

ca. 1180   **186**

In the land of Greece the Jews are subject to a grievous «exile» *(galut)* and are enslaved in body. There are youths among them who are expert in the use of divine names, and who invoke demons who serve them like slaves. There are so many congregations among them that Palestine could not contain them if they migrated thither.

L. Grünhut. *Die Rundreise des R. Petachjah aus Regensburg.* Jerusalem, 1904-5. p. 36, tr. 49. (Text also in Eisenstein, *Osar Masáot.* New York, 1926. p. 56; tr. Adler, *Jew. Travellers*, 91.) On the term *bahurîm*, see Krauss, *Studien*, 66, n. 2. Cf. the ed. of E. Carmoly, *JA*, XIX, 1831, 408 f. Following the word «names» this text has the following addition: «among them being them R. Shabbetai.» These three words are apparently an interpolation, but it is, nevertheless, relevant to note that Carmoly has identified the individual named with a Byzantine Jew who visited Spain in the 13th c., and who is mentioned by Nahmanides (*ca.* 1260) in his sermon *Torat Adonai Temimah*, ed. Jellinek. Leipzig, 1853. p. 28: «Some time ago we had here a Greek who had acquired this knowledge [palmistry] from the mystics (*hassidim*) of Germany. His discourse before the Gentiles on physiognomy was quite remarkable. His name was R. Shabbetai the Greek.» Cf. *id., Beiträge zur Geschichte der Kabbala.* Leipzig, 1852. II, 5.

The latter individual, in turn, was believed to be the same as the commentator on the Mishnah, cited by Abraham b. David of Posquières (latter 12th c.) as «the Greek rabbi» in his strictures (*Hassagot*) on Maimonides' *Mishneh Torah, s. Matnot 'Aniyim*, v, 11, etc., by I. M. Jost. «Beiträge zur Geschichte der Juden im byzantinischen Reiche (1100-1450).» *Israelitische Annalen*, I, 1839, 154, n. Somewhat more plausible is the suggestion of Gross, who would identify the anonymous scholar with the commentator Isaac b. Malkīzedek of Siponto; *Monats.*, XXII, 1873, 458 f.

[1183-5   **187**

A dialogue-polemic against the Jews, attributed to Andronikos I.

PG, CXXXIII, 797-924 (Latin version). The work cannot be earlier than the 14th c.; Krumbacher, *Gesch. d. byz. Litt.*, 91; Nau, *PO*, VIII, 737-40; Williams, *op. cit.*, 181-87. Correct, accordingly, J. Guttmann, *EJ*, II, 825; *Eshkol*, II, 1011].

ca. 1185 **188**

.... He who raises his voice [above the cantor's in reading the Scriptural lesson] is to be commended. In France I saw R. Jacob of blessed memory raise his voice as high as the cantor's, while in Greece and Lombardy the reader reads and the cantor remains silent. May their strength persist · · · ·

Ephraim b. Isaac of Regensburg in a responsum to Joel b. Isaac *ha-Levi* of Bonn, cited in Isaac b. Moses, *Or Zaru'a,* II, 20a, s. 42. The latter custom contrasts to an even greater degree with the modern procedure in which the professional reader's voice is the only one heard. See I. Elbogen. *Der jüdische Gottesdienst in seiner geschichtlichen Entwicklung.* 3rd ed., Frankfort, 1931. pp. 170 f.

Yavan and *Lombardia* may refer to different parts of Italy (no. **136n.**), but the fact that the latter appears occasionally (no. **104**) as a designation of s. Italy, perhaps justifies us in understanding the former as denoting the Empire.

1185 **189**

.... If someone had secured food somewhere, he would sell it only at a high price. Alas, such barbarian inhumanity! The Jew and the Armenian from the neighboring Krania and Zemenikos they supplied with food measuring out a due quantity and more, but to a citizen of the besieged city, only the minimum ...

Eustathios, Account of the siege of Thessalonica, s. 113. *PG,* CXXXVI, 112; tr. Tafel, *Komnenen und Normannen.* 2nd ed., Stuttgart, 1870. p. 173.

See O. Tafrali. *Thessalonique depuis les origines au quatorzième siècle.* Paris, 1919. p. 190; Miller, *Eng. Hist. Rev.,* XXXII, 168.

1185 **190**

.... The former [Andronikos Dukas] was beheaded, and was carried across to Pera into the Jews' cemetery ...

Nikétas Choniates (contemporary): Χρονικὴ Διήγησις, *PG,* CXXXIX, 649. See G. Finlay. *History of Greece,* ed. H. F. Tozer. Oxford, 1877. III, 313. The map of a Venetian traveller of the Turkish period, *EL,* VIII, facing 400, shows the «Sepulture dei Giudei» near the district of Cassim Pacha; cf. no. **191.** (A discussion of the local cemeteries in a forthcoming work is promised by Galanté, *Documents,* 60, n. 2.)

ca. 1200   **191**

.... There is a little suburb *(gorodok)* in Constantinople adjoining the *Ispiganskoi* [i. e., εἰς Πηγάς] quarter, in the Jews' quarter *(po stranye zhidov)* ...

Anthony of Novgorod, *Kniga Palomnik,* ed. Loparev, 3, 64, 72; tr. Ehrhard, *Romania,* LVIII, 49. See Millingen, *Byz. Cp.*.210, and map facing p. 19 (= *Dict. d'arch. chr.,* II, 1389.) Cf. no. **192.**

[1200   **192**

.... This miracle took place after the matins and before the beginning of the Mass. When the priests who were at the altar and all the people who were in the church saw it, they exclaimed with fear and joy, «God, in His mercy, has manifested Himself to us Christians ... God wishes to have us live now as in the reign of Constantine, and even better. God will lead all the accursed Jews (and Moslems) to baptism, and they will live in holy union with the Christians. War will be waged only against those who refuse to receive baptism; and willingly or not, God will compel them to be baptized. There will be an abundance of goods on the earth».....

God performed this sacred miracle in the year 6708, during my lifetime, on Sunday, May 21, on the feast of the emperor Constantine and his mother Helena, during the reign of Alexios [III] .....

Anthony, 13-15, 47 f., 77; tr. Ehrhard, *l.c.,* 54 f. In the chapel of the Blachernae Palace he was shown the icon of Christ which Theodore gave Abraham as a surety (no. **2n.**); pp. 21, 55, 82, tr. Ehrhard, *l. c.,* 58. The mistaken notion that the latter was a money-lender by profession appears in the title of the abridgement of the story by S. Baring-Gould. *Historic oddities and strange events: First series.* London, 1899. pp. 103-20: «Abram the usurer».

ca. 1200   **193**

Joseph of Constantinople, author of ʿ*Adat Deborim.*

The ms., II. Firkowicz 153, is in the Leningrad Public Library. See the analysis of its contents by Harkavy, *Hadashim gam yeshanim* (*Hamispah,* 1885), pp. 11-13. It cites the Hebrew and Arabic works of the following: Aaron b. Moses, b. Saadia, Mishael b. ʿUzzīel, Hai, Jonah b. Janah, and Moses b. Jikatilla. The Masoretic portion, based on Mishael b. Uzzīel's Arabic treatise, has been analyzed and cited by L. Lipschütz. *Ben Asher-Ben Naftali. Der Bibeltext der tiberischen Masoreten. Eine Abhandlung des Mischael ben Uzziel veröffentlicht und untersucht.* Bonn, 1935.

The *terminus ad quem* for the date of composition is furnished by the Karaite scribe, Judah b. Jacob of Gagry (on the Black Sea), who completed the ms. in 1207. (Mishael is dated in the 11th c. at the latest). Joseph himself, however, was not a Karaite; Poznanski, *ZfhB,* XX, 1917, 80. See further, Mann, *REJ,* LXXII, 1921, 163.

Among the glosses cited by Harkavy, note in particular ὁ ἦχος employed in the ecclesiastical sense, that is, corresponding to *taʿam* and Arabic *lahn;* Lipschütz, *op. cit.,* text-part, p. 13, n. 9.

ca. 1200   **194**

... I have heard that you desire to return *(lahazor)* to Byzantium *(Romaniah)*, on account of the aggravation caused by this people. Beware lest you do that, for you would be leaving a peaceful place to go to «places upset by troops» ...

Maimonides to Pinhas b. Meshullam, communal judge at Alexandria; *Qobes teshubot ha-Rambam.* Leipzig, 1859, I, no. 140, end, p. 27a. Cf. Mann, *Jews in Egypt,* II, 307, n. 2 (misled by the verb *lahazor* to infer that the addressee had come originally from Byzantium). The same document, *op. cit.,* p. 25b, makes it clear that Pinhas was a Provençal; cf. Marx, *HUC An.,* III, 1926 = n. 24. Apparently he had come to Egypt by way of the Empire; Assaf, *Moaznayim,* III, 1935, 429. (Hence, one need not suppose *Romaniah* to denote France, as does Eppenstein, *Schriften* of the Gesellschaft zur Forderung der Wissenschaft des Judentums, XI, pt. 2. Leipzig, 1914, p. 95, n. 2.

*ca. 1200?   **195**

A copy of a legal code by Judah b. Barzillai was brought to Worms from the Empire *(Yavan)*.

Anon. ms., *Ha-Assufot* (14th c.), 110a, cited by Luzzatto, *Magazin,* VI, 1878, 15; Gross, «Das handschriftlichen Werk Assufot. Analecten». *l. c.,* X, 77. A work entitled *Sefer ha-Dīn(īm)* by the author in question has survived only in part; it was composed in the early 12th c.

196

.... Then they spent the night before the tower [of Galata] and in the Jewry, which is called *Estanor* [i. e., Stenon] where there was a very pretty and very rich suburb ... (Ensi le herbergièrent la nuit devant la tour et en la juerie que l'on apele l'Estanor, ou il avoit mult bone vile et mult riche).

Geoffroi de Villeharbouin. *Conquête de Constantinople,* ed. and tr. M. N. de Wailly. Paris, 1882. p. 88. See E. Pears. *The Fall of Constantinople.* London, 1885. pp. 300f.

For the sake of rectifying an obvious inaccuracy reference must be made to an account of the supposed destruction of the Jewish quarter by the Crusaders in that year, as given in W. C. Hazlitt. *The Venetian Republic.* London, 1915. I, 281f. This is based on a misunderstanding of Niketas' (*PG,* CXXXIX, p. 933) circumlocution, τῷ τῶν ἐξ Ἀγαρ συναγωγίῳ, which can only refer to the well-known mosque. Cf. F. C. Hodgson. *The early history of Venice.* London, 1901. pp. 384-86.

Appendix A
Karaites in the Empire.

The earliest reference is in the letter of 1028, with respect to three Karaites from Attaleia; no. **132.** Within the same generation there appear the first signs of the existence of a community in the capital, as manifested by the life and activities of Tobiah b. Moses, who acted as its leader, and who had apparently been born there *ca.* 1020. (See Seligman, *JE,* XII, 166f., whose tale of how Tobiah abandoned Rabbinism and consequently suffered persecution, is, however, utterly unfounded; cf. Poznanski, *Osar Yisrael,* V, 12-14, *id., REJ,* LXXII, 1921, 190, no. 28). He is known to have been among the disciples of Yeshuah b. Judah of Jerusalem, the sect's leading scholar of the day; see Markon, *EJ,* IX, 42f. We also have a letter written by him before 1048, during his sojourn in that city; Gottheil and Worrell, *Fragments,* 142-48. Another one, presumably later, was written in Egypt; Mann, *Texts,* I, 372-74, 383-85.

Tobiah returned to Cp., and there prepared Hebrew translations of his master's Arabic works, as well as those of other Karaite authorities; Frankl, *Monats.,* XX, 157, XXI, 83f.; *id., Jahresberichte* of the Berlin Lehranstalt für die Wissenschaft des Judentums, V, 1887, 10-3;

Poznanski, *REJ,* XXXIV, 97, 185, XLIV, 186; Markon, *EJ,* IX, 325. Two liturgical poems are also attributed to him; Davidson, *Osar,* IV, 383. Finally, for the period of his leadership there is a record of comunication between this community and the one in Jerusalem. The authorities of the latter were consulted with regard to the problem of the Jewish calendar, which at times involved communities outside of Palestine in difficulties. The responsum advised in a conciliatory tone that in the event of doubt arising, they were to follow the Rabbinite practice; no. **125 n.**

The New Year of 1096 or 1097 witnessed a difference in the date of observance between the two groups in Cp., but we are not told how it affected their relations; no. **154.** In a similar instance more details are given, but although the date and place of the events are unknown, there seems to be no objection to Mann's suggestion, viz., the eleventh century. It appears, however, that the capital, rather than Thessalonica, was the scene of the bitter conflict. The affair led to the filing of slanderous charges by the Karaites with the civil authorities, who levied a heāvy fine on the opposing group; no. **125.**

It is probably to this period that we should assign a certain Jacob b. Simeon, who translated Yeshuah b. Judah's work on the forbidden marital degrees *(Sefer ha-ʿArayot).* This individual's provenance is known only by inference from his Greek glosses; M. Schreiner, *Jahresb.* of the Berlin Lehranstalt, XVIII, 1900, 70, i-ix. Even more obscure is the identity of other translators, whose names have not been preserved. See the translation of the commentary of Salmon b. Yeruhīm on Ruth, ed. Markon, in *Sefer zikkaron le-kebod Poznanski,* pp. 91f. See also the fragment of a translation of the commentary of Yaft b. ʿAlī on Ex.-Lev.; Poznanski, *REJ,* LXXII, 186, no. 7; Frankl, *Monats.,* XX, 157, XXI, 216, 274.

A commentary on the entire Old Testament was written by Jacob b. Reuben. This has been published in part, and has been cited in the present work; nos. **121 n., 147 n.** The author has been assigned to the 11th c. by Poznanski, *JE,* VII, 41, but more recently Markon, *EJ,* VIII, 852 f., has preferred the following century. An argument for the former dating is furnished by his comment on a passage in Dan., *op. cit.,* 18, in which he mentions the horn which was sounded in Ramleh when a Byzantine vessel anchored off the coast of Palestine to dispose of a cargo of captives, thus reflecting a situation in the city named which was probably terminated by the time of the Seljuq conquest; see B. Segal, *Ziyon.* V, 1933, 16. For a selection and tr. see A. Neubarer and S. R. Driver.

The fifty-third chapter of Isaiah according to the Jewish interpreters.
Oxford-London, 1876-77. I, 56-61, II, 61-63. It is also relevant to
recall the strictures of Tobiah b. Eliezer on Karaite exegesis; no. **164.**

A more important scholar was Judah b. Elijah Hadassī, who
lived in the capital in the middle of the 12th c. His brother Nathan,
who was one of his teachers, presumably also lived there; Skoss, *EJ,*
VII, 773-78. His legal compendium in rhymed prose, *Eshkol ha-Kofer,*
was begun in 1148, and several references have been made to it
above; see notes to nos. **1,59, 101, 125, 177.** In one passage, in addition to furnishing an interesting piece of folklore, he refers apparently
to the visit of a group of Oriental Karaites; no. **168.** He expresses
the earliest known opposition to astrology (*op. cit.,* 31a, 151b); cf. L.
Loew. *Gesammelte Schriften.* Szegedin, 1890. II, 125f. Some selections
from his work are given in tr. by J. Hamburger, in Winter and
Wünsche's *Jüd. Lit.,* II, 90-3. A list of 27 liturgical poems is credited
to him; Davidson, *op. cit.,* IV, 392.

As for the arrival of Shemaria Alexander in Cp. this may have
occurred either in the same century or in the following one; no. **154.**

When Benjamin visited the city, he found 500 Karaites residing
there, or $^1/_4$ the number of Rabbinites. The two groups lived in adjacent
quarters, separated by a fence. Elsewhere he notes the existence of this
sect only in Cyprus (no. **182**). Hence it may be assumed that numerically
they were not as strong in the Empire as in Palestine, Egypt, or Mesopotamia. See also Brutzkus, *Zeit. f. b. Gesch. d. J. in Deutsch.,* III, 106.

The Greek glosses in the writings mentioned above have been
noted in the studies cited in each instance. To these must be added
the excellent Study of Hadassī's material by Frankl, *Monats.,* XXXI,
1882, 82f., XXXIII, 1884, 448-57, 513-99, supplemented by Bacher,
JQR, VIII, 431-44. For the purposes of the present work the significance of these glosses lies in the fact that whereas those of the
Rabbinite writers reveal contact only with the colloquial language,
the Karaite scholars show, in varying degree, acquaintance with the
philosophic terminology. In the present state of research, however, it
is impossible to say whether they actually read the classical philoso-
phers or the manuals of their own time. See Frankl, in Ersch and
Gruber's *Encyklopädie,* 2nd s., XXXIII, 18.

In the first half of the 13th c. the leader of the Karaites of Cp.
was Aaron b. Judah *baʿal ha-derashot.* See Poznanski, *Evreiskaya
Entsiklopediya,* I, 22, and Mann, *Texts,* II, 140f. On the subject in
general, Mann, *ib.,* II, 287-91.

Appendix B

Texts

Letter in Cambridge University Genizah Collection — T.-S. 13 J 34[3]

(See no. **129**)

1. . . . . חק . . . .
2. נאספו . . . . לח. חללו . . . . . . כמשמעתו מאת מחסה
3. ומעוז לבני ישראל נצח . . . . נו הרב המונהק שלום עצום ורב
4. מאת אלהים צורנו וממנו בני הקהלות הקדושות אשר בנא אמון מאושש[ות]
5. ובשחי כניסי[ו]ת[א] מחכנשות לצורם סקדישוה וסעכודתו ל[א פו]רשוה
6. ומיחודו לא משוה ואם בכל עת הצרים מחרגשים ואליהם . . . . .
7. עיניהם מעשישים ורוחוחם מבקשים ומהונם למו פרשישים ואל המזבח[ות]
8. לשחוט מגישים ולולי הנערץ בסוד קדושים הנקדש במקהלות חרשישים
9. אזי חיו נואשים ומחים פורשים. כד' לולי ײ שהיה לנו וג' אזי חיים
בלעונו וגו'
10. . . . חמיד אנו שואלים מלפני אלהינו להשפיר נחלחנו בחי רבנו חרב ולפאר
11. וסננו בחיו יראה זרע יאריך ימים וחפ [..] ועפע ײ אלהינו ב[.] ה[ו] יצלח והוא . . .
12. יען המשאל בחסדו ואמונחו. מגמח שורים. אלה להדר ככודו חודיע[ו]
13. שאירע באילו הימים סביאת חמשח שבוים אלינו מארץ אסטצניילו והם עדי[ן]
14. נערים ונפלו בידי אכזרים אלפים הוגיעונו והציקו את רוחוחינו עד
שהגיעו את
15. נפשנו עד סוה ונחעזרנו עליהם בשליט המדינה ולא הועיל עד שש[יח]דנ[ו] למו
16. כרביח מאח זהובים וקבצנו בענינן מאנשים ונשים ונערים ונחולוה מז[ה]כ[ ]
17. ונחשח ופשחים חי וטחי וכרים וכסחוח וזולחם עד ש[..]כ[ ]לל לנו מ[א]ה . . . .
18. נחקבץ בסכנח נפש מכאב לבנו ו . . . . . נו על אילו הנערים . . .
19. וכל הגוים חומחים ממנו ואומרים אשרי העם שככה לו אשרי העם ש[י א]להי[ו]
20. נחבטלו מעסקיחם ושקדו לילה ויומם עד שחצילו אילו השבויים מידי אכז[רי]ם
21. ועזר אלחינו כשראה ע[צ]ם חאו[ח]נ[ו] בחצלחם והעלינום אל שכונתנו בש[לו]מ[ה]
22. ולא נשלמה שמחחנו בהם כי נפלו כולם בחולי. קשה. האלהים .' . . . .
23. נר . . . . ו[ ]חח או . . . .

Remarks by Elīsha bar Shināya
(See no. 131)

··· الروم الذين يستنكرون فى ديارهم من اليهود ··· ويصونوهم ويمكنوهم من
اظهار دينهم وبنا كنايسهم (157ۈ) ·· يقول اليهودي فى بلادهم اننى يهودي
ونظهر دينه وصلاته ولا يكلم ولا يمنع ولا يعترض (158ۈ) ··· حتى ان اليهود
يدخلون هياكل بلد الروم (202ۈ) ··· وذاك ان ببلد الروم في قطب ملكهم
وزعم خلايق كثيرة من اليهود قد صبروا علي المذلة والبغضة منهم ومن
جميع الناس (213ۈ)·· ··

BIBLIOGRAPHY

I. Encyclopedias. Bibliographical Works. Lexica.

BARDENHEWER, O. *Geschichte der altkirchlichen Literatur.* Freiburg, 1932. v. V.

BAUMSTARK, A. *Geschichte der syrischen Literatur.* Bonn, 1922.

BELOT, J. B. *Vocabulaire arabe-français.* 11th ed., Beyrut, 1920.

BEN YEHUDAH, E. *Millon ha-lashon ha-'ibrit.* Jerusalem-Berlin, 1908-. vv. I-VIII.

BROCKELMANN, C. *Geschichte der arabischen Literatur.* Weimar, 1898-1902. 2vv. *Supplement.* Leyden, 1936-.

DAVIDSON, I. *Osar ha-shirah ve-ha-piyut.* New-York, 1924-33. 4vv.

DELEHAYE, H. *Bibliotheca hagiographica graeca.* Brussels, 1909.

Dictionnaire d'Archéologie Chrétienne et de Liturgie. Paris, 1907-. vv. I-XIII.

DU CANGE, C. DU FRESNE. *Glossarium ad scriptores mediae et infimae latinitatis,* ed. Fabre, L. Niort, 1883-7. 10vv.

ΕΛΕΥΘΕΡΟΥΔΑΚΗ, Ἐγκυκλοπαιδικὸν Λεξικόν. Athens, 1928-31. 12vv.

Enciclopedia Italiana di scienze, lettere, ed arti. Rome, 1929-37. 36vv. *Appendice,* 1934-.

Encyclopedia of Islam, ed. Houtsma, M. T. *et al.* Leyden-London, 1913-36. 4vv. *Supplement,* 1931-.

Encyclopedia Judaica. Berlin, 1928-. vv. I-X.

Eshkol. Ensiqlopediah Yisreelit. Berlin, 1929-. vv. I-II.

JASTROW, M. *A dictionary of the Targumim, the Talmud Babli, and Yerushalmi, and the midrashic literature.* (Reprint) New York-Berlin, 1926.

Jewish Encyclopedia. New York, 1901-6. 12vv.

Jüdisches Lexikon. Berlin, 1927-30. 5vv.

KRUMBACHER, K. *Geschichte der byzantinischen Literatur von Justinian bis zum Ende des oströmischen Reiches (527-1453).* 2nd ed., revised by Ehrhard, A., and Gelzer, H. Munich, 1897.

LIDDELL, H. G., *Greek-English Lexicon.* Oxford, 1901. New ed., revised by Jones, H. S., and Mc Kenzie, R. Oxford, 1925-.

SMITH, R. P. *A compendious Syriac dictionary,* ed. Smith, J. P. Oxford, 1903.

Μεγάλη Ἑλληνικὴ Ἐγκυκλοπαιδεία. Athens, 1926-. vv. I-XXIII.

SOPHOCLES, E. A. *Greek lexicon of the Roman and Byzantine periods (B.C. 146 to A.D. 1100).* (Reprint) Cambridge (U.S.A.), 1914.

248

II. Byzantine History and Related Subjects.

AMARI, M. *Storia dei musulmani di Sicilia,* 2nd ed., revised by Nallino, C. A. Catania, 1933-5. vv. I-II.

BROLO, L. di. *Storia della chiesa in Sicilia nei primi dieci secoli del cristianesimo.* Palermo, 1884. v. II.

BURY, J. B. *A history of the later Roman empire, 395-800.* London-New York, 1889. v. II.

BURY, J. B. *A history of the Eastern Roman empire.* London, 1912.

Cambridge Mediaeval History. Cambridge, 1932. vv. II, IV.

CHALANDON, F. *Les Comnène. Étude sur l'empire byzantin au XIe et au XIIe siècles.* Paris, 1900-12. 2vv.

DÖLGER, F. *Beiträge zur Geschichte der byzantinischen Finanzverwaltung besonders des 10. und 11. Jahrhunderts.* Leipzig-Berlin, 1927. (*Byzantinisches Archiv,* IX).

DÖLGER, F. *Regesten der Kaiserurkunden des oströmischen Reiches (565-1453).* Munich-Berlin, 1924-5. I, pts. 1-2.

DVORNIK, F. *Les légendes de Constantin et de Méthode vues de Byzance.* Prag, 1933.

GAY, J. *L'Italie méridionale et l'empire byzantin, 867-1071.* Paris, 1904.

HEYD, W. *Histoire du commerce du Levant,* tr. F. Raynaud. (Reprint) Leipzig, 1923. 2 vv.

IORGA, N. *Histoire de la vie byzantine.* Bucharest, 1934. vv. II-III.

MARQUART, S. *Osteuropäische und ostasiatische Streifzüge.* Leipzig, 1903.

MARTIN, E. J. *A history of the iconoclastic movement.* London, 1932.

MILLINGEN, A. VAN. *Byzantine Constantinople.* London, 1899.

RAMSAY, W. M. *Historical geography of Asia Minor.* London, 1890.

RUNCIMAN, S. *Byzantine Civilisation.* Cambridge, 1932.

  » *The emperor Romanus Lecapenus and his reign. A study of tenth-century Byzantium.* Cambridge, 1929.

SCHLUMBERGER, G. *L'épopée byzantine à la fin du dixième siècle.* Paris, 1896-1905. 3 vv.

TAFRALI, O. *Thessalonique au quatorzième siècle.* Paris, 1912.

USPENSKI, F. I. *Istoria Vizantiskoi Imperii.* Leningrad, 1927. II, pt. 1.

VASILIEV, A. *L'histoire de l'empire byzantin.* Paris, 1932. 2 vv.

  » *Byzance et les Arabes.* Brussels, 1932. v. I.

VOGT, A. *Basile Ier, Empereur de Byzance (867-886), et la Civilisation byzantine à la fin du IXe siècle.* Paris, 1908.

WILLIAMS, A. L. *Adversus Judaeos. A bird's-eye view of Christian Apologiae until the Renaissance.* Cambridge, 1935.

ZACHARIÄ VON LINGENTHAL, K. E. *Geschichte des griechischrömischen Rechts.* 2nd ed., Berlin, 1892.

ZOLOTAS, G. Ἱστορία τῆς Χίου. Athens, 1924. v. II.

III. Sources: editions, translations, and commentaries.

A. Jewish.

AARON B. ELIJAH. *Gan*ʿ*Eden,* ed. Savsakan, J. Eupatoria, 1866.

ABRAHAM IBN EZRA, (selections) ed. and tr. Rosin, D. *Die Reime und Gedichte des Abraham Ibn Ezra.* Breslau, 1885-7. vv. I-II. *(Jahres-Bericht des Jüdisch-theologischen Seminars «Fraenckelsche Stiftung»).*

ADLER, E. N. *Jewish Travellers.* London, 1930.

APTOWITZER, V. «Seder Elia». *Jewish Studies in memory of G, A. Kohut.* New York, 1935. pp. 5-39.

ASCOLI, F. I. «Iscrizioni inedite o mal note, greche, latine, ebraiche, di antichi sepolcri giudaici del Napolitano». *Atti* of the 4th International Congress of Orientalists. Florence, 1880. Pt. I, 239-52.

BENJAMIN OF TUDELA. *Sefer Masa* ʿ*ot,* ed. and tr. Adler, M. N. *The itinerary of Benjamin of Tudela.* London, 1907. (Reprinted from *JQR,* XV-XVII, 1904-6.)

BRANN, M. [Notes on a ms. *Mahzor Romaniah.*] *Monats.,* LXII, 1918, 276 f.

BRODY, H., AND WIENER, M. *Mibhar ha-shirah ha-*ʿ*ibrit.* Leipzig, 1922.

CASSUTO, U. «Una lettera ebraica del secolo X.» *Giornale della Società Asiatica Italiana,* XXIX, 1918-20, 97-110.

» «Iscrizioni ebraiche a Bari». *Rivista,* XV, 1934, 316-22.

» «Nuove iscrizioni ebraiche di Venosa.» *Archivio storico per la Calabria e la Lucania,* IV, 1934, 1-9.

» «Ancora nuove iscrizioni ebraiche di Venosa», *l.c.,* V, 1935, 179-84.

» «Hebrew inscriptions in Southern Italy» (Hebrew) *Sefer [J.] Klausner.* Tel Aviv, 1937. pp. 240-42.

CASTELLI, D., ed. *Il commento di Sabbetaï Donnolo sul libro della creazione.* Florence, 1880 = *Sefer Yesirah* with commentaries, Warsaw, 1884. pp. 11-48.

CONLEY, A. «Bodleian Gewizah Fragments, IV.» *JQR,* XIX, 1906, 250-54.

DAVIDSON, I. «*A qerobah* by R. Amittai b. Shefatiah.» (Hebrew) *Abhandlungen zur Erinnerung an H. P. Chajes.* Vienna, 1933. pp. 181-94.

EHRENREICH, H. L., ed. *Sefer ha-pardes le-Rashi.* Budapest, 1924.

ELEAZAR B. NATHAN. *Sefer Raben,* ed. Albeck, S. Warsaw, 1904.

FREIMANN, A. «The commentary of R. Hillel on the Baraita of R. Ishmael», (Hebrew) *Sefer zikkaron le-kebod S. A. Poznanski.* Warsaw, 1927. pp. 172-80.

250

250

GEIGER, A., and HEILBERG, S. L. *Nite'é Na'amanim.* Breslau, 1847. v. I.
GINZBERG, L. *Ginzé Schechter.* New York, 1928. v. I.
GRAETZ, H. «Die alten jüdischen Katakombeninschriften in Süditalien
nach Prof. Ascoli». *Monats.,* XXIX, 1880, 433-51.
GREENUP, A. W., ed. «The commentary of Meyuhas b. Elijah on Exo-
dus.» (Hebrew) *Hasofeh,* XIII, 1929, 1-81, 121-82.
 »   with TITTERTON, C. H. *The commentary of Meyuhas b. Eli-*
jah on Genesis. London, 1909.
GROSS, H. «Das handschriftliche Werk Assufot.» *Magazin,* X, 1883, 64-87.
 »   «Jesaya b. Mali da Trani.» *ZfhB,* XIII, 1909, 46-58, 87-92,
118-23.
HADASSI, JUDAH B. ELIJAH. *Eshkol ha-Kofer.* Eupatoria, 1836.
 »   ed. Bacher, W. «Inedited chapters of Jehudah Hadassi's
'Eshkol Hakkofer'.» *JQR,* VIII, 1906, 431-44.
HARKAVY, A. *«Hadashim gam yeshanim,* II.» *Hamispah,* 1885, 11-13.
Zikkaron la-rishonim ve-gam la-'aharonim. Berlin, 1887, v. I.
(Verein Mekize Nirdamim, IX).
ISAAC B. ABBA MARI. *Sefer ha-'Ittur,* ed. Katz, M. Vilna, 1873-5. 2vv.
ISAAC B. MOSES. *Or Zaru'a,* ed. Lehren, A. Zhitomir, 1862. 2vv.
JELLINEK, A., ed. *Qontres ha-Rambam.* Vienna, 1878.
JOSEPH B. SIMON QARA. [Commentary on Job.] *Monats.,* VI, 1857,
270-74, VII, 255-63, 345-58.
JUDAH B. SAMUEL *he-hasid. Sefer ha-hasidim,* ed. Wistinezki, J. Berlin,
1893. Repr., ed. Freimann, J. Frankfort, 1924.
KAHANA, D. *Sifrut ha-historiyah ha-yisreelit.* Warsaw, 1922. v. I.
KAUFMANN, D. «Ein Brief aus dem byzantinischen Reiche über eine
messianische Bewegung der Judenheit und der zehn Stämme
aus dem Jahr 1096.» *BZ,* VII, 1898, 83-90.
 »   «Letter sent to Constantinople by Alafdhal's ex-Minister
of finances.» *JQR,* X, 1898, 430-34.
 »   «Beiträge zur Geschichte Ägyptens aus jüdischen Quellen.»
ZDMG, LI, 1897, 444-47.
 »   «Aus Abraham b. Asriel's '*Arugat ha-Bosem.*» *Monats.,*
XXXI, 1882, 316-24, 360-70, 410-22.
KOKOVTZOV, P. K. *Evreisko-Khazarskaya Perepiska v X Vek.* Lenin-
grad, 1932.
KOUKOULÉS, PH. «Γλωσσάριον Ἑβραιοελληνικόν.» *BZ,* XIX, 1910, 422-29.
KRAUSS, S. «Un nouveau texte pour l'histoire judéo-byzantin.» *REJ,*
LXXXVII, 1929, 1-27 = «Ein neuer Text zur byzantinisch-
jüdischen Geschichte» *Byz.-neugr. Jahrb.,* VII, 1930, 57-86.
LIPSCHÜTZ, L. *Ben Asher-Ben Naftali. Der Bibeltext der tiberischen*
Masoreten. Eine Abhandlung des Mischail b.' Uzziel veröffent-
licht und untersucht. Bonn, 1935.

LUZZATO, S. D. [Citations from Shabbetai Donnolo's *Sefer ha-mazzalot.*] *Kerem Hemed,* VII, 1843, 61-67.

MANN, J. *The Jews in Egypt and in Palestine under the Fātimid Caliphs.* London, 1920-2. 2 vv.

» «The Messianic movements during the first Crusades.» (Hebrew) *Hateq̣ufah,* XXIII, 1924, 243-61, XXIV, 335-58.

» *Texts and studies in Jewish history and literature.* Cincinnati-Philadelphia, 1931-5. 2 vv.

MARCUS, J. «Studies in the chronicle of Aḥimaaz.» *Proceedings* of the American Academy for Jewish Research, V, 1933-4, 85-93.

MARMORSTEIN, A. «Nouveaux renseignements sur Tobiya ben Eliézer.» *REJ,* LXXIII, 1921, 92-97.

» «Sur un auteur français inconnu du treizième siècle. (OR. BRIT. MUS. 2853).» *l. c.,* LXXVI, 1923, 113-31.

MOSCONI, JUDAH B. MOSES. «*Eben ha-Ezer*», introd., ed. Berliner, A. *Osar Tob.* Berlin, 1878. pp. 01-010.

MUNK, S. «Notice sur Abou'l Walid Merwan ibn-Djanah et sur quelques autres grammairiens hébreux du Xᵉ et du XIᵉ siècle.» *JA,* LII, 1850, 10-18.

NEUBAUER, A. *Catalogue of the Hebrew manuscripts in the Bodleian Library.* Oxford, 1886-1906. 2 vv. and *Supplement;* v. II with Cowley, A.

» «Un chapitre inédit de Sabbetai Donnolo.» *REJ,* XXII, 1891, 213-18.

» «The early settlement of the Jews in southern Italy.» *JQR,* IV, 1892, 606-25.

» «Egyptian Fragments.» *l. c.,* IX, 1896, 29-36.

» *Mediaeval Jewish chronicles and chronological notes.* Oxford, 1895. 2 vv. (*Anecdota Oxoniensa :* Simitic series, I, v-vi).

PAPADOPOULOS - KERAMEUS, A. «Γλωσσάριον Ἑβραιοελληνικόν.» *Festschrift zu Ehren des Dr. A. Harkavy.* Petrograd, 1908. pp. 68-90, 177.

Pesiqta Rabbati, ed. Friedmann, M. Vienna, 1889.

PETAHIAH OF REGENSBURG. *Sibbub,* ed. and tr. Grünhut, L. *Die Rundreise des R. Petachja aus Regensburg.* Jerusalem, 1904-5.

POZNANSKI, S. «Eine wertvolle hebräische Handschrift.» *ZfhB.* XVI, 1913, 178-84.

REINACH, T. «Un contrat de mariage du temps de Basile le Bulgaroctone.» *Mélanges offerts à M. G. Schlumberger.* Paris, 1924. I, 118-32.

SALZMAN, M., ed. and tr. *The chronicle of Aḥimaaz.* New York, 1924.

SASSOON, D. S. *Ohel Dawid.* London, 1932. v. I.

SCHECHTER, S. «Notes on Hebrew Mss. in the University Library of Cambridge.» *JQR,* IV, 1891, 90-101.

SCHECHTER, S. «An unknown Khazar document.» *l. c.,* III, 1912, 181-219.

SCHIRMANN, J. «Zur Geschichte der hebräischen Poesie in Apulien und Sizilien.» *Mitteilungen* of the Forschungsinstitut für hebräische Dichtung. II, 1933, 96-147.

» *Mibhar ha-ha-shirahʿibrit be-Italiah.* Berlin, 1934.

SCHWAB, M. *Rapport sur une Mission de Philologie en Grèce: Epigraphie et Chirographie.* Paris, 1913. (*Nouvelles Archives des Missions Scientifiques et Littéraires,* n. s., X).

STARR, J. «The epitaph of a dyer in Corinth.» *Byz.-neugr. Jahr.,* XII, 1936, 42-49.

» «A fragment of a Greek Mishnaic glossary.» *Proc.* of the Amer. Acad. for Jew. Res., VI, 1935, 353-67.

» «On Nahrai b. Nissim of Fustāt.» (Hebrew) *Zion,* I, 1936, 436-53, II, 92.

STEINSCHNEIDER, M. *Donnolo: Fragmente des ältesten medizinischen Werkes in hebräischer Sprache,* Berlin, 1867.

» «Donnolo. Pharmakologische Fragmente aus dem 10. Jahrhundert.» *Archiv für pathologische Anatomie und Physiologie und für klinische Medizin,* XXXVIII, 1868, 65-91; XXXIX, 296-336; XL, 80-124; XLII, 51-174 (Repr. with the Hebrew fragment, Berlin, 1872).

TOBIAH B. ELIEZER. *Leqah Tob.* Gen.-Ex., ed. Buber, S. Vilna, 1880.

» Lev.-Dt., ed. Padua, A. M. Vilna, 1884.

» Cant., ed. Greenup, A. W. Hertford, 1896; repr. London, 1909.

» Ruth, ed. Bamberger, S. Mayence, 1887.

» Lam., ed. Nacht, J. Frankfort, 1895; ed. Greenup. London, 1908.

» Eccl., ed. Feinberg, G. Berlin, 1904.

» Esther, ed. Buber, S. *Sifré d'Agadta ʿal Megilat Esther.* Vilna, 1886. pp. 85-112.

B. Greek and Latin.

ANASTASIOS THE SINAITE. «Anagogicarum contemplatum in Hexaemeron.» *PG,* LXXXIX, 931-33 (Latin version).

ps.-ANASTASIOS. Polemic, *l. c.,* 1228-38.

ANNA COMNENA, Ἀλεξιάς, ed. Reifferscheid, R. Leipzig, 1864. v. I, tr. Dawes, E. A. S. *The Alexiad.* London, 1928.

Annales Cavenses, ed. Pertz, G. H. Hannover, 1839. (*MGH:* Script.,III).

«Anonymus Barensis.» *Chronicon,* ed. Muratori, L. A. *Rerum Italicarum Scriptores.* Milan, 1725, v. V.

ATTALEIATES, MICHAEL. Ἱστορία, ed. Bekker, A. I. Bonn, 1853 (*CSHB,* L).

253

BARDY, G., ed. and tr. *Les Trophées de Damas. PO,* XV. Paris, 1927.

BARING-GOULD, S. *Historic oddities and strange events. First series.* London, 1889.

BARTOLF DE NANGIS. «Gesta Francorum Iherusalem expugnantium.» *Recueil des historiens des Croisades: Historiens occidentaux.* Paris, 1866. v. III.

Basilika, ed. Heimbach, W. E. *Basilicorum libri LX.* Leipzig, 1833-70. 6 vv. v. VII, ed. Mercati, J. and Ferrini, E. C. Leipzig, 1897.

BAUDRI (Baldricus) of Bourgueil. «Historia Jerosolimitana», ed. Thurot, C. *Recueil des historiens des Croisades: Historiens occidentaux.* Paris, 1879. v. IV.

BEKKER, A. I., ed. «Theophanes continuatus.» Bonn, 1838 (*CSHB,* XXXIII); repr., *PG,* CIX.

BENESHEVICH, V. N. «On the history of the Jews in Byzantium, 6-10th centuries.» (Russian) *Evreiskaya Mysl,* II, 1926, 197-224, 305-18.

BOAK, A. E., tr. «The Book· of the Prefect.» *Journal of Business and Economic History,* I, 1929, 600-19.

CLEUS, J., ed. Life of St. Nilos, jr. *Acta Sanct.,* Sept., VII, 282-342. Paris-Rome, 1867; repr. *PG,* CXX, 15-165.

Corpus Iuris Civilis, ed. Krueger, P., Schoell, R., and Kroll, W. (Reprint) Berlin, 1928-9. 3 vv.

COZZA-LUZI, G. *La cronaca siculo-saracena di Cambridge con doppio testo greco.* Palermo, 1890.

CUMONT, F. «Une formule grecque de rénonciation au judaïsme.» *Wiener Studien,* XXIV, 1902, 466-69.

»   «La conversion des juifs byzantins au IXe siècle.» *Revue de l'instruction publique en Belgique,* XLVI, 1903, 8-15.

DAVREUX, J. «Le Codex Bruxellensis Graecus II 4836 (De haeresibus).» *Byzantion,* X, 1935, 91-106.

DELEHAYE, H., ed. Life of St. Constantine. *Acta Sanct.,* Nov., IV. Brussels, 1925. 627-56.

DOANIDOU, S. I. «Ἡ παραίτησις Νικολάου τοῦ Μουζάλωνος ἀπὸ τῆς ἀρχιεπισκοπῆς Κύπρου. Ἀνέκδοτον ἀπολογητικὸν ποίημα.» Ἑλληνικά, VII, 1934, 109-50.

DÜMMLER, E. *Auxilius und Vulgarius.* Leipzig, 1866.

EUSTATHIOS. Account of the siege of Thessalonica by the Normans, ed. Bekker. Bonn, 1842 (*CSHB,* XLVII); repr., *PG,* CXXXVI; tr. Tafel, G. L. F. *Komnenen und Normannen.* 2nd ed., Stuttgart, 1870.

»   Epistles, ed. Tafel (repr.), *PG,* CXXXVI, 1244-1334.

FICKER, G. *Erlasse des Patriarchen von Konstantinopel Alexios Studites.* Kiel, 1911.

254

GAETANO, O., ed. Life of Bishop Zosimus of Syracuse. (Latin version) *Acta Sanct.*, Mar., III, 835-40. Paris, 1865.

GENESIOS, JOSEPH. Βασιλείαι, ed. Bekker. Bonn, 1834 (*CSHB*, XXII); repr. *PG*, CIX.

GOODSPEED, E. J. «Pappiscus and Philo.» *American Journal of Theology*, IV, 1900, 796-802.

GREGORIOS. Life of St. Lazaros, ed. Delehaye. *Acta Sanct.*, Nov., III, 524-42. Brussels, 1910.

GREGORIOS ASBESTAS, ed. and tr. de Stoop, E. «Het Antisemitisme en te Byzantium onder Basilius den Macedonier.» *Verslagen en Mededeelingen* of the Koninklijke Vlaamsche Academie voor Taal en Letterkunde. Ghent, 1913. pp. 451-92.

HEFELE, C. J. *Histoire des conciles,* tr. with revisions, Leclerq, H. Paris, 1907-09. v. III.

HOFERER, M. *Ioannis Monachi Liber de Miraculis.* Würzburg, 1884.

IVANOV, Y. *B'lgarski Starini iz' Makedoniya.* Sofia, 1931.

JOHN OF DAMASCUS. Πηγὴ γνώσεως. *PG,* XCIV; tr. Allies, M. H. *St John Damascene on Holy Images.* London, 1898.

ps.-JOHN OF DAMASCUS. Epistfes. *PG.* XCV.

KEDRENOS, G. Σύνοψις ἱστοριῶν, ed. Bekker. Bonn, 1838. v. II (*CSHB,* XXXV); Repr., *PG,* CXXI-I.

KRAUSS, S. «Eine byzantinische Abschwörungsformel.» *Festskrift i Anledning af Professor D. Simonsens 70-aarige Fodselsdag.* Copenhagen, 1923. pp. 134-57.

LABRIOLLE, P. de *Les sources de l'histoire du montanisme.* Paris-Fribourg, 1913.

LAMPROS, S. P. «Ὁ βίος Νίκωνος τοῦ Μετανοεῖτε.» Νέος Ἑλληνομνήμων, III, 1906, 129-228; repr. Galanopoulos, M. E. Βίος, πολιτεία, εἰκονογραφία, θαυμάτα καὶ ᾀσματικὴ ἀκολουθία τοῦ ὁσίου καὶ θεοφόρου πατρὸς ἡμῶν Νίκωνος τοῦ «Μετανοεῖτε.» Athens, 1933.

LATYSHER, V. V. *Neizdannie gretcheskie agiografitcheskie teksti. Zapiski* of the Akademiia Nauk (Petrograd), historical-philological class, s. 8, XII, 2. Petrograd, 1914.

«LEO GRAMMATIKOS.» Χρονογραφία, ed. Bekker. Bonn, 1842. (*CSHB,* XLVII).

MANSI, J. D. *Sacrorum conciliorum nova et amplissima collectio.* Florence, 1765. vv. XI, XIII, XIV.

MC GIFFERT, A. C., ed. *Dialogue between a Christian and a Jew.* Marburg, 1889.

MICHAEL CHONIATES. Μιχαὴλ Ἀκόμινατου τὰ σωζόμενα, ed. Lampros, S. P. Athens, 1879-80. 2 vv.

MONFERRATOS, A. G., ed. *Ecloga Leonis et Constantini cum Appendice.* Athens, 1889; tr. Freshfield, E. H. *A manuel of Roman law: the Ecloga.* Cambridge, 1926.

MONNIER, H. *Les Novelles de Léon le Sage.* Bordeaux-Paris, 1923. (*Bibliothèque des Universités du Midi*, XVII).

NAU, F. «Le texte grec des récits utiles à l'âme d'Anastase (le Sinaite).» *Or. Chr.*, III, 1903, 56-90; tr. abstract, *id., Revue de l'Institut catholique de Paris*, VII, 1902.

NIKEPHOROS, patriarch of Cp. *Opuscula historica*, ed. de Boork. Leipzig, 1880.

NIKETAS CHONIATES. Χρονικὴ Διήγησις, *PG*, CXXXIX.

«Petri Ducis Venetiarum Epistula», ed. Weiland, L. *MGH:* Legum Sectio IV. Hannover, 1893. v. I.

PITRA, I. B. *Iuris ecclesiastici graecorum historia et monumenta.* Rome, 1868. v. II.

RAUSCHEN, G., ed. *Die Legende Karls des Grossen.* Leipzig, 1890.

RHALLÉS, G. A., and POTLÉS, M. Σύνταγμα τῶν Θείων καὶ ἱερῶν κανόνων. Athens, 1852-9. 6 vv.

SCHWAB, M. «Sur une lettre d'un empereur byzantin.» *JA*, CXLIX, 1896, 498-509.

SCOTT, S. P., tr. *The Civil Law.* Cincinnati, 1932. v. XVII.

ps.-SYMEON MAGISTER. Χρονογραφία, ed. Bekker. Boon, 1838 (*CSHB,* XXXIII); repr. *PG*, CIX.

THEODOSIUS. Account of the siege of Syracuse, tr. Josaphat, ed. Muratori, *Rerum Ital. Script.*, I, pt. 2.

THEOPHANES. Χρονογραφία, ed. de Boor, K. (with tr. of Anastasius Bibliothecarius) Leipzig, 1883. 2 vv.

TRINCERA, F., ed. *Syllabus graecarum membranarum.* Naples, 1865.

VILLEHARDOUIN, G. de. *Conquête de Constantinople*, ed. and tr. de Wailly, M. N. Paris, 1882.

VOELL, W. and Justell, R., edd. *Bibliotheca Iuris canonici.* Paris, 1661. 2 vv.

ZÉPOS, J. and P., edd. *Jus Graecoromanum (ex editione C. E. Zachariä a Lingenthal).* Athens, 1931. vv. I-VI.

ZIGABÉNOS, EUTHYMIOS. Πανοπλία δογματική, *PG*, CXXX.

ZONARAS, JOHN. Ἐπιτομὴ ἱστοριῶν, ed. Büttner-Wobst, J. Bonn, 1897. v. III (*CSHB*, XLVI).

C. Arabic, Syriac, etc.

AGAPIUS (Mahbūb). *Kitāb al-ʿUnwān (Histoire Universelle)*, ed. and tr. Vasiliev. *PO*, VIII, fasc. 3. Paris, 1904.

ANTHONY OF NOVGOROD. *Kniga Palomnik*, ed. Loparev, C. M. Petrograd, 1899 (*Pravoslavnyi Palestinskii Sbornik*, XVII, 3 no. 51); tr. Ehrhard, M. «Le livre du pèlerin d'Antoine de Novgorod.» *Romania*, LVIII, 1932, 44-65.

AL-AZDĪ (AL-HALABĪ), JAMĀL AD-DĪN ABŪ'L HASAN ʿALĪ B. DĀFIR, *Kitāb ad-dūwal almunqatīʿa,* ed. Wüstenfeld, F. *Geschichte der Fatimiden-Chalifen nach arabischen Quellen.* (*Abhandl.* of the Göttingischen K. Gesellschaft der Wissenschaften, XVI-II) Göttingen, 1881.

BAR HEBRAEUS. *Makhtebhānūth zabhnē,* ed. Bedjan, P. Paris, 1890; tr. Budge, E. A. W. *The Chronography of Gregory Abu'l Faraj.* London, 1932.

AD-DIMASHQĪ. *Nukhbat ad-dahr fī ʿajāʾib al-bahr wa l-bahr (Manuel de la Cosmographie du Moyen Age),* ed. Mehren, A. F. Petrograd, 1866; tr. id., Copenhagen, 1874.

ELĪSHA BAR SHINAYĀ. *Al-burhān ʿalā sahih al-ʾimān,* Vatican codex arabicus 180; tr. Horst, L. *Beweis der Wahrheit des Glaubens.* Colmar, 1886.

IBN KHURDĀDHBAH. *Kitab al-masalik waʾl-mamālik (Livre des Routes et des Royaumes),* ed. and tr. de Goeje, M. J. Leyden, 1889. (*Bibliotheca Geographicorum Arabicorum,* VI).

AL-JAHĪZ, ed. FINKEL, J. *Three essays of Abu ʿOthman ʿAmr ibn Bahr al-Jahiz (d. 869).* Cairo, 1926; tr. Recher, O. *Exzerpte und Übersetzungen aus den Schriften des Philologen und Dogmatikers Gahiz aus Baçra.* Stuttgart, 1931.

AL-MASʿŪDĪ. *Kitāb murūj adh-dhahab wa-maʿaʾdin al-jawāhir (Les Prairies d'Or),* ed. and tr. de Meynard, C. B., and de Courteille, P. Paris, 1861. v. II.

MATTHEW OF EDESSA. *Chronique,* tr. from the Armenian, Dulaurier, E. Paris, 1838. *(Biblothèque Historique Arménienne).*

MICHAEL THE SYRIAN. *Makhtebhānuth zabhnē (Chronique),* ed. and tr. Chabot, J. B. Paris, 1899-1910. vv. II-IV.

NASIR-I-KHUSRAU. *Diary of a Journey through Syria and Palestine, 1047 A. D.,* tr. from the Persian, Le Strange, G. *(Palestine Pilgrims' Text Society).*

PEETERS, P. «Histoires monastiques géorgiénnes.» *Analecta Bollandiana,* XXXVI-II, 1917-19, 8-68.

SIMON OF VLADIMIR AND SUZDAL. Lives of the monks of the Pechera monastery, ed. Abramovich, D. *Kievo-Pecherskii Paterik.* Kiev, 1930.

IV. Special Studies.

A. Byzantine-Jewish History and Literature.

ANDRÉADÈS, A. M. «Οἱ Ἑβραῖοι ἐν τῷ Βυζαντινῷ κράτει.» Ἐπετηρὶς Ἑταιρείας Βυζαντινῶν Σπουδῶν. VI, 1929, 20-43.

» «Περὶ τοῦ ἂν ὑπῆρχον Ἑβραῖοι ἐν Κρήτῃ, ὅτι οἱ Βενετοὶ κατέλαβον τὴν Κεφαλόνησον.» Πρακτικὰ Ἀκαδημίας Ἀθηνῶν. IV, 1929, 32-37.

ANDRÉADÈS, M. A. «Les juifs et le fisc dans l'empire byzantin.» *Mélanges Charles Diehl*. Paris, 1930. I, 7-29.

» «Sur Benjamin de Tudèle.» *BZ*, XXX, 1930, 458-61.

» «The Jews in the Byzantine Empire.» *Economic History*, III, 1934, 1-23.

AUERBACH, M. *Die Erzählung von den vier Gefangenen*. Berlin, 1928. (*Jahresbericht* of the Berlin Rabbiner-Seminar, 1925-7).

BACHER, W. «Notes critiques sur la Pesikta Rabbati,» *REJ*, XXXIII, 1896, 40-46.

» «Bari in der Pesikta rabbathi.» *Monats.*, XLI, 1897, 605-09.

BEES, NIKOS A. «Übersicht über die Geschichte des Judentums von Jannina (Epirus).» *Byz.-neugr. Jahrbücher*, II, 1921, 159-77.

» «Οἱ Ἑβραῖοι τῆς Λακεδαιμονίας καὶ τοῦ Μυστρᾶ» Νουμᾶς 1905, Nr. 166.

BEES, NIKOS A. — MÜLLER, N. Die Inschriften der jüdischen Katakombe am Monteverde zu Rom. Leipzig, 1919.

CARO, G. «Ein jüdischer Proselyt (?) auf dem Thron von Byzanz.» *Monats.*, LIII, 1909, 576-80.

DENDIAS, M. A. «Λευκὰς ἢ Ἄρτα; Ἑρμηνεία ἑνὸς χωρίου τοῦ ὁδοιπορικοῦ τοῦ Βενιαμὶν τοῦ ἐκ Τουδέλης.» Ἠπειρωτικὰ Χρονικά, VI, 1931, 23-28.

DÖLGER, F. «Die Frage der Judensteuer in Byzanz.» *Viertel.*, XXVI, 1933, 1-24.

EPSTEIN, A. «Studien zum Jezira-Buche und seiner Erklärer.» *Monats.*, XXXVII, 1893, 266-9, 458-62.

» «Recherches sur le Séfer Yecira.» *REJ*, XXVIII, 1894, 61-78, 96-108.

FERORELLI, N. *Gli ebrei nell' Italia meridionale dall' età romana al secolo XVIII.* Turin, 1915. (Repr. from *Archivio Storico per la Napoletane*, XXXII-III, 1907-8).

GRÉGOIRE, H. «Le 'Glozel' Khazare.» *Byzantion*, XII, 1937, 225-66.

JANIN, R. «Les juifs dans l'empire byzantin.» *Echos d' O.*, XV, 1912, 126-33.

JUSTER, J. *Les juifs dans l'empire romain*. Paris, 1914. 2 vv.

KAUFMANN, D. *Gesammelte Schriften*. Frankfurt, 1910-15. 3 vv.

KRAUSS, S. *Studien zur byzantinisch-jüdischen Geschichte*. Leipzig, 1914.

» «The names Ashkenaz and Sefarad.» (Hebrew) *Tarbiz*, III, 1932, 423-30.

» «Die hebräischen Bennenungen der fremden Völker.» *Jewish studies in memory of G. A. Kohut*. New York, 1935. pp. 379-412.

» «Zu Dr. Mann's neuen historischen Texten.» *HUC An.*, X, 1935, 265-96.

LEWIN, L. «Eine Notiz zur Geschichte der Juden im byzantinischen Reiche.» *Monats.*, XIX, 1870, 117-22.

LEWY, R. «Kleine Beiträge zur Volkskunde und Religionswissenschaft.» *Archiv für Religionswissenschaft*, XXV, 1927, 194-206.

MANN, J. «Are the Ashkenazim the Khazars?» (Hebrew) *Tarbiz*, IV, 1933, 391-94.

» «Varia on the Gaonic Period, v.» *l. c.*, V, 286-301.

MARX, A. «Studies in Gaonic history and literature.» *JQR*, I, 1910,61-104.

MERCANTI, G. «Un antisemita bizantino del secolo IX che era siciliano.» *Didaskaleion*, IV, 1915, 1-6.

MIESES, M. «Les juifs et les établissements puniques en Afrique du Nord, xii.» *REJ*, XCIV, 1933, 82-86.

MOŠIN, V. «Les Khazares et les Byzantins d'après l'Anonyme de Cambridge.» *Byzantion*, VI, 1931, 309-25.

NEUBAUER, A. «Abou Ahron le babylonien.» *REJ*, XXIII, 1891, 230-32.

PARKES, J. *The conflict of the church and synagogue*. London, 1934.

PERLES, F. «Jüdisch-byzantinische Beziehungen.» *BZ*, II, 1893, 569-84.

POZNANSKI, S. «*Skapernea* und *Drmudana*.» *ZfhB*, XVII, 1914, 18f.

SALFELD, S. «Das Hohelied bei den jüdischen Erklärern des Mittelalters: Tobia b. Elieser.» *Magazin*, V, 1878, 141-44.

SONNE, I. «Alcune osservazioni sulla poesia religiosa ebraica in Puglia.» *Rivista*, XIV, 1933, 68-77.

» «Notes sur une *Keroba* d'Amittai publiée par Davidson.» *REJ*, XCVIII, 1934, 81-84.

STARR, J. «Byzantine Jewry on the eve of the Arab conquest (565-638).» *Journal of the Palestine Oriental Society*, XV, 1935, 280-93.

» «An iconodulic legend and its historical basis.» *Speculum*, VIII, 1933, 580-03.

» «An Eastern Christian Sect: the Athinganoi.» *Harvard Theological Review*, XXIX, 1936, 93-107.

» «The place-name *'Italiya-Antaliyah*.» *Rivista*, XVII, 1937/8, 475-478.

USPENSKI, F. «The itinerary of Benjamin of Tudela.» (Russian) *Annaly*, III, 1923, 5-20.

B. Miscellaneous Writings on Jewish Subjects.

APTOWITZER, V. «Untersuchungen zur gäonischen Literatur.» *HUC An.*, VIII-IX, 1931-2, 373-441.

» «R. Chuschiel und R. Chananel.» *Jahresbericht* of the Vienna Israelitisch-Theologische Lehranstalt, XXXVII-IX, 1929-32, 3-51.

ARONIUS, J. *Regesten zur Geschichte der Juden im fränkischen und deutschen Reiche bis zum Jahre 1273*. Berlin, 1902.

ASSAF, S. *Ha-ʿonashin aharé hatimat ha-Talmud*. Jerusalem, 1922.

BARON, S. W. *A social and religious history of the Jews*. New York, 1937. 3 vv.

BRUTZKUS, J. «The earliest notices of the Jews in Poland (10-11th cc.).» (Yiddish). *Historishe Shriften* of the Yidisher Visenshaftlichen Instituts: *Historishe Sektzie*. Warsaw, 1929. I, 55-71.

» «Der Handel der westeuropäischen Juden mit dem alten Kiev.» *Zeitschrift für die Geschichte der Juden in Deutschland*, III, 1931, 90-110.

CARO, G. *Sozial- und Wirtschaftsgeschichte der Juden*. 2nd ed. Frankfort, 1924. v. I.

DUBNOW, S. *Weltgeschichte des jüdischen Volkes*, tr. Steinberg, A. Berlin, 1929. vv. III-IV.

EPPENSTEIN, S. «Beiträge zur Geschichte und Literatur im gaonäischen Zeitalter.» *Monats.*, LV, 1911, 324-29, 620-28, 729-42; repr., same title, Berlin, 1913.

GRAETZ, H. *Geschichte der Juden*. 7th ed., revised by Eppenstein, S. Leipzig, 1909. vv. IV-VI.

MANN, J. «The Responsa of the Babylonian Geonim as a source of Jewish history.» *JQR*, IX, 1918, 165-71.

POZNANSKI, S. «Meswi al-Okbari.» *REJ*, 1897, 116-91.

STARR, J. «Le mouvement messianique au début du huitième siècle.» *REJ*, CII, 1937, 89-100.

WINTER, J. AND WÜNSCHE, A., edd. *Die jüdische Literatur nach Abschluss des Kanons*. Trier, 1894-6. vv. II-III.

ZUNZ, L. *Zur Geschichte und Literatur*. Berlin, 1845.

» *Gesammelte Schriften*. Berlin, 1875-6. vv. I, III.

C. Miscellaneous Studies.

ANDRÉADÈS, A. M. «La population de l'empire byzantin.» *Bulletin de l'Institut Archéologique Bulgare*, IX, 1935, 117-26.

BROWN, H. F. «The Venetians and the Venetian quarter in Constantinople down to the end of twelfth century.» *JHS*, XL, 1920, 68-88.

GOEJE, M. J. «International haandelsverkeer in de middeleeuwen.» *Verslagen en medeelingen: Afdeeling Letterkunde*, of the Koninklijke Academie van Wetenschappen, 4th s., IX, 1909, 245-69.

OSTROGORSKY, G. «Löhne und Preise in Byzanz.» *BZ*, XXXII, 1932, 293-333.

PACE, B. «I barbari ed i bizantini in Sicilia.» *Archivio storico siciliano*, n. s., XXXVI, 1911, 20-24.

TOMASCHEK, W. «Die Handelswege im 12. Jahrhundert nach den Erkundigungen des Arabers Idrisi.» *Sitzungsberichte (philos.-hist. Classe)* of the Vienna Kaiserlichen Akademie der Wissenschaften, CXIII, 1886, 285-373.

INDEX